Practicing Transnationalism

Practicing Transnationalism

American Studies in the Middle East

EDITED BY EILEEN T. LUNDY
AND EDWARD J. LUNDY

University of Texas Press Austin

Requests for permission to reproduce material from this work should be sent to:
Permissions
University of Texas Press
P.O. Box 7819
Austin, TX 78713-7819
http://utpress.utexas.edu/index.php/rp-form

♾ The paper used in this book meets the minimum requirements of
ANSI/NISO Z39.48-1992 (R1997) (Permanence of Paper).

Library of Congress Cataloging-in-Publication Data
Names: Lundy, Eileen T., editor. | Lundy, Edward J., editor.
Title: Practicing transnationalism : American studies in the Middle East / edited
    by Eileen T. Lundy and Edward J. Lundy.
Description: First edition. | Austin : University of Texas Press, 2016. | Includes
    bibliographical references and index.
Identifiers: LCCN 2016004934 | ISBN 978-1-4773-0928-5 (cloth : alk. paper) |
    ISBN 978-1-4773-1073-1 (pbk. : alk. paper) | ISBN 978-1-4773-0929-2
    (library e-book) | ISBN 978-1-4773-0930-8 (nonlibrary e-book)
Subjects: LCSH: United States—Civilization—Study and teaching—Middle
    East. | United States—Study and teaching (Higher)—Middle East. |
    Education, Higher—Middle East. | Educational exchanges—Middle East. |
    Transnationalism.
Classification: LCC E175.8 .P735 2016 | DDC 973.071/1—dc23
LC record available at http://lccn.loc.gov/2016004934

doi:10.7560/309285

Contents

Foreword

In August 2003, we arrived in Amman, Jordan, as Fulbright scholars and lecturers to join the faculty of the American studies program at the University of Jordan (UJ). Established two years earlier in the Faculty of Graduate Studies, the program had just moved to the English Department. We soon learned, to our surprise, that this was the first graduate American studies program in an Arab university in the Middle East. For the two years before we arrived at the University of Jordan, we had been teaching in the American studies undergraduate program (American Language and Literature) at Bilkent University in Ankara, Turkey, where the twenty-five-year-old American Studies Association of Turkey and a network of both graduate and undergraduate programs flourished throughout the country, complete with well-funded yearly conferences and an annual journal, the *Journal of American Studies in Turkey*. In the Bilkent program where we taught, three of our Turkish colleagues had PhDs in American studies, two from the United States and one from a Turkish university. By contrast, the professor named to direct the program in Jordan, Tawfiq Yussef, held a doctorate in English and had taught the only American literature course in the English Department, an undergraduate course. The range of American studies was new to him and to all the local faculty. The first phase of an emphasis on comparative and transnational subjects in American studies was in full swing in the United States, energizing scholars and raising questions both philosophical and practical. Thanks to the conferences at the American University of Beirut (AUB) sponsored by the Center for American Studies and Research (CASAR) there, Professor Yussef and other directors and professors already or soon to be involved in American studies programs had a source for information and assistance.

The American studies program in Jordan depended on yearly visiting Fulbright professors to help add their expertise. One or two Fulbrighters per year helped, but the program had to recruit faculty from other parts of the university and, at times, from other universities to teach some of the required courses for the master's degree. In American universities not only in the United States but also in the Middle East—American Universities of Beirut, Cairo, and Sharjah and Georgetown at Qatar—professors with expertise in subjects related to the Americas, other than literature and history, could be found within the institution. But in universities such as the University of Jordan and the University of Bahrain (UOB), this was not the case.

After several years' residence in the English Department, the program at the University of Jordan moved to the Faculty of International Studies, where the area studies programs had begun to cluster.

In January 2004, we attended a conference in Cairo, funded by the Egyptian Fulbright program, designed to explore the status of American studies in the Middle East and North Africa (MENA). Most of the participants were professors either of American literature or of American history, government, philosophy, or cultural studies. We met Professor Mohammed Dajani Daoudi, who presented student work from the newly founded graduate American studies program at al-Quds University in Ramallah, the second graduate program of its kind in an Arab university. We would later meet Professor John Hillis, chairman of the English Department at the University of Bahrain, who was the leading force in the opening of the first minor in American studies in an Arab university, in 1998.

From then on, we began to hear of American studies programs opening throughout the Middle East and to meet professors from some of those programs at the biannual conferences at AUB. As a result of the AUB conferences, a network of scholars and teachers gradually formed, sharing ideas and expertise as they worked to understand and adapt the ideas of comparative and international studies into their own programs.

Even as the invasion of Iraq occurred, along with the revelations of the horrors of Guantánamo and Abu Ghraib, other programs in American studies began and grew. As we worked in our own program at the University of Jordan and as we attended the AUB conferences every other year, the questions accumulated: What is the impetus for this growth? Who are the people delivering these programs? What has happened to them over the years?

When our two-year tenure at the University of Jordan ended, we applied to and received grants as senior scholars with the American Center for Oriental Research (ACOR) in Amman, Jordan, to investigate these and other programs. We traveled to each of the programs, interviewed students and faculty, observed classes and conferences, sat in on seminars, and attempted to assess the situations as we sought answers to our questions and formulated others. We had six months to do this, January to July 2006. After we returned to the United States, we continued to attend the AUB conferences and to maintain contact with as many of our colleagues as possible.

What we found was great variety among the programs, from the well-researched and well-funded program at AUB's CASAR, under the direction of Professor Patrick McGreevy, to the one office and yearly conference administered by Professor Hyatt at the American Center at Queen Arwa University. What we also found was that in a number of programs in American studies in the Middle East, local professors, sometimes with the help of Fulbright scholars and lecturers, often were on a learn-as-you-go course, having roots in American literature and history, perhaps, but faced with the broad spectrum of courses to staff and the challenges brought by the newly developing emphasis on comparative and transnational studies as it was evolving internationally.

The University of Bahrain, the University of Jordan, al-Quds University in Ramallah, CASAR at the American University of Beirut, CASAR at the American University of Cairo (AUC), the American Center at Queen Arwa University in Yemen, the American University of Sharjah (AUS), the Georgetown School of Foreign Service at Qatar, and, while not an Arab university an active member of the American studies network in the Middle East, the University of Tehran in Iran were the programs we visited. And just at the end of 2008, Munifiyeh, a university just outside Cairo, launched a well-researched program under the direction of Professor Osama Madany. In all, we visited ten programs in ten years during a time of rising anti-American feeling. This is a phenomenon of historical interest and importance, one to be explored and recorded.

The first two chapters address questions raised by the historical phenomenon of the rise of ten American studies programs in ten years during a time of international tensions. The three following chapters identify significant contexts in which these programs grew; the political, the academic liberal education tradition; and the skewing of media messages to the West. Following the chapters on contexts, two chapters offer views of cultural interactions in the cultural contact zones of literature and music, part of the world of cultural politics. And, finally, the last three chapters offer insights into the actual delivery of the developed curricula as American professors presented some of the challenges that rose from the classroom, the proving ground of any educational idea or ideal.

Eileen T. Lundy

Acknowledgments

We would like to thank the following for their many kinds of support as we worked on this project:

To the Fulbright Commission who brought us to Jordan and especially to Alain McNamara, Director of the Binational Fulbright Program in Jordan, and his wife, Kathy Sulivan, for their wise guidance and introduction to Jordanian society;

To our colleagues and students in the American Studies Programs we visited in the Middle East, who welcomed us to their programs, gave of their time, and shared their experiences; we especially wish to thank our colleagues and students in the Department of English and the American Studies Program at the University of Jordan for all that they taught us;

To the administrators and staff of the American Center for Oriental Research in Amman, Jordan, especially Director Barbara Porter and Associate Director Chris Tuttle for providing facilities and financial support for our research;

To Patrick McGreevy, Founder of the Center for American Studies and Research at the American University of Beirut, for providing the opportunity for scholars in American Studies in the Middle East to gather and share their ideas;

To the Ecco Foundation headed by the late Elizabeth "B. J." Warnock Fernea for a travel grant enabling us to visit the American Studies Program at the University of Tehran, Iran. And to B. J. herself for her support and faith in us as we set out on this project;

To Annes McCann Baker for her friendship, her wisdom, and her editorial advice along the way and to Virginia Hagerty for her invaluable assistance in the final editing stages of the manuscript;

To Jim Burr and his fellow editors at the University of Texas Press for encouraging us to pursue the project and for working with us through the revisions and editing processes;

And finally, our gratitude to the chapter authors for the knowledge and experience they shared with us, their cooperation through the readings and revisions, their patience and goodwill throughout the process.

Thank you all.

Practicing Transnationalism

Introduction

American studies programs began to crop up in the Middle East in 1998, just as the last century ushered us into the twenty-first. The programs began amid a plethora of questions and challenges. How should they proceed to develop, especially during the times that saw the US invasion of Iraq and the 2006 devastating bombing of Lebanon by Israel, a neighboring country seen to be in strong alliance with the United States, during the days when news of the US atrocities in Abu Ghraib and Guantánamo filled the media reports? This raises the question "Why then?" as well as the question of how to proceed.

Patrick McGreevy, from his vantage point as founding director of the Center for American Studies and Research at the American University of Beirut, discusses in chapter 1 the esteem American higher education still held in the Middle East at this time. But, again, why 1998 and the years immediately following, why then? Why begin American studies programs at that time? Once again, the power of the United States, the superpower both economically and militarily, had been demonstrated, so some came to the study of the United States to better understand the enemy influencing so many parts of their lives: foreign relations, technology, movies, television, music, clothing, fast food, and so forth. And some came because they admired the ideals set forth as America's—freedom, democracy, free speech—even though they knew the United States did not always live by these ideals, even though they knew those ideals were not owned exclusively by the United States.

At the same time, the field of American studies was changing, moving beyond a postcolonial and postnational focus to take a transnational turn. This turn presented the challenge of profoundly rethinking the field. But the two movements, the growth of new programs in the Middle East and the transnational turn in the field, were developing simultaneously. In addition, the first American studies program in the Middle East—a minor in American studies at the University of Bahrain—was housed in the English Department. The second, the master's degree program in American studies at the University of Jordan, after its first two years in the Graduate Studies Department soon found itself in an English Department as well. While this helped draw to the programs students versed in the English language, it also placed the programs under the direction of professors prepared in American literature and in the cultural and historical studies informing the literature, giving them an affinity with the older paradigms in American studies. These professors, with the help of Fulbright professors, were faced with the challenge to learn new paradigms as they built the programs just as those emphases for the field were evolving from an early literature and history base, so the questions multiplied.

How would they design and deliver curricula that reflected the recognition not only of the many cultures and colors of US Americans but also of the influences of the effect of what Mary Louise Pratt called the "contact zones," those borderlines and borderlands where cultures abut, interchange, and exchange characteristics (1992, 2001)? This mixing and abutting of cultures raised the question of the meaning of the word "America" itself. Whose America? America where? America in those contact zones with other cultures? Which cultures of America? And also, which of the Americas? North, Central, or South, not just the United States? In our travels to the ten programs in the Middle East, almost exclusively, the term "America" was being used synonymously with "United States of America."

The program builders in the rapidly increasing number of American studies sites in the Middle East had taken on quite a challenge. Perhaps the greatest challenge of all was that of coming to terms with the meanings and implications of transnationalism in the field. Cousin of globalization, this transnational idea, introduced to the field but not well understood at the time these programs were forming, became a test ground for the programs. The term itself was elusive at that time, having been used in many different ways. Even in 2011, the term "transnational" in the introduction to *Re-framing the Transnational Turn in American Studies* (Fluck, Pease, and Rowe 2011) was called "this promiscuous signifier" and "a mobile category" for its many interpretations and applications. In 2013, however, the description of the program philosophy of the new master's in transnational American studies carried this clear working definition of the term and its intents:

> Over the last decade, the discipline of American Studies has undergone a major transformation as a result of globalization and the ascendancy of US economic and military supremacy. Whereas the field once thought that its mission was to better understand the "American character" in American literature and everyday life, the field today is far more concerned with understanding the interdependencies between domestic politics and culture and US engagements abroad. This new focus has led many American Studies programs to focus on transnational and comparative understandings of American culture. (*MA in Transnational American Studies* 2013–2014)

But for the programs emerging between 1998 and 2008, that definition was not yet so clear. And so the questions mounted again: Who would staff these programs? How would faculty prepare themselves for these changes? Who would offer leadership across the region of the MENA to help reeducate faculty for the evolving emphases? Who locally would be prepared to draw together discrete courses in a curriculum into a comprehensive program called American studies? What challenges would students, professors, and scholars in the Middle East face as the paradigm for American studies continued to evolve and change? Could American studies programs develop transnationally and comparatively, avoiding direct or implied messages of American exceptionalism? Could American studies programs develop independent of the tentacles of American imperialism? Could these programs develop without becoming either anti-American or pro-American? The following chapters propose to explore the questions and challenges to those programs, the ones we have seen from the vantage point of our two-year experience in the program at the University of Jordan in Amman, our association over several years with American studies colleagues through the biannual conferences held at the Center for American Studies and Research at the American University of Beirut, and from our visits to all of the programs during our time as senior fellows at the American Center for Oriental Research, also in Amman, Jordan. These chapters propose to delineate the questions (chapters by McGreevy and Noori), to describe the contexts and implications of events surrounding the growing programs (chapters by Anderson and Lucas), to provide examples of cultural exchanges across the contact zones (chapters by Elayyan and

McDonald), and to offer a view of several practical classroom situations that serve to demonstrate the stages of implementation of comparative and transnational teaching in action in Bahrain, Qatar, and Jordan (chapters by Cavell, Sampsell-Willmann, and Lundy).

The authors of the following chapters are professors who worked directly or indirectly in the programs that developed over the growth period of 1998–2008. Most taught in the programs; three provide context for the programs as they grew. The scholar-teachers write from the experience of having been there, of having worked in the opening days of the programs, and of having faced the challenges not only of a new program but also of an evolving shift in the grounding of the programs. Theirs are valuable voices in the history of these phenomenal years. Betty Anderson, with her placement of AUB as the flagship university for liberal education in the Middle East; Luke Peterson, with his linguistic analysis of the distortion of media messages to the West, using as an illustration the famous case of Gilad Shalit; and Scott Lucas, with his early recognition of the changing place of US America in its position of influence in the Middle East, all situate the programs in the contexts that exerted influence on them. In the ground of these contexts and of the conflicts mentioned earlier, these programs grew rapidly. These events may, for a time, be swallowed in importance by the mounting urgencies of the conflicts following the Arab Spring and with the rise of the Islamic State of Iraq and the Levant (ISIL). But these chapters carry the words of a representative group of scholar-teachers active in American studies during the beginning years and represent their thinking during that time.

Growth of the Programs

Soon after the programs began in Bahrain under the direction of John Hillis and in Jordan under the direction of Tawfiq Yussef, al-Quds University in Ramallah opened the second graduate program, this one under the direction of Mohammad Dajani Daoudi. After 9/11 Prince Alwaleed Bin Talal Bin Abdulaziz al-Saoud of Saudi Arabia bestowed an endowment of ten million dollars to be shared equally by the two American Universities in Beirut and in Cairo to establish Centers for American Studies and Research. AUB would begin with a minor in American studies and by 2013 instituted a graduate degree in transnational American studies. Early on, AUC had a minor in the catalog, but a transition between leadership personnel coupled with a move to a newly built campus outside the city slowed the development of its program. Other programs followed rapidly: American University of Sharjah, a minor in American studies in the Department of International Studies; Georgetown University of Foreign Service at Qatar, a minor in the English Department; and the University of Tehran, a graduate degree in the Faculty of European and North American Studies. The Center for American Studies at Queen Arwa University in Sana'a, Yemen, was originally planned as a two-year program but actually developed as a granting agency for lecture series and research grants.

Attesting to the interest in and growth of American studies programs, two sections of the AUB CASAR December 2005 conference, "America in the Middle East, the Middle East in America," consisted of papers and roundtable discussions on topics related to teaching American studies in the Middle East. A year earlier, in January 2004, the Fulbright Program in Cairo had hosted a meeting of professors from various countries in the Middle East, who were then and continue to be engaged in studies of America, in literature, history, philosophy, and other subjects. Seventy-five professors from thirty Arab universities attended, seventy-two of them Arab professors and three Americans, all three of us at one time Fulbright scholars teaching in the graduate program at the University of Jordan, an obvious demonstration of interest and potential commitment.

The American studies program at the University of Jordan began with the understanding that Fulbright professors would come, one or more each year, to teach in the program. This plan continued but led to a major challenge: How would Jordanian professors of English linguistics and American literature, with the help of local professors of history, economics, and political science from other parts of the university or, at times, from other universities, prepare themselves to teach topics as they reflected America, its influence on Jordan and the region, and Jordan's view of those elements of American culture? How would they equip themselves to lead Jordan's view of those elements of American culture? How would they equip themselves to lead students in comparative and transnational studies of the United States in the Middle East and the Middle East in the United States? These questions were further complicated by the fact that the program, originally housed in the Graduate Studies Faculty and developed by a Fulbright professor, Christopher Wise, had been moved to the English Department and, after several years, to the International Studies Faculty, with Fulbright professors coming and going each year. The Middle Eastern Partnership Initiative paired the University of Jordan with the University of North Carolina and enabled several professors to spend six weeks in the United States in the summer, studying with American studies scholars. On several occasions, UNC, as part of the MEPI program, sent scholars to lecture to students in the program at UJ. MEPI, initiated during the Bush administration, soon ended, as did, therefore, the opportunities for exchange of scholars. The frequent shifting of location for the program challenged what expertise had been built as well as the continuity of the program. But it was AUB CASAR, under the leadership of Professor Patrick McGreevy, that led in providing opportunities for professors in American studies programs to gather biannually in Beirut at conferences designed to further explore the implementation of American studies programs.

During our two years at the University of Jordan, the United States, the so-called "unrivaled superpower," found itself mired in sand and blood in Iraq and Afghanistan and looked upon with disarray and disgust in many parts of the Middle East for its unconditional support of Israel, even as it occupied more and more Palestinian land. Also, the continuing news of prisoner abuse and then the news of governmental incompetence revealed during the days following Hurricanes Katrina and Rita presented a view not of a superpower but of misguided, misplaced, and ill-conceived uses of power. As our Jordanian students studied US America, they and many Jordanians found themselves divided between opposition to the actions of America, especially in the Middle East, and their long-standing ties with America in higher education, diplomacy, trade, aid, and the ideals, at least, of peace and justice.

This dilemma provided them with enough reason to study America in order to clarify their own stances in the search for knowledge, wisdom, and understanding in international relations between the various societies of the Middle East and those in America. But there was another compelling reason for the study.

Said's Question

The reason was stated simply and clearly by Edward Said in *Peace and Its Discontents: Gaza—Jericho, 1993–1995* when he asked: "Is there today a major Arab or Islamic contribution to the study of America, or to research on Europe, contributions that would change the nature of the subject the way European and American contributions to the study of Arabs or Islam dominate those fields, much more even than Arab contributions?" (1995, 96). This challenged universities in the Middle East to promote the study of America in the Middle East and from the various perspectives in the Middle East, not merely to pass on American views of America. But what would this entail? It would be much more than our limited experience could delineate fully. We needed the views and voices of Arab professors and students as well as those of American scholars and professors and of American expatriates who had lived or taught (or both) in the Middle East. And as we began to gather these voices, we found that within Said's major challenge lay many others, some minor, some more daunting.

Teaching Jordanian university students an American studies curriculum demanded we see through the eyes of the students. Basic approaches that we had taken for granted frequently needed to be explained carefully, concepts such as the geographical immensity of the United States as compared with their relatively compact nation; the various ways in which US Americans deal with the sacred and the secular, sometimes in ways that surprise us; public discussion in the university classroom of topics related to religion and politics; the awareness of many Muslims' deep sensitivity to material that even tangentially touched Islamic values; the recognition of the many cultures within the United States, within Jordan, and within other Middle Eastern regions; and the exploration of similarities and differences in the family structures of the Americas and of Middle Eastern countries, especially the differences between tribal societies and other societal organizations.

American Studies: Interdisciplinary, International, Transnational—the Major Challenge

But it was the comparative, reciprocal, international, and emerging transnational nature of American studies that presented the greatest challenge to scholars, professors, and students alike. The first gathering of American studies professors in Arab universities decided that this reciprocal quality should be central to American studies programs in the Middle East. Participants in the 2004 Cairo conference referred to earlier position papers to guide the structures, philosophy, and policies of the programs in formation in many, if not most, of the universities represented.

One of the position papers emerging from the conference stated the necessity of a reciprocal quality in American studies if those studies were to contribute positively to Arab-American relations. It reads:

> As with all sensitive issues loaded with emotional overtones and in situations when one side is seen as the potential colonizer and the other side the potentially helpless colonized, balance is to be sought at all costs. Giving equal weight to the concerns and the legitimate needs of both sides can be one of the ways to achieve this balance.
>
> Another way is to give both parties the same chances to express themselves with the means available, be they technological, financial, or otherwise. There is a possibility of creating a context where American Studies complements and enriches Arab students on the express condition that American Studies be taught in a spirit of reciprocity. (Cairo Group 2004, 1–2)

Papers and discussions at one of the CASAR conferences at AUB echoed the ideas of reciprocity expressed by the Cairo Group in 2004, adding considerations of moving toward transnational frameworks in the programs. Those early Cairo voices for the reciprocal nature of American studies found that they were being joined by many voices in the field speaking for a transnational framework wherever American studies was being taught.

Amy Kaplan, in her presidential address to the American Studies Association in 2003, articulated the need to study America as a "relational and comparative concept": "We have the obligation to study and critique the meanings of America in their multiple dimensions, to understand the enormous power wielded in its name, its ideological and affective force, as well as its sources for resistance to empire." And she suggested ways to do this:

> 1) To study more about the differences among nation, state and empire . . .
>
> 2) To study how meanings of America have changed historically in different international contexts. Through the studies of political, literary and cultural images, we must understand how "America" is a relational, a comparative concept, how it changes shape in relation to competing claims to that name and by creating demonic others. . . .
>
> 3) To investigate the phoenix-like issue of American exceptionalism . . . by conducting studies of comparative exceptionalisms. (2003, 10–12)

Setting Kaplan's ideas into the context of American studies in the Middle East, an enormous challenge, confronted the developers of the programs there. The programs were new. They had not experienced a gradual transition from a literature and history base through postcolonial and postnational stages into the comparative and transnational situation now before them. They were jumping in in media res. And this is where AUB's CASAR delivered and continues to deliver a distinct and valuable service to those programs in the MENA: the education or reeducation of professors engaged in building the programs. Beginning in 2005, with the first conference titled "America in the Middle East, the Middle East in America," AUB brought in participants not only from universities with degree-granting programs or minors but also from universities where courses in American literature, history, or culture were being taught. The conferences flowed from research and development at AUB as they reflected and incorporated the trends and strains of American studies research internationally. The conferences drew major scholars in the field as keynote speakers, panelists, and forum participants where they presented their research, raised questions and challenges, and engaged in discussions with the other participants. These conferences have provided a major educational setting where those working in the MENA can bring their questions and join in the challenging discussions. AUB's CASAR has become the hub of American studies in the Middle East and North Africa.

So to Edward Said's question "Is there today an Arab or Islamic contribution to the study of America?" the answer is yes. The challenges are many, major among them the constant and continuing political and military upheavals in the region. Amazingly, many of the programs survive the violence. During the daily devastation of the 2006 bombing of Beirut, AUB continued to stay open, as did CASAR and their American studies program. Professor John Hillis, director of the American Studies Center at the University of Bahrain, wrote in an e-mail in 2013 that in spite of the expulsion of students and faculty during the 2012 uprisings (most were eventually reinstated), "the center has experienced something of an explosion in the numbers of students who have signed up for the minor." Hillis also comments that the program is under greater scrutiny than in its earlier years and that he is meeting difficulties staffing all the courses, especially those in US–Middle East relations or America's role in international affairs. In 2013 AUB inaugurated its graduate degree program in transnational American studies. The program at the University of Jordan is now housed in the International Studies Faculty. However, not all programs may be proceeding as well, and the continuing and, in some cases, escalating conflicts may make their future even more difficult.

Another challenge faced by and continuing to face American studies programs in the MENA is what John Carlos Rowe calls "the embattled institutional situation of the field." He contrasts this phenomenon with the "intellectual energy of American Studies scholarship" (Fluck, Pease, and Rowe 2011, xiv). In the universities that house American studies programs in the Middle East, AUB, AUC, AUS, al-Quds, and the University of Tehran appear to have been managing coherent programs. AUB, al-Quds, Bahrain, and the University of Tehran regularly sent professors, and sometimes students as well, to the CASAR conferences in Beirut to explore the scholarly developments and to incorporate them into their programs. Representatives from the University of Jordan's English Department continued to attend those conferences even after the program had moved to another department. The English Department still offered undergraduate courses in the introduction to American studies and in American literature. The gathering of faculty and courses into a comprehensive program of comparative and transnational studies still challenges many programs. Lists of courses about US America constitute a minor or a major of some programs still striving to situate themselves in the new and shifting framework. One program, the Georgetown School of Foreign Service at Qatar, at the time of our visit, was in only its second year of development and, with competing goals being expressed, had not yet established a fully formed program of study. Toward the end of 2008, under the direction of Professor Osama Madany, the American studies program opened at the University of Minufiya just outside Cairo. Professor Madany, a regular attendee at the AUB CASAR conferences, where he met many scholars in the field, called upon some of those scholars during the months of preparation to advise on the formation of the program at this university. As a result, this program promises to be one to watch.

The Chapters

Considering the challenges and questions facing the directors and faculties of American studies programs developing in the MENA between 1998 and 2008, we soon saw that the quality and preparedness of those designing and teaching in the programs determined how the challenge would be met, how the questions would be answered. That is why we asked a number of those professors to offer their experiences, interests, and concerns so that readers might see who were some of the deliverers of the programs to students and what were their involvements during these years of development.

The chapters fall into four parts that fit into two major categories: "Questions and Challenges," "Contexts and Implications," then "Cultural Encounters" and "Classroom Encounters." Thus, the first two parts lay out the challenges, and the second two show professors working to meet those challenges practically.

In the first part, "Questions and Challenges," Patrick McGreevy in Beirut and Neema Noori, at that time in Sharjah, explore the many questions program leaders face. Those challenges pose what McGreevy calls "the American question." Noori raises questions about the presence and uses of American-style higher education as he saw it in Sharjah and as he found it reflected in the answers to his interviews and surveys. Motivated by the question of use of education as an arm of cultural imperialism in the Middle East, Noori conducted extensive interviews with professors and students not only in Sharjah but also in surrounding areas.

In the second part, "Contexts and Implications," Betty S. Anderson's chapter serves as a link between parts 1 and 2. This second part deals with two important aspects of the contexts in which American studies programs reside in the Middle East, and Anderson's chapter uses the history of the American University of Beirut to explore the place American higher education has taken in the Middle East. Her chapter both posits questions and provides context for that role. The continuing prestige of the American University of Beirut and the contracting of American universities in several countries in the Middle East attest to some desire for American educational curricula and approaches, such as the liberal arts foundation for specializations, the emphasis on English as the language of instruction, the exploration of comparative studies, the opportunity to further the understanding of American cultures, the study of the reaches of American power, and more. The American-based universities in Qatar form an "Education City" a half-hour or more car trip from the city center. AUC has chosen to locate away from the teeming city center of Cairo, where its original campus had been a landmark for years. But the American University of Beirut remains in the heart of the city, near the Corniche, on the shores of the Mediterranean, an academic respite in the midst of the bustle, tensions, and conflicts so often part of that city's life. Through civil war, the destruction of much of the city's infrastructure by Israel, through skirmishes, tensions, and conflicts, AUB continues, as do the American studies program and the biannual conferences on American studies in the Middle East. Anderson offers a thorough view of AUB and insight into the attraction of American universities in the region, even as their proliferation raises the question of the extension of empire.

The third part, "Cultural Encounters," deals with the arts, particularly music and literature, where the emphasis on transnational studies and explorations has revealed the power of the arts in fostering cultural understandings. Hani Ismail Elayyan, past chair of the English Department at the University of Jordan, specialized in teaching a course called America and the Arabs as part of the American studies program at UJ. The course proposed to explore America's influence on Arabs in Arab lands, but Hani expanded that expectation to include American poets writing in Arabic in America and the entrance of Arab American literature written in Arabic into the stream of American literature. He offers the work of three poets as examples of the immigrant's longing for home while striving to develop allegiances to the new homeland. David McDonald in his chapter demonstrates the power of shared influences in music between the United States and the Middle East, using hip-hop protest music in Palestine as his controlling example. McDonald presents a powerful demonstration of the transnational nature of music not only to cross borders but also to diminish those borders to the point of disappearance in the exchange of the art, as well as to deal directly through art with the social and cultural pressures of the Palestinian-Israeli conflict, the very heart of much of the unrest in the Middle East.

Finally, the last part, "Classroom Encounters," deals with the professors and their students in classroom experiences, teaching challenges, understandings, and misunderstandings. Research and development in American studies programs everywhere serve to inform the formation of the programs and, of utmost importance, the implementation of those programs in the classroom. Colin Cavell, a resident of Bahrain for more than ten years at the time of this writing, shows us the challenges he faced in teaching American politics to his students in Bahrain. Those challenges rose from obvious discrepancies between the values and policies inherent in America's official documents and the realities so close by in the general area of the Middle East. Comparisons between the history of politics and political movements in America with those of the world the students saw around them presented interesting if delicate challenges.

Kate Sampsell-Willmann, a social photographer and historian, uses an event from her teaching in a university in the Gulf region to demonstrate the power of the visual in social photography. She uses the work of the American photographer Lewis Hine, who, during the days of the Great Depression and the rise of industrialization in the United States, exposed in his photographs the exploitation of poor laborers and their children. Students in a Service Learning group at the university approached Sampsell-Willmann and asked her to work with them in a project in which they would explore through photographs the laborers in their city, Doha, an excellent comparative project following upon the work of Hine and one initiated by the Emirati students themselves. But it does not have a happy ending, thus presenting not only the power of social photography but also the challenges and tensions sometimes revealed in comparative studies.

Finally, Edward Lundy takes us into his classrooms in American literature and American culture at the University of Jordan. He writes of being told by the students of unwritten laws and boundaries for what he and the students might discuss, yet they found ways to proceed with those discussions with impunity. He writes of tribal boundaries that influence students' relations with one another, of the spiritual quality of much poetry that is not based in religion, of insights into cultural challenges in the history of the United States, and of students' responses to all of these discussions. He takes you there with him as he lists what he and the students learned together.

These chapters do not pretend to offer a full and comprehensive description of the status of American studies in the Middle East in the period 1998–2008. Rather, they represent views of the programs during those important beginning years. Most of all, they offer the words of those engaged in comparative and transnational studies of America as they were emerging in the region at that time. Some of these voices speak from studied scholarly experience in the field, deeply engaged in the emerging paradigms. Others have learned on the job and with the leadership and help of colleagues experienced in the work of American studies. The words of these scholars attest to the ongoing work to build programs that, long ago, departed from the idea of a program of study that would tell others who and what America is to the idea of America as a relational concept. All are asking the questions and challenges that constitute "the American question": what does the transnational power of America mean to people outside the United States? These chapters present glimpses of how those professors and scholars with their students and colleagues are confronting and exploring that question.

We tread unsteady ground in American studies programs in the Middle East today. Also, the shifting tectonic plates of current events have thrust American studies into a transnational frame where, perhaps, these programs should have been long before now. We face the challenge, but, knowing professors and scholars such as the authors of these chapters, those who came with ideas and questions to the CASAR conferences, and other leaders and practitioners in American studies internationally, we trust that this shifting ground will produce a landscape of study more varied, interesting, authentic, and productive for international understanding than the flat plain of American exceptionalism.

References

Cairo Group. 2004. "Position Paper, Focus Group I." American-Egypt Fulbright Bi-national Commission, Arab-American Studies Conference, Cairo, January 23–26.

Fishkin, Shelley Fisher. 2011. "Redefinitions of Citizenship and Revisions of Cosmopolitanism—Transnational Perspectives: A Response and a Proposal." *Journal of American Studies* 3, no. 1: 1–11.

Fluck, Winfried, Donald E. Pease, and John Carlos Rowe, eds. 2011. *Reframing the Transnational Turn in American Studies*. Hanover, NH: Dartmouth College Press.

Kaplan, Amy. 2003. "Violent Belongings and the Question of Empire Today: Presidential Address to the American Studies Association, October 17, 2003." *American Quarterly* 56, no. 1: 10–11.

Lundy, Edward. 2005. Unpublished student survey, the University of Jordan.

MA in Transnational American Studies. 2013–2014. Catalog description, the American University of Beirut.

Pease, Donald E. 2009. *The New American Exceptionalism*. Minneapolis: University of Minnesota Press.

Pratt, Mary Louise. 1992. *Imperial Eyes: Travel Writing and Transculturation*. London: Routledge.

———. 1999. "Arts of the Contact Zone." In *Ways of Reading*, edited by David Bartholomae and Anthony Petrosky. 5th ed. New York: Bedford/St. Martins.

———. 2001. "The Contact Zone Revisited: Violence, Reconciliation, and Co-existence." Presented at the Border and Transcultural Research Circle conference, University of Wisconsin, Madison.

Said, Edward. 1995. *Peace and Its Discontents: Gaza—Jericho, 1993–1995*. London: Vintage Books.

PART I

QUESTIONS AND CHALLENGES

CHAPTER 1

The American Question

PATRICK MCGREEVY

In the summer of 2006, as US-made bombs rained down on Lebanon, President George Bush repeatedly insisted that it was premature to demand an end to the killing, and Condoleezza Rice called the suffering "the birth pangs of a new Middle East" (2006). Lebanon's share of these pangs included more than a thousand dead, a million displaced, infrastructure destroyed, and beaches and harbors polluted with oil. These events were on my mind as I prepared to teach fall-semester American studies courses at the American University of Beirut, but in a sense they merely intensified the already existing context for such teaching. On the one hand, such events obviously demonstrate that teaching American studies is not the same everywhere. On the other hand, the US role in this war points to a concern that confronts people almost everywhere because the power of the United States is palpable almost everywhere. I propose to call this concern the American question.

US leaders have wielded political and military power in an increasingly overt way since September 11, 2001, particularly in the greater Middle East, upping the ante from earlier moments when US global power came into focus, such as at the end of World War II and at the end of the Cold War. The conflicts in Afghanistan, Iraq, and indeed Lebanon also reveal the limits of US military might, but—despite the success of the Democratic Party in the November 2006 elections—there is little evidence of a fundamental change in the global projection of US political and military power. People throughout the world are also aware of the economic and cultural power of the United States. Many point to US domination of the key institutions of the global economy or to the ubiquity of Coke, Pepsi, and Starbucks. US cultural products—television, film, music, fashion, language, and the Internet—permeate almost everywhere. Perhaps the United States is simply the most powerful and successful among a network of entities that currently dominate the globe, but those who consider this network a monster believe its head is in the United States (Hardt and Negri 2000, 2004). The ongoing PEW worldwide surveys ("US Image Up Slightly" 2005) show a remarkably uniform unease about US hegemony that both supporters and opponents are increasingly willing to name "empire" (Bacevich 2002; Fergusson 2004; Kaplan 2004).

Scholars and teachers of American studies would want to complicate this picture in a number of ways. First, the fact that US political and cultural leaders have appropriated the word "America" seems to many living in the other countries of the Americas a hegemonic act. The recent debates in American studies about the appropriate name for the interdiscipline—should it, for example, be US studies or studies of the Americas?—have not removed the name but rather turned it into a kind of question (Lenz 1999; Pease and Wiegman 2002; Radway 1999; Rowe 1998). Second, people outside of the United States are not passive. What they do with the America they confront is unpredictable; resistance is possible; influences are multidirectional. Third, there is a growing scholarly awareness that countries, despite their obvious importance, are not neat containers of culture. American studies began as the interdisciplinary study of the culture and history of the United States. Where its practitioners once saw a culture, they now see cultures, and they recognize that individuals may identify with—and feel loyalty to—communities smaller or larger, older or newer, than the national one. For those of us teaching American studies outside the United States today, the global ubiquity of America points not just to the state but also to these complex and protean realities.

In nineteenth-century Europe, the transnational presence of Jewish people amid a rising tide of ethnic nationalism elevated to prominence the issue of how Jews were, and should be, related to non-Jews. Although the so-called Jewish question was first mentioned in the mid-eighteenth century, it became salient a century later, particularly in response to debates over Jewish emancipation (Abraham 1992; Berman 1980; Bernstein 1996; Marx [1843] 1967; Sartre [1945] 1962; Ungvári 2000; Yaffe 1996). Some believed that Jewish people were assimilable into European nations or that they were capable of living alongside fellow citizens in modern pluralistic states. Others argued that Jews were essentially different from and incompatible with Christians. Non-Jews with such beliefs generally opposed emancipation and favored maintaining traditional restrictions on Jews. Jews who believed in essential differences sometimes also favored segregation, perhaps in autonomous provinces or even in an independent state. The "Jewish question" was a protean phrase. It could encompass almost every aspect of Jewish life in modern European countries. It was a name for a perceived state of affairs, but it could also refer to a specific question about that state of affairs. In the context of a particular country, for example, nationalists might ask, "What does the presence of a non-Christian minority—that we cannot imagine as part of our national community—mean to the project of nation building?" Such a question assumes that it is possible unambiguously to identify what a "Jew" is and that there are no "borderlands" around Jewishness (Anzaldúa [1987] 1999). Because European nation building relied on the identification of an essentialized national subject, nationalists frequently named Jews as alien, essentializing them, in turn, and associating them with subversive transnational conspiracies.

In referring to the "American question," I do not intend to imply that US Americans are the victims of a similarly virulent demonization. Nor is there any equivalence between the claim of an international hegemony attributed to a dispersed stateless minority and one attributed to the world's most powerful country. The American question, I suggest, is like the Jewish question in only one important way: it arises in response to a transnational presence that, in the view of many people in many places, poses fundamental cultural, economic, and political challenges. Although the American presence includes such things as products, media, and military forces—while the Jewish presence took the form of a Diaspora of people—the American question confronts not only people outside the United States but also those within it; indeed, the transnational turn among US-based Americanists is, in part, an attempt to wrestle with the American question.[1] Similarly, the Jewish question—once problematized—confronted European Jews themselves, providing an impetus for, among other things, Zionism. Moreover, we must ask a parallel set of questions about what and who is "American."

Like the Jewish question, the American question is a name for a perceived state of affairs, but it can also refer to a specific question. Because there are so many perspectives on that state of affairs, the specific question might be asked in many ways. In one form, it could simply be "What does the transnational presence of American power mean to people outside the United States politically, economically, and culturally?" The moment of European nationalism constellated the Jewish question; what is the moment that constellates the American question? It seems to be a global one. We cannot separate the American question from such questions as "What kind of world do we have?" and "What kind of world is possible?"

Teaching American studies outside the United States today is different from, say, teaching Swedish studies, precisely because it is both animated and burdened by the American question. It bids us ask further questions. What does it mean that people perceive and name a presence "American"? Is American studies now inseparable from questions of politics, economics, and culture almost everywhere? The American question, for those of us teaching American studies in places like the Middle East, can seem to be the very air we breathe. For this reason, we must interrogate the American question itself, lest we unwittingly accept the normalcy of American ubiquity and allow it to undergird a new exceptionalism. In identifying the American question as a transnational concern, we must be careful to examine what this concern conceals. Both supporters and critics of US power may use a number of different words to name this concern—words like "anti-Americanism," "globalization," and "empire." Michael Hardt and Antonio Negri (2000, 2004), for example, argue that the exclusive focus on US power obscures the networks of global power within which the United States is only one actor. Projecting America as not only ubiquitous but also omnipotent hides the real limits of American power and the important roles of other entities and hegemonic states. In Lebanon, for example, one cannot help but be aware of the regional power of Syria, Iran, Saudi Arabia, and Israel. Moreover, the ongoing tragedies of Iraq and Afghanistan present the perfect demonstration of the limits of US power. To the extent that the American question is based on a perception of omnipotence, it can also obscure the deep divisions within US society. In the 1840s and 1850s, the United States directed its power against Native American groups and Mexicans in an orgy of expansion before its internal tensions erupted in civil war. Are there similar tensions concealed beneath the current global projection of US power? Although the American question cannot be separated from American studies classrooms outside the United States, those classrooms must also be sites for its interrogation: teaching America cannot be separated from thinking America.

In what follows, I will address two questions about teaching American studies outside of the United States: Why are we teaching American studies? How might we approach this task in a world where one is never far from American power? My perspective obviously has been shaped by the experience of developing a center and teaching American studies at the American University of Beirut. Like our counterparts in other regions, we have continually faced the American question, but our particular institutional, local, and regional contexts have also presented us with distinct challenges and opportunities. In addressing these two fundamental questions, I will try to be clear about what is particular to our situation and what may apply more generally in order to highlight the ways that the American question intersects with more local concerns.

American Studies: Why?

What impulses propel universities to establish American studies centers and programs outside of the United States? Why are courses offered? What motivates students to take courses and pursue degrees in American studies? The answers to these questions depend upon the time and the place. During the first two decades of the Cold War period, when most American studies scholars inside the United States envisioned a unitary national culture defined as exceptional to all others, the US government supported the teaching of American studies in allied countries such as Turkey, Germany, and Japan. The demand for American studies, even then, was not separate from the presence of US power. On the other side of the Iron Curtain, at places like Lajos Kossuth University in Hungary, American studies was pursued for very different reasons. The interest, in both kinds of places, was a response to US success, but in Hungary it stemmed partly from a desire to understand an adversary—the sort of motivation, perhaps, that inspired Condoleezza Rice to take up Russian studies or that inspires the Lebanese University to offer Hebrew-language courses (primarily to people who intend to monitor Israeli media).[2]

Through the awarding of Fulbright positions and public diplomacy efforts such as the Middle East Partnership Initiatives and other grants, the US government still influences the success of American studies programs in many countries. The fact that so many Fulbright appointments are in the field of American studies seems to indicate that the Council for International Exchange of Scholars is itself responding to the American question. At the same time, every Fulbright appointment—indeed every American studies program, course, and even lecture (even if highly critical of the United States)—increases the presence that evokes the American question.

Increasingly, governments outside the United States have begun to initiate American studies centers and programs. In November 2006, the Australian federal government endowed the new US Studies Centre at the University of Sydney with twenty-five million dollars. The center is a joint initiative with the American Australian Association, a non-profit organization whose goal is "to encourage stronger ties across the Pacific, particularly in the private sector" (n.d.). At the association's in-augural dinner, attended by Prime Minister John Howard and News Corporation chief Rupert Murdoch, Chairman Malcolm Binks said that "the centre will make a contribution to the enhancement of the al-ready outstanding relationship between our two countries" ("Sydney to Host" 2006). Although the center will include an academic compo-nent offering master's and PhD degrees, its promoters clearly are con-cerned primarily with enhancing economic and political ties between allies. Hence, the center's inception must be understood in relation to the economic, political, and military power of the United States.

A very different initiative is the new master's program in North American studies at the University of Tehran in Iran, which began op-erating in 2006. US-Iran relations have been nearly the opposite of US-Australian ones, particularly during the administrations of Mah-moud Ahmadinejad and George Bush. Although Barack Obama has shifted to a more conciliatory rhetoric, it is not clear if the fundamen-tals of the relationship have changed. The Iranian desire to understand the United States is a direct response to US power, policies, and rheto-ric. After President Bush labeled Iran as one of the three countries that constituted the "axis of evil" (2002), and after unleashing US military might on one of the other two countries so named—which happened to be next door—the American question began to assume a striking im-portance in Iran. Although it may be present almost everywhere, the American question is not an equally pressing concern in all places.

The University of Tehran's center is one of at least five new American studies programs that have opened in the Middle East since the turn of the century.[3] One of them, at the University of Jordan in Amman, heavily relies upon visiting Fulbright teachers. The Center for American Studies and Research at AUB and a second center at AUC were estab-lished with endowments from Prince Alwaleed Bin Talal Bin Abdulaziz al-Saoud of Saudi Arabia. Shortly after the World Trade Center attacks, Prince Alwaleed offered New York City ten million dollars in aid, but when the prince suggested that the United States should have a more balanced policy regarding the Israeli-Palestinian conflict, Mayor Rudy Giuliani turned down the offer. A few weeks after the US invasion of Iraq, in response to what he referred to as a growing "gap" between the United States and the Arab world, the prince then provided the funds to establish the two centers ("Prince Alwaleed Bin Talal" 2003). The founding document of CASAR at AUB simply states that the center is dedicated to "increasing mutual understanding between the United States and the Arab World, and increasing knowledge of the United States in the Arab World" through teaching, research, and outreach. Because, for al-Qaeda, the 9/11 attacks were themselves a response to the American question, CASAR was connected to the American question at birth. The prince wanted to support academic discourse that could counter mutual demonization, but he also wanted to make the United States itself an object of Arab knowledge.

In 2003 AUB formed a steering committee and initiated an elaborate planning process to explore what American studies could be in Beirut (*Final Report of the Steering Committee* 2004). In order to formulate some preliminary plans, the committee organized a series of remarkably open discussions, including a stakeholders retreat (attended by scholars from several Lebanese universities, journalists, members of parliament, ambassadors, and representatives from nongovernmental organizations), an open forum to which all AUB students and faculty members were invited, and a workshop with seven international experts in American studies. The single clearest recommendation to surface from these sessions was that CASAR must make it perfectly clear that it is an independent academic project and not an organ of US public diplomacy. It is difficult to gauge the extent to which this concern is unique to Beirut or the Arab world, but to be perceived as promoting a US government agenda in Beirut, after the invasion of Iraq, and especially after the 2006 summer war, would guarantee the failure of any academic project. CASAR has received complaints and pressure from groups and individuals on both ends of the political spectrum in Lebanon, the Middle East, and beyond.[4] Hence, at CASAR, the consensus has been to identify the program's mission as neither pro- nor anti-American, but rather as a strictly academic one of pursuing knowledge about American–Middle Eastern encounters in an atmosphere of freedom.

Because Lebanon has the highest proportion of Christians of any Arab country, and because it is connected to a worldwide diaspora (which includes the largest percentage of Arab Americans), and because so many of its people speak French and English, it is a very distinct Arab country. The American University of Beirut is an example of this distinctiveness. Its leaders have never tried to conceal that Americans founded it. Indeed, partly because of AUB's role in empowering Arabs, the term "American" still has enormous cachet in the Arab world. There are dozens of primary, secondary, and higher-education institutions with the word "American" in their official names.[5] As historian Ussama Makdisi (2002) has shown, because of the positive influence of institutions such as AUB, and because of the perception that the United States was anticolonial compared to Britain and France (especially at the end of World War I and after the Suez Crisis of 1956), the United States enjoyed a relatively positive image in the region until approximately 1967. Indeed, a 2005 Gallup poll still showed that nearly as many Lebanese people had a favorable as an unfavorable opinion of the United States—39 percent to 41 percent, respectively. After the summer war, it had become 28 percent favorable to 59 percent unfavorable (Mann 2006).

Despite this increasing negativity, the word "American" still has many positive connotations. When civic leaders in North Sioux City, South Dakota, decided to refer to their high-technology initiative as the Silicon Prairie, or when their counterparts in Portland, Oregon, called theirs the Silicon Forest, they were hoping to capture something of the aura of California's Silicon Valley because the word "silicon" had come to signify innovation and the prosperity that flows from it. What does the word "American" mean in the Arab world? Its resonance is simply one aspect of the American question. In the realm of higher education, it seems to connote success. Its very proliferation indicates that "American" suggests the best kind of education—one that stresses rigor, science, mathematics, reason, and critical thinking. It also serves as a foil to the presumably corrupt institutions where success is based not on ability or effort but on *wasta* (connections) or wealth. Partly because of this perception, it also connotes prestige. Jean Baudrillard suggested that the US flag is "simply the label of the finest international enterprise" (1988, 85). This is a kind of capital that is remarkably enduring despite the anger most people feel at recent US policies and actions in the region.

Such considerations help us understand why at least some AUB students take courses in American studies. I have even spoken with young Hezbollah supporters who would like nothing better than a chance to study or live in the United States. Students are attracted to American studies for other reasons as well, but all of them are related to the American question. Like Hungarians during the Cold War, many want to understand their enemy. More, it seems, want to learn how to influence the most powerful country's policies and actions. They often ask, "How does the Israeli lobby do it?"

Because America is present in the Middle East in multiple ways, students come to the classroom with knowledge and experience of it. America's reputation and indeed its myths are present as well. In my own classes, I have always been surprised how many students believe that anyone who works hard can become wealthy and successful in the United States. In Lebanon, however, conceptions and misconceptions of the United States are never universally shared. In fact, like the United States itself, Lebanon is a society characterized by disagreement. Some students fail to distinguish between the actions and attitudes of leaders and those of ordinary Americans. Most Arabs do not make this mistake, if only because they feel alienated from their own leaders. A more common idea is that the United States has a unitary culture and that its people universally feel a profound sense of unity and loyalty. Although at one level they know about the fissures in US society—along racial lines, for example—it seems easy to forget about them and speak of the simple America they often learn of in Hollywood films and through US public diplomacy efforts or the equally simple version presented by some Arab critics of the United States.

Partly because of these perceptions, people teaching American studies in the Middle East frequently report that students seem to have learned about the United States primarily via American television, Hollywood films, and popular music. Yet this summary ignores the fact that students may also experience US power directly or indirectly via the new Arabic media. A good example of the former was Lebanon's summer war of 2006. As the relentless bombing raids continued, US leaders blocked international attempts to bring the bloodshed to a halt. This experience of being so often on the wrong end of the stick of US hard power provides Arabs with a certain perspective on the United States that, to borrow a phrase from W. E. B. DuBois, we might call the vantage or "ground of disadvantage" (1982, 241).

Those who teach American studies in the Middle East and North Africa have equally diverse motivations. Some are natives of the region who, like the students discussed above, may be attracted by the success and prestige of the United States. Others are interested in the tradition of dissent in the United States and particularly in African American resistance with its own interesting connections to the Arab world.[6] Some MENA scholars have a profound grasp of—and a challenging perspective on—contemporary American studies. Like their counterparts in the United States, they are fascinated by the intriguing complexity of the issues involved, but the US presence in the MENA is never far from their consciousness. There are US citizens, and a few Europeans, who teach American studies in the MENA. Their motivations and perspectives are also complex. Most have some critical distance from US government policies and actions. They may suffer—or benefit—from what Edward Said called the perspective of the exile. "Most people are principally aware of one culture, one setting, one home," Said wrote in his 1999 memoir, *Out of Place*. "Exiles are aware of at least two, and this plurality of vision gives rise to an awareness of simultaneous dimensions, an awareness that—to borrow a phrase from music, is contrapuntal." An awareness of "contrapuntal juxtapositions," he suggested, can "diminish orthodox judgment and elevate appreciative sympathy" (216). Although this sensibility can make expatriates acutely aware of their own limitations, students often expect professors who are US citizens to synecdochically embody America, as if it were their job alone to provide an answer to the American question. In summary, when we ask "Why American studies?"—for those teaching American studies, for donors and administrators initiating programs, and for students taking courses—the answer is the presence of American power in all its forms. American studies is a response to the American question.

American Studies: How?

Given this situation, what options are open to those of us teaching American studies outside of the United States? My suggestions are based on how my own teaching has evolved in response both to the American question and to ongoing debates within American studies. I have two proposals: that American studies be envisioned as an *encounter* and that it be constantly *comparative*.

The missionaries who founded the Syrian Protestant College saw themselves as representatives of a civilization and a religion that were superior in every way to their local counterparts. In 1920 the college became the American University of Beirut and slowly developed into a hybrid institution—both American and Arab—where, as one student recently put it, "Occidental and Oriental streams of thought could meet and debate and reshape each other" (Nahle 2004). Some still believe that American studies should be more like the nineteenth-century Syrian Protestant College than the contemporary AUB. They see the United States as a model of success, both material and moral. American studies, from this perspective, becomes a one-way transfer of information and influence. As noted above, some of our students may be among those expecting or even clamoring for such an American studies curriculum. It is American studies from a single perspective—a perspective from which the United States appears as an exception to all other countries—an American studies program that does not ask disturbing questions about the meaning of America, in short, an arm of US soft power. Decades of scholarly debate within American studies point in a very different direction: that we examine America from many different perspectives, including those of people outside the United States because they also experience America in complex and sometimes direct ways. My first suggestion, therefore, is that we envision American studies as an encounter, not only in our classrooms, but also in our research and community-outreach activities. In an environment permeated by the American question, this approach has the most potential to contribute to intercultural understanding.

This is not to suggest that academic values must be sacrificed. Indeed, those values demand such an approach. If we are committed to relentlessly employing the power of thinking and questioning, and encouraging our students to do the same, we must remain as open to their thinking as we expect them to be to ours. Communities of scholars and scientists work because the process of critical dialogue produces more wisdom than even the most brilliant mind operating in isolation. It is through interaction and conversation that thinking evolves. Hence, it is our very commitment to freedom of the mind, and its implication that each of us must be willing to reevaluate our previous judgments and commitments, that can save us from the arrogance of seeing American studies as a one-way transferal of knowledge and expertise. Particularly those of us who have spent long periods in the United States must be open to the possibility of being reshaped. It is often those most different from us who can best challenge us in this way.

One way to implement the strategy of American studies as encounter is curricular. Our Introduction to American Studies course at AUB approaches America as a story of human encounters. Beginning in the early seventeenth century, North America, Europeans, Africans, and native peoples interacted in mutually influencing, if asymmetrical, ways.

This intercultural reality later expanded to include Latinos, Asians, and even Arabs. The stories that political and cultural elites developed to understand their nation, its history, its distinctiveness, and its destiny ignored these realities. The American question often intrudes into the classroom when we examine the fact that, despite these upbeat stories, the United States was born of a vast conquest and that its economic success came partly at the expense of African slaves. At the mention of these things, a certain percentage of our students are ready to launch into an anti-American rant that totally demonizes the United States and its people. They ask: "What is wrong with 'the American people'? Why are they aggressive, greedy, and racist?" I usually respond: "Are you including black, Latino, Asian, and Arab Americans in that judgment?" US citizens may be uniquely powerful, but they are not essentially evil. We must insist on thinking clearly. Here it is also important to point out how people have worked to overcome racism and injustice through struggles such as the civil rights movement, the women's movement, and the gay rights movement.

Yet when we speak about these successes, or when we show how the checks and balances of US institutions eventually can correct some of the worst abuses of power, do we run the risk of appearing to draw an unflattering contrast to Arab societies and institutions? Are we presenting the United States, once again, as a model? Even when trying to critique the United States, are we innocent of a kind of public diplomacy? The American question twists us this way. Yet we must resist the exceptionalist notion that equality before the law, critical thinking, and struggling for justice are uniquely American ideas. Moreover, I do not attempt to conceal my own commitment to such ideas. That is part of what I bring to the encounter.

My second suggestion is that American studies, particularly outside of the United States, must be constantly comparative. This emphasis implies that our inquiry is not simply about America, but also about fundamental questions such as the following: How does nationalism work? What about other kinds of community loyalty and identity? How does power operate? How does culture circulate? Hence, we take the American presence in the Middle East, and the Middle Eastern presence in America, as central. Recognizing such transnational realities helps us to interrogate the American question itself, for it shows us that although power and culture circulate in asymmetrical ways, the circulation is never one way or unquestioned. Examining how US power works in relation to a place like Lebanon makes very clear the limits of that power, if for no other reason than that there are a host of other regional and global actors competing for hegemony.

Because American power is present almost everywhere, we might conclude that American studies cannot escape being part of that hegemony, that the study of America and the power of America are part of a single imperialism. Such an argument would be a kind of inverse of Edward Said's suggestion that European knowledge of the "Orient" was not innocently separate from European imperial power (1978). When people outside of the United States acquire knowledge about America, does it increase the power of the United States? The people who established the new master's program at the University of Tehran certainly do not believe so. Edward Said himself also disagreed with this view of American studies. He repeatedly recommended that AUB institute an American studies program and urged other universities in the Arab world to do the same. His advocacy was obviously a response to the American question. American studies is needed, he wrote, because "the United States is by far the largest, most significant outside force in the contemporary Arab world" (1994, 356). Said argued that Arabs needed to understand how ordinary Americans felt and thought—to grasp American culture—as his sister, Jean Said Makdisi, recalls, in order to "get the facts of the Palestinian question through to the American public, and to create more sympathy for the Palestinians." In general, she continues, Edward Said believed that Arabs "were going about their efforts in all the wrong ways, in large part because of their misunderstanding of the nature of American society, politics, and policymaking." Said wanted to make the United States an object of Arab knowledge by employing "the highest possible academic standards" to inform an Arab response "based on the reality of the USA and not on mere emotional backlash" (2006).

For Edward Said, knowledge and power were always connected, but his commitment to academic integrity meant that the nature of that connection must be open to debate. Hence, he believed that the American studies classroom must allow "debate on the nature and institutions of the US" (ibid.). If the exile's experience of multiple cultures can "diminish orthodox judgment and elevate appreciative sympathy," then classrooms that create intercultural encounter may foster intercultural understanding that is counterhegemonic and promotes social justice. Edward Said had such an objective in mind when, along with Israeli pianist and conductor Daniel Barenboim, he promoted musical collaborations between young Israelis and Palestinians. Eventually, Said and

Barenboim published a record of their conversations on music, culture, and politics. Their conversations, like the experiences of the young Palestinian and Israeli musicians, were open-ended encounters. Music, culture, and politics were connected, Said suggested, in a way that, "I am happy to say, neither of us can fully state, but we ask our readers, our friends, to join us in trying to find out" (Barenboim and Said 2002).

We have no way of knowing how our students will make use of the intercultural understanding they may gain in our classrooms, but teaching American studies as an encounter that is constantly comparative, I suggest, offers the best hope of directly addressing the American question without allowing it to overwhelm the experience of thinking and learning.

Notes

This is a revised and updated version of a paper that appeared in *Journal of American Studies in Turkey* 24 (Fall 2007): 15–27.

1. The transnational turn is evident not only in books and articles too numerous to list, but also in the establishment of the International American Studies Association, the journals *Comparative American Studies* and *Review of International American Studies*, and transnational initiatives such as the 2004 American Studies Association Conference in Atlanta.

2. Only the biblical version of Hebrew is taught at Lebanese University.

3. Al-Quds University (Jerusalem, Palestine), the University of Jordan (Amman), the American University in Cairo (Egypt), the American University of Beirut (Lebanon), and the University of Tehran (Iran); several other programs, such as Georgetown's new School of Foreign Service in Doha (Qatar), have substantial American studies components. In addition, the center at the University of Bahrain opened in 1997.

4. These complaints tend to come from both poles of the political spectrum in Lebanon and the region. They usually arrive as e-mails, notes, phone calls, or requests for meetings. The substance is usually a charge of pro- or anti-Americanism. The complaints come from embassy staff, journalists, politicians, students, and interested individuals.

5. Universities include the American University of Beirut, the American University of Sharjah, the American University of Kuwait, the American University in Cairo, the American University in Dubai, the Lebanese American University, the American Intercontinental University (Dubai), the American University of Science and Technology (Lebanon), Lebanese American University, American Middle East University (Jordan), and Arab American University (Palestine/West Bank); in addition, the US State Department website lists twenty-one primary and secondary schools in the MENA with the word "American" in their name (http://www.state.gov/m/a/os/c1701.htm).

6. See Trafton 2004 and McAlister 2005, especially chapter 2, "The Middle East in African American Cultural Politics, 1955–1972" (84–124).

References

Abraham, Gary A. 1992. *Max Weber and the Jewish Question: A Study of the Social Outlook of His Sociology.* Urbana: University of Illinois Press.

American Australian Association. n.d. http://www.americanaustralian.org.

Anzaldúa, Gloria. [1987] 1999. *Borderlands/La Frontera.* 2nd ed. San Francisco: Aunt Lute Books.

Bacevich, Andrew. 2002. *American Empire: The Realities and Consequences of US Diplomacy.* Cambridge, MA: Harvard University Press.

Barenboim, Daniel, and Edward W. Said. 2002. *Parallels and Paradoxes: Explorations in Music and Society.* New York: Pantheon Books.

Baudrillard, Jean. 1988. *America.* London: Verso.

Berman, Russell. 1980. "Recycling the 'Jewish Question.'" Special issue 3, "Germans and Jews." *New German Critique* 21 (Autumn): 113–127.

Bernstein, Richard J. 1996. *Hannah Arendt and the Jewish Question.* Cambridge: Policy Press.

Bush, George W. 2002. State of the Union address, January 29.

DuBois, W. E. B. 1982. "Worlds of Color" (1924). In vol. 2 of *Writings of W. E. B. DuBois in Periodicals Edited by Others,* edited by Herbert Aptheker. Millwood, NY: Kraus-Thomson.

Fergusson, Niall. 2004. *Colossus: The Price of America's Empire.* New York: Penguin.

Final Report of the Steering Committee for the Center for American Studies and Research (CASAR). 2004. Faculty of Arts and Sciences, American University of Beirut, June.

Hardt, Michael, and Antonio Negri. 2000. *Empire.* Cambridge, MA: Harvard University Press.

———. 2004. *Multitude: War and Democracy in the Age of Empire.* New York: Penguin.

Kaplan, Amy. 2004. "Violent Belongings and the Question of Empire Today: Presidential Address to the American Studies Association, October 17, 2003." *American Quarterly* 56, no. 1: 1–18.

Lenz, Gunter. 1999. "Towards a Dialogics of International American Studies: Transnationality, Border Discourses, and Public Culture(s)." *Amerikastudien/American Studies* 44, no. 1: 5–23.

Makdisi, Jean Said. 2006. Personal communication, December 4.

Makdisi, Ussama. 2002. "'Anti-Americanism' in the Arab World: An Interpretation and a Brief History." *Journal of American History* 89, no. 1: 1–48.

Mann, William C. 2006. "Poll Finds War with Israel Hurt US Image in Lebanon." *Daily Star* (Beirut), November 15.

Marx, Karl. [1843] 1967. "On the Jewish Question." In *Writings of the Young Marx on Philosophy and Society,* edited and translated by Loyd David Easton and Kurt H. Guddat, 216–248. Garden City, NY: Doubleday.

McAlister, Melani. 2005. *Epic Encounters: Culture, Media and US Interests in the Middle East since 1945.* Berkeley: University of California Press.

Nahle, Randy. 2004. "AUB: A Bridge between East and West." Founders' Day 2004 prizewinning essay, December 6. http://staff.aub.edu.lb/~webinfo/highlights/2004/speeches/Founders_Nahle.pdf.

Pease, Donald, and Robyn Wiegman, eds. 2002. *The Futures of American Studies*. Durham, NC: Duke University Press.

PEW Global Attitudes Project. 2006. PEW Research Center, November 30. http://www.pewglobal.org.

"Prince Alwaleed Bin Talal Endows a New Center for American Studies and Research." 2003. *Main Gate* (Summer–Fall).

Radway, Janice. 1999. "What's in a Name? Presidential Address to the American Studies Association, 20 November 1998." *American Quarterly* 51, no. 1: 1–32.

Rice, Condoleezza. 2006. "Special Briefing on Travel to the Middle East and Europe." US Department of State, July 21. http://www.state.gov/secretary /rm/2006/69331.htm.

Rowe, John Carlos. 1998. "Post-nationalism, Globalism, and the New American Studies." *Cultural Critique* 40 (Fall): 11–28.

Said, Edward W. 1978. *Orientalism*. New York: Pantheon Books.

———. 1994. *Culture and Imperialism*. London: Vintage.

———. 1999. *Out of Place: A Memoir*. New York: Alfred A. Knopf.

Sartre, Jean-Paul. [1945] 1962. *Reflections on the Jewish Question*. New York: Grove Press.

"Sydney to Host US Studies Centre." 2006. University of Sydney, November 14. http://www.usyd.edu.au/news/84.html?newsstoryid=1448.

Trafton, Scott. 2004. *Egypt Land: Race and Nineteenth-Century American Egyptomania*. Durham, NC: Duke University Press.

Ungvári, Tamás. 2000. *The "Jewish Question" in Europe: The Case of Hungary*. East European Monographs, no. 556, Atlantic Studies on Society and Change, no. 99. Boulder, CO: Social Science Monographs.

"US Image Up Slightly, but Still Negative: American Character Gets Mixed Reviews." 2005. PEW Global Attitudes Projects, June 23. http:/pewglobal .org/reports/display.php?ReportID=247.

Yaffe, Martin D. 1997. *Shylock and the Jewish Question*. Baltimore: Johns Hopkins University Press.

CHAPTER 2

The Politics of American-Style Higher Education in the Middle East

NEEMA NOORI

Paradoxically, the decline of America's popularity in the Middle East has done nothing to diminish the regional appetite for institutions that bear the label "American." Since the US invasion of Iraq in 2003, the number of institutions serving up an American-style[1] curriculum has grown spectacularly and now includes the following: the American University of Kuwait, the American University of Sharjah, the American University of Qatar, Georgetown University in Qatar, George Mason University in Ras al-Khaimah, the American University of Dubai, and the soon-to-be-launched Abu Dhabi Branch of New York University (NYU). The robust growth of Western-style universities in the Gulf and the wider Middle East cannot be attributed to the calculated strategies of American foreign policy makers. Similarly, there's scant evidence to suggest that the largely elite population who sends their children to American-style universities views their proliferation as being politically motivated. The apolitical nature of these institutions is a taken-for-granted assumption that is rarely challenged. This chapter tests the validity of this assumption by examining the political implications of higher education American style in the Middle East by questioning the extent to which American-style institutions in the Middle East further US interests.

With the belief among some social scientists that the world has entered a phase of global politics in which the international order will be dominated by empires, scholarly work on the subject of empire has surged. Conventional treatises of empire have long highlighted the necessity of interlocutors, individuals capable of bridging the cultural, linguistic, and institutional gaps separating the imperial heartland from the periphery. Though there is an extensive literature on the relationship between state formation and education, comparatively little has been written about the relationship between empire and institutions of higher education: the institutions responsible for training cohorts of elites capable of mediating between imperial cores and peripheries.

Universities that claim to deliver on the promise of offering an American-style education are staffed by American instructors or instructors who are trained in the United States. Similarly, the textbooks are authored and published in the United States. The guiding principles of the institution, informing everything from admission requirements to the range of majors offered, are derived from an American model. Therefore, based on these attributes, it would be logical to conclude that these institutions advance American interests by encouraging students either indirectly or directly to see the world from an American point of view. However, by emulating an American style of education, these institutions set in motion countervailing forces that have the potential to undermine American interests in surprising ways. By encouraging classroom debate and critical thinking skills, American pedagogical philosophies are potentially counterhegemonic. The liberal arts dimension of an American curriculum, which exposes students to a diverse range of fields outside their major course of study, broadens their worldviews in an unpredictable and potentially subversive fashion.

I investigate these competing claims by interviewing a wide range of faculty members and students at American-style universities in the Middle East located primarily, but not exclusively, in the Persian Gulf region to determine the extent to which faculty members are conscious of the delicate role they play as de facto representatives of empire. I also rely on my own three years of experience as an assistant professor at an American university in the region, the American University of Sharjah. Though many of the emergent campuses have been heavily influenced by more established institutions in the region such as the American University of Cairo and the American University of Beirut, this project focuses on second-generation American universities in the region. Contemporary Western-style universities open their doors in a radically different international political order and therefore need to be distinguished from their predecessors, founded by missionaries a century ago.

Cultural Imperialism in Historical Perspective

In a recent article criticizing Azar Nafisi's *Reading Lolita in Tehran*,[2] Hamid Dabashi cites Thomas Babington Macaulay's infamous "Minute on Indian Education" speech of 1835, arguing that Nafisi's book was akin to the same imperialist project. Dabashi writes, "Azar Nafisi is the personification of that native informer and colonial agent, polishing her services for an American version of the very same project . . . by seeking to recycle a kaffeeklatsch version of English literature as the ideological foregrounding of American empire, *Reading Lolita in Tehran* is reminiscent of the most pestiferous colonial projects of the British in India."[3] In the infamous speech cited by Dabashi, Macaulay, a British colonial officer, derides the cumulative achievements of Middle Eastern and South Asian civilizations. Macaulay observes, "It is, I believe, no exaggeration to say, that all the historical information which has been collected from all the books written in the Sanskrit language is less valuable than what may be found in the most paltry abridgements used at preparatory schools in England. In every branch of physical or moral philosophy, the relative position of the two nations is nearly the same." Having asserted the intellectual and general cultural superiority of European civilization, he boasts that the English language will do for the subcontinent what Latin did for post-Renaissance Britain, which is to serve as a vessel for the transmission of knowledge and to act as a civilizing force. In the passage below, Macaulay highlights the role he envisions for the British-educated Indian elite:

> I feel with them, that it is impossible for us, with our limited means, to attempt to educate the body of the public. We must at present do our best to form a class who may be interpreters between us and the millions whom we govern; a class of persons, Indian in blood and colour, but English in taste, in opinions, in morals, and in intellect. To that class we may leave it to refine the vernacular dialects of the country, to enrich those dialects with terms of science borrowed from the Western nomenclature, and to render them by degrees fit vehicles for conveying knowledge to the great mass of the population.[4]

By targeting the elite, inculcating students with Western values, and offering English-only instruction, are Western-style universities guilty of cultural imperialism? Social scientists have long recognized that material power, a combination of military strength and economic dynamism, is on its own not enough to make others accept the legitimacy of a given world order. The leading country's ability to influence secondary powers is enhanced by getting other countries to internalize the norms and values of the leading power. When hegemonic powers succeed in making the elite in secondary states accept the existing institutional framework, as laid out by the hegemon, the costs of managing the system or governing the empire decline precipitously. "The ability to generate shared beliefs in the acceptability of legitimacy of a particular international order—that is, the ability to forge a consensus among national elites on the normative underpinnings of order—is an important if elusive dimension of hegemonic power."[5]

In a comparison of British colonial interventions in Egypt and India, Ikenberry attributes Britain's largely peaceful and long-lasting administration of India to its success in socializing the elite to accept British values. In colonial India the system of higher education was modeled after the British system. Universities established in Calcutta, Bombay, and Madras all "adopted London's examination procedures." In Egypt, on the other hand, the British relied on coercion and placed less emphasis on educational reform to socialize a loyal cadre of elites to help them "govern." Curiously, to counter the spread of nationalism, British officials abandoned the strategies that had worked so well on the subcontinent and "opposed the expansion of the university system."[6] Absent any institutional mechanism to train and socialize the Egyptian elite, the British were reliant on material force to maintain control. Lacking a reliable cadre of elites to administer the territory, the British experience in Egypt was both shorter and costlier. To illustrate this point, Ikenberry observes that between 1896 and 1906, the number of British officials serving in Egypt more than doubled, from 286 to 662. In addition to these officials, the British were forced to hire 50,000 village-level informants for surveillance purposes, to pass on information to the colonial administration.

> The imposition of foreign rule unadorned by a corpus of beliefs and norms led to a period of occupation that was both difficult and relatively short-lived. Britain's experience of formal empire in India, though it also ended in acquiescence to nationalism, was far more durable and left a deeper impression on Indian society. The distinguishing feature of British hegemony in India was that Britain succeeded in building and socializing a new political elite, allowing it to penetrate and reshape Indian political culture.[7]

Education and the exercise of power have always gone hand in hand. History textbooks, for example, often provoke contentious debates over their telling of sensitive events. When Taliban fighters in Afghanistan target state schools, they do so principally because these schools are agents of the state, an important component of Kabul's efforts to centralize state power. For the West, on the other hand, because private seminaries in Pakistan and Afghanistan stand accused of producing radical militants, they are thought to be as much of a threat to building a stable political order as are the poppy fields that fuel the drug trade and provide the capital for Taliban arms expenditures. Primary and secondary public school teachers are indeed agents of the state tasked with the important duty of nurturing devotion and a strong sense of responsibility on the part of the citizenry. Hence, it is not at all surprising that so much of the United States' reconstruction aid in both Afghanistan and Iraq is earmarked toward rehabilitating the educational sector. For example, the Middle East Partnership Initiative, a US government–sponsored aid program whose aim is to promote political liberalization in the Middle East initially, targeted three issue areas for reform: education, women's empowerment, and entrepreneurialism.[8] Not surprisingly, most of the grant money allocated for women's empowerment and entrepreneurialism ends up funding initiatives that take the form of instructional workshops held locally or in the United States.

Degrees of Imperialism

It is undeniably accurate to assert that exporting the American model of education is a form of cultural imperialism. There are elements of the model such as the language of instruction, the textbooks used, and the curriculum that can be accused of having the sort of pernicious effect underlined by Hamid Dabashi in his critique of *Reading Lolita in Tehran*. However, in my interviews with administrators, instructors from a variety of disciplines, and students, it became clear that when the model is not fully exported, it may, in the words of one of my informants, contain the worst elements of the Western system and the worst elements of the local system. When, for example, the exported model is deprived of a robust liberal arts program and when the program is conceived of in a purely instrumental fashion, students are not equipped with the tools that allow them to challenge prevailing orthodoxies or assumed wisdom. Many of the institutions that have recently emerged offer stripped-down versions of the American model that lack general education requirements. Public perceptions that the American model offers students a practical, nontheoretical hands-on approach to education are partly responsible, as is the prevailing trend in American universities, which sees a diminution of the centrality of liberal arts in higher education.

Accreditation boards similarly play a definitive role in regulating and shaping educational practices. The process of seeking accreditation arguably adds an additional mechanism for the West to influence the curriculum of Western-style universities in the region. It would be logical to assume that foreign accreditation bodies have the potential to act as a particularly invasive force. On the surface, the necessity of meeting a set of standards established by a foreign body appears very much like the British effort to reform Indian educational practices by establishing colonial universities. Interestingly, American accreditation boards demand that universities have a student governance program in place as a prerequisite for accreditation. Having an active and engaged student body is as important as having a strong liberal arts core in protecting academic freedom on the campus and determining the political autonomy of the institution. These boards also stipulate that universities have mechanisms in place allowing for faculty to participate in the governance of the institution.

Accreditation boards, to the extent that they concern themselves with these elements of the certification process, enhance the institutional features that are most likely to promote freedom and institutional autonomy. Far from suggesting that the intervention of foreign accreditation boards stifles local autonomy or that they standardize or homogenize education offerings in ways that contribute to American hegemony, my research suggests quite the opposite. The universities with accreditation are in fact the ones in which instructors report higher levels of academic freedom. Though they are often depicted as a source of unwelcome intervention by administrators and faculty members who loathe the additional work, accreditation does provide some defense of academic freedom. The desire to maintain accreditation does make it harder for administrators to fire instructors for what they say in the classroom.

Defining the Model of American Education

The globalization of the American model of higher education inevitably gives rise to an attempt to define it. What is the American model of higher education? Is it distinguishable from the British or the Canadian model? And are any of its core attributes muddled or lost in the process of transferring a set of institutions and practices that were developed in a cultural and political environment very different from that of the Middle East? Clearly, regional understandings of the model, viewed from a distance, are just as important as American perceptions of what the American model of higher education entails. It is also important to recognize that the core institutional features of the model are not fixed. Therefore, local understandings of the model are determined by distant perceptions and real-time changes in American academia. For example, American universities in the United States increasingly emphasize the importance of broader civic engagement or public service in their curricula. And, as will become clearer later in this chapter, American-trained instructors in the region are pushing local institutions to adopt these changes.

The structure of the curriculum is one characteristic that makes the institution decidedly American. Students at American-style universities are required to meet general education requirements, meaning that students in the humanities are given the opportunity to take classes in math, physics, and biology, while engineering students have to take courses in history, literature, and sociology. General education requirements in the humanities and social sciences are the courses whose crucial task is to impart critical and analytical thinking skills. The pedagogical style is similarly distinctive. Professors trained in and working at American-style universities are expected to employ collaborative teaching methods. Rather than lecture exclusively, they are expected to engage students in discussion through a pedagogical style referred to as student-centered learning. Increasingly, an American education emphasizes engagement with the community through service learning or other forms of volunteerism. Student life is an exceptionally important ingredient on the typical American campus. Associational life is composed of a rich mix of academic clubs, political organizations, and social outlets. More important, there is a commonly held view that students should have a voice in how the university is run. The conventional mechanism that makes this possible is the student council or the student government, with elections held on a yearly basis to fill the various posts that constitute such student governments.

What do American universities look like once they are exported to the Middle East? What practical changes do American universities in the Gulf face when they attempt to emulate these characteristics? In my conversations with students, faculty members, and administrators in the

Gulf and elsewhere in the Middle East, I received unexpected answers to this question. And in an age characterized by America's cultural, political, and economic dominance, is one making a political statement by enrolling at an "American university"? Western-style universities typically partner with a more established university in the West. The partnership provides a convenient transmission belt for the transfer of admission requirements, credit hours, majors, policies, and procedures from the more established university to the emergent institution. The structure of the curriculum retains the liberal arts requirements typical of most American institutions. Since the language of instruction is English, most Western universities must, out of necessity, develop robust English-language instruction programs for nonnative English speakers. This initial, often yearlong introduction to the university serves two purposes: first, it equips students with the skills to take courses at the university; second, it socializes students, helping prepare them for this new experience where for the first time students are in a coeducational environment.

Student life on campus is in the words of one informant "carefully choreographed." At al-Akhawayn University in Morocco the Student Affairs Office, the department in charge of managing student activities, is the second most important administrative division within the university. At AUS the Student Affairs Office is one of only two administrative divisions within the university to be staffed by Emirati citizens. And though it is not the second most important administrative division on campus, it wields almost exclusive authority over all matters that pertain to student life. This includes the formation of student clubs. At AUS the student organizations that receive the bulk of funding are those that are organized according to nationality. Students who deviate from the script and attempt to form interest-based clubs are often turned away. Once a year AUS hosts what is known as Global Day, a two-day festival in which each of the university's nationality-based clubs is given money to prepare a stall showcasing important elements of each country's national culture. The pavilion designs are outsourced and built over a ten-day period leading up to Global Day. The raucous two-day event includes dance performances that are held in the university's main auditorium. Over the course of the event, the various pavilions engage in what can best be described as a friendly competition to see whose pavilion can draw the bigger crowd or to see whose music speakers can generate the loudest sound. One of my faculty informants used the occasion to examine whether Global Day in some fashion represented a microcosm of social relations in the United Arab Emirates (UAE). She challenged her students to make sense of Global Day by asking the following questions: "What's the purpose, multiculturalism or pluralism? Is it designed to promote a collective identity? Or is it designed to promote the fragmentation of identity? What does Global Day say about the treatment of culture in the UAE?" The top-down administrative planning of student associational life on campus does mirror larger trends and patterns in UAE society. Though tolerant of the cultural practices of other nationalities, the UAE places limits on some forms of social interaction and has increasingly made it more difficult for residents to gain citizenship. For example, Emirati women who marry foreign men risk not being able to pass citizenship rights to their children. They are also deprived of many of the financial perks that are ordinarily given to newlyweds.

When universities open in the Middle East, there is a decidedly political and normative role to be played by exposure to Western higher education. To illustrate this point, many faculty members assume that they have a personal responsibility to introduce students to American culture. One informant pointed out that we shouldn't forget that this is "the *American* University of Sharjah," with emphasis on the word "American." However, the limit of what is considered to be the appropriate form of politics is reached quite quickly, and the domain of the permissible is under constant negotiation. Most students are guarded to begin with when it comes to organized political activity on campus. For students transferring from AUC or AUB, the atmosphere is repressive by comparison. For example, in the fall of 2007 after the controversial Danish cartoons had been printed, a group of students went to the Student Affairs Office for permission to organize a protest meeting on campus. Employees provided the students with several forms that had to be filled out for approval. Though not formally discouraged from pursuing collective action, the students became increasingly cautious about going forward with their plans and eventually backed out. Another student informant confirmed that the need to obtain official permission deters student political activism along with many other forms of student engagement.

More serious and troubling is the commonly held perception that very little is possible. Many students and faculty members assume that the campus is a no-politics zone or an arena where the discussion of politics should be kept to a minimum, and it should never under any circumstances be a place to engage in a critique of local politics. One informant at Zayed University in Abu Dhabi freely criticizes social and cultural trends in Dubai but feels uncomfortable critiquing the same phenomena as they apply to Abu Dhabi. Other faculty members on occasions that demand discussion of "sensitive" issues with local relevance, such as labor rights, locate analogues in other countries. For example, to stir debate on migrant labor rights, an AUS professor might point out failures of the American system to protect the rights of migrant workers.

Academic Freedom

Do administrators signal or more overtly communicate what can and cannot be said in the classroom? Though neither students nor faculty members are ever directly informed about the need for discretion in discussing matters of political sensitivity at AUS, most members of the university community are guarded about what they openly discuss. For faculty, the lack of tenure and the short-term structure of contracts engender some level of insecurity. At AUS and Zayed University new faculty hires are initially presented one- and two-year contracts, with the understanding that they will almost automatically be extended unless serious "mistakes" are made. At al-Akhawayn University in Morocco, faculty members are hired on the basis of a one- or two-year contract. According to one informant, "Tenure is nonexistent, and because one is consistently up for review, faculty are easily pushed around because the turnover rate is so very high. Faculty are seen as replaceable cogs." The scarcity of tenure at American-style universities in the region is a very real threat to academic freedom. At AUS, for example, in lieu of tenure assistant professors are granted what is called a rolling contract, which means that after every four years, their performance is reviewed. If the review committee's evaluation is positive, their contract is renewed for an additional four years. More serious in the UAE and elsewhere is the ever-present knowledge that university instructors are from time to time fired for what they say in the classroom. Also, since most students are nonnative English-language speakers, one is always afraid that what is communicated in the classroom may be misinterpreted. However, as was indicated earlier, accreditation provides a defense of academic freedom by erecting a bulwark against the arbitrary termination of faculty contracts.

For universities that have entered the competitive field of higher education in the Gulf to make a profit, the pressure to maintain high enrollments promotes censoring of one sort or another. Even at supposedly nonprofit institutions such as al-Akhawayn and AUS, the status of the university is, perhaps unfairly, contested by students and faculty who cynically question high tuition rates and cost-cutting measures undertaken by the university because they assume that the university is secretly a moneymaking enterprise. According to an informant at al-Akhawayn University, self-sufficiency becomes a euphemism for seeking profitability. All of this serves to diminish the already low status of the liberal arts components of the university.

For students, two factors impede academic freedom. First, for noncitizens, the majority in many of the Western universities in the Gulf, the knowledge that one is an unprotected foreign resident acts as a strong deterrent in preventing students from speaking freely in the classroom. Whether out of respect for local citizens or out of fear, international students censor their comments in the classroom. One of my student informants claimed to be very conscious of who was in the classroom. To illustrate this point, one student made the following observation, in reference to having Emirati citizens in the classroom: "It's easier to speak freely when there are no locals." Emirati citizens, on the other hand, often censor or moderate their public stances on contentious issues when they constitute the minority in a classroom. It is a commonly observable phenomenon in group dynamics for a group in the minority to adopt a defensive or conservative stance. Also, not surprisingly, both faculty and students are likely to become more tight-lipped in the presence of members of the royal family. It is important to point out, however, that having someone from a prominent family who willingly and openly engages in a critique can encourage open discourse in the classroom. Both because of the elite makeup of the student body and because of the large number of royal family members in circulation throughout the Gulf, it is not at all unusual to have a handful in one classroom.

The Politics of Choice

Why do students from the Middle East choose to attend American-style universities? In a world in which American president George Bush famously declared, "You are either with us or against us," is the decision to attend an American-style university tantamount to picking sides in the war against terror? Most non–Gulf Cooperation Council (GCC) students select AUS because their parents are stationed in the UAE and it is the most highly regarded institution in the Gulf. They apply to AUS because of the institution's reputation and because acquiring a degree from an accredited English-language university enhances one's job-search prospects.

Many families opt to send their students to American-style universities for the simple reason that their children can acquire a Western education without being in the West and without being exposed to Western values. Though coeducational, the university has rules in place that set limits on interaction between the sexes. Female guards ensure that women do not wear "suggestive" clothing and that the sexes do not touch one another. Though not strictly enforced, dress codes must be observed by both faculty and students. For example, male faculty members are discouraged from wearing shorts on campus.

Curiously, for many students, the single most important barrier to attending AUS is its coed status. To illustrate this point, one student laughingly observed that many more conservative members of her family disapproved of her attending that "American university." "Due to its coed status, they see us as brainwashed," she continued. The university is known more for its coed status than its Americanness. One faculty informant at AUS remembers a conversation with a student's family in which the father was asked why he consented to having his daughter sent to AUS. He replied that Sheikh Sultan's stamp of approval removed any doubts he may have had. It is quite possible that for many GCC students, the university's affiliation with Sharjah's ruler makes the institution an acceptable place.

The Absence of the Local

Aside from the institution's diversity, one unusual characteristic of AUS, Zayed University, and many other American-style universities in the Gulf is the dearth of GCC citizens. None of the faculty members at AUS are native Emiratis. In fact, the few Emiratis employed at AUS are concentrated within two administrative posts: Public Affairs and Student Affairs. The Public Affairs division is responsible for visa applications and all other matters that pertain to the university's relationship to the UAE government. The largest proportion of the faculty, at 42 percent, is from the United States, while the second-largest group is from Canada, at 14 percent. The composition of the student body is as follows: 19 percent are from the UAE, 12 percent from Jordan, 9 percent from Palestine, 7 percent from Pakistan, and 5 percent each from Iran, Saudi Arabia, and Egypt. In fact, most institutions of higher education in the GCC share similar patterns. Having high numbers of nonnative faculty members adds to the institution's disengagement from the community. At informal faculty gatherings, one of the more common topics of conversation involves summer travel plans. And indeed during the summer, most GCC universities are deserted. The lack of rootedness is primarily a product of the Gulf's political economy, one in which expats make up a large proportion of the general population.

Gated enclosures contribute to the extraterritorial feel of second-generation American-style universities in the Middle East. Due to security reasons, the elite makeup of the student body, and its coed status, these institutions are under heavy security and are often built apart and sequestered from the wider urban community. Paradoxically, despite tenuous relations with the community, it's quite possible that American-style universities do more to engage local society than more established government-affiliated universities in the GCC. Given the elevated importance of service learning in American higher education, faculty trained in the United States increasingly incorporate service-based learning projects into their curricula. For example, at AUS professors organize clean-up crews of local beaches, and the Student Affairs Office provides support for children's hospitals and sponsors blood drives. According to a faculty informant at Zayed University, given the small size of the local population, when she proposed developing a community outreach program for her students, the question that naturally arose was "What community? Are you going to visit a senior seminar for Emiratis, or are you going to visit a labor camp for migrant workers?" The latter of course would be off-limits because of its political sensitivity. Her strategy was to begin working with Emirati citizens; she then hoped to branch out to other communities over time.

The Emirati American founder of a nongovernmental women's shelter in Dubai, Sharla Musabih, came to give a presentation to discuss the challenges of operating an independent women's shelter in the UAE. Having been vilified in the press, she was quite surprised to have been invited to a local university.[9] In her words, national universities were for the longest time completely disengaged from the community and would never have invited her to discuss such a sensitive set of issues. In truth, the students who had proposed the idea of inviting her were initially reluctant. In the end, they decided to invite her without seeking official permission from the administration. It is quite surprising then that universities that lack strong ties to the community may in reality be more engaged in community affairs than government-affiliated universities that have been around for a much longer period of time.

Language

In an article discussing the increasing marginalization of Western-educated Arab liberals, Jon Alterman contends that what was once a class of legitimate and trusted interlocutors is now seen as sellouts. "Elites often serve as a lubricant between foreign and domestic systems, using commonalities in travel, education, and language to bridge national divisions." He goes on to say:

> Many heirs to the liberal elite tradition in the Arab world live and work in Washington, DC. They often fill posts in the World Bank and other international institutions, work for the US government, or labor in academia. They despair of the misdirection of the Arab world, and they speak movingly of the need for change. We notice their accents when they speak English, and we hail them as authentic voices for change in the Middle East. But what Washington doesn't hear is that many of these people have accents when they speak Arabic as well. Their speech marks them as Arabs who have left, who have fundamentally compromised or been compromised. One colleague used the evocative phrase "native aliens" to describe them; their most valuable commodity is that they simultaneously hold Western ideas and non-Western passports.[10]

One of the more destructive consequences of nineteenth- and twentieth-century British imperialism was its effect on native languages. This is indeed one of the concerns most shared by those I interviewed. One faculty informant stated the problem in succinct terms: "Language is a major issue for me. By depriving students of an academic command of their mother tongue, we are doing something very brutal. How can they reclaim their heritage? We are denying them a form of cultural competence. How can one expect to have a professional command of English when one lacks a strong command of Arabic? They are in some cases nonlingual."

Most students never have the opportunity to develop professional fluency in their native language. In fact, because of minimal general education requirements, native Arabic speakers rarely develop professional fluency in English. Those who major in the humanities or the social sciences take more writing-intensive courses and therefore have a better chance of becoming highly competent users of the English language. Hence, graduates of American-style universities may find that they are best suited for work in the West or in Western companies but that they lack the "cultural competence" to work in domestically rooted places of employment. This may be less of a problem in a globalized world, but it does present challenges for students who want to work in fields where professional fluency in Arabic is expected. For example, in my first year at AUS, in my capacity as internship coordinator, I assigned two Emirati students to an internship at the UAE Ministry of Foreign Affairs in Abu Dhabi. The students, both of whom were strong and hardworking with an excellent command of English, had a miserable time. They were criticized for lacking an adequate knowledge of Arabic. Their supervisor very bluntly made it clear that they had no future at the ministry. Though Alterman questions the ability of local elites to effectively advocate for change in a political environment where Westernized elites lack legitimacy, I worry that having been deprived of the opportunity to develop professional fluency in Arabic, they may have trouble thriving locally.

Conclusion

Over the past decade, the US government has been strangely ambivalent toward the expansion of "American universities" overseas. In August 2007 the House Committee on Science and Technology held a series of hearings on this subject. "Lawmakers questioned whether university ventures, all of which are indirectly or directly subsidized by taxpayers, might be undermining America's economic competitiveness by helping other countries develop scientific and technological work forces."[11] More recently, a *New York* magazine article pejoratively titled "The Emir of NYU," takes NYU to task for opening a branch campus in Abu Dhabi. The article criticizes NYU for putting financial considerations ahead of maintaining the university's reputation. A *New York Times* article raises a similar set of concerns, asking the following questions: "Will the programs reflect American values and culture, or the host country's? Will American taxpayers end up footing part of the bill for overseas students? What happens if relations between the United

States and the host country deteriorate? And will foreign branches that spread American know-how hurt American competitiveness?" The same article quotes a California lawmaker, Dana Rohrabacher. "I'm someone who believes that Americans should watch out for Americans first," he said. "It's one thing for universities here to send professors overseas and do exchange programs, which do make sense, but it's another thing to have us running educational programs overseas."[12] Curiously, very little of this debate examines the political ramifications of exporting the American model of education. More important, the defensive posture adopted by these pieces overlooks the vast potential gains that may accrue from the proliferation of American universities overseas and the international adoption of the American model of higher education.

It is naive to assume that the expansion of the American universities in the Middle East will not have political consequences. Even the minimalist branch institutions with minuscule student populations, lacking in general education requirements, fulfill a political function. Universities without robust liberal arts programs, which constitute the majority, lack the capacity to engender the analytical tools that enable students to question authority and to think critically about the practical education that they receive. Ironically, to the extent that these institutions offer a technical education devoid of general education requirements, they may even limit the capacity of "American" universities to realize their potential for imperial gains. How can a university socialize a new generation of elites when the candidates recruited for elite training are not taking courses that expose them to Western values? And, it is important to remember, as Ikenberry points out, that "the surge of anti-imperialism that eventually led to the demise of the British empire, for example, was rooted in the same liberal notions of justice and representative government that initially served to facilitate British rule."[13]

Notes

1. The phrase "American-style university" was first used in a report prepared by Shafeeq Ghabra and Margreet Arnold for the Washington Institute for Near East Policy. They use the label "American-style" to refer to American, Australian, British, and Canadian universities that have recently opened their doors in the Middle East, all of which, they argue, are distinguished by their student-centered focus, having English-speaking faculty trained in the West, and instruction promoting critical thinking and analysis. *Policy Focus* 71 (June 2007): 1.

2. Azar Nafisi, *Reading Lolita in Tehran* (New York: Random House, 2003).

3. Hamid Dabashi, "Native Informers and the Making of the American Empire," *al-Ahram Weekly*, 797, 1–7 June 2006.

4. Thomas Babington Macaulay, "Minute 2 February 1835 on Indian Education," in *Macaulay, Prose and Poetry*, edited by G. M. Young (Cambridge, MA: Harvard University Press, 1957), 721–724, 729, http://www.fordham.edu/halsall/mod/1833macaulay-india.html.

5. G. John Ikenberry and Charles A. Kupchan, "Socialization and Hegemonic Power," *International Organization* 44, no. 3 (1990): 289.

6. Ibid., 309, 312.

7. Ibid., 313.

8. For more on this, see Zakia Salime, "Women, Freedom, and Democracy in the 'Broader Middle East': The Civil Society Mandate" (paper presented at the SSRC Conference Asian Connections, February 21–24, 2007).

9. The local press has repeatedly accused her of selling victims' stories to foreign journalists. She has even been accused of confiscating and selling for adoption babies born at the shelter.

10. Jon B. Alterman, "The False Promise of Arab Liberals," *Policy Review* 125 (June–July 2004): 77–85.

11. *Diverse Issues in Higher Education* (June 1, 2006).

12. Henry Jameson, "The Emir of NYU," *New York*, April 13, 2008; Tamar Lewin, "Universities Rush to Set Up Outposts Abroad," *New York Times*, February 10, 2008.

13. Ikenberry and Kupchan, "Socialization and Hegemonic Power," 294.

PART II

CONTEXTS AND IMPLICATIONS

CHAPTER 3

The American Liberal Education System and Its Development at the American University of Beirut

BETTY S. ANDERSON

The 1897–1898 course catalog for the Syrian Protestant College (SPC) in Lebanon states that "the Collegiate Department gives a liberal education in language and literature, science, history, and philosophy, leading to the degree of Bachelor of Arts." Despite implying that an alteration in the educational program had occurred, with this first mention of the term "liberal education," no curricular changes actually took place in that year, or for years thereafter, for that matter. Students continued to complete a prescribed curriculum, locked in place since at least 1880. As an example, in this 1897–1898 academic year, the school required of all senior students in the Collegiate Department that they take classes in Arabic, French, English literature (reading *Hamlet* and *Paradise Lost*), logic, economics, history (covering English constitutional history and the history of philosophy), psychology, astronomy, botany, geology, and an informal course on the Bible, conducted by the president.[1] President Daniel Bliss also taught the capstone moral philosophy course, using Mark Hopkins's work *The Law of Love and Love as a Law: Moral Science, Theoretical and Practical.* Only in 1906 did the faculty begin to offer course electives, and even then their numbers did not grow substantially until after 1920, when the board of trustees voted to rename the school the American University of Beirut.

In the 1950–1951 academic year, AUB further codified its curricular goals when it chose the Columbia University Core Curriculum as the program all students needed to complete before entering into courses focused on their more specialized majors. Begun in 1919 at Columbia, the new freshman Contemporary Civilization class rejected both the previous American focus on education based on the Greek and Latin classics and the more recent call for teaching solely in professional and preprofessional fields. Instead, as history professor Harry J. Carman declared, "In introducing the general survey course, Columbia has operated on the assumption that it is not the fundamental business of the College to turn out specialists in a narrow field, and that an individual is, after all, not well educated unless he or she has at least some conception of the broad field of intellectual endeavor."[2] The class work for the course used the great books of Western civilization as a means for laying out why that civilization had been so successful by the twentieth century. Over the following decades, course requirements expanded to include literature humanities, music humanities, and art humanities, all with the pronounced goal of giving students a broad base of knowledge in the humanities and social sciences and teaching them the methods by which to critically analyze any type of data presented to them. As a Harvard report of 1946, *General Education in a Free Society*, summarized, the primary goal of this type of education was to teach students how to think: "By *effective thinking* we mean, in the first place, logical thinking: the ability to draw sound conclusions from premises."[3] After World War I, American universities, including SPC/AUB, typically required of all students that they complete a similar type of core curriculum in their first years of study, while finishing a specific major in the last two.

Arising as a result of dramatic change in American society in the late nineteenth and early twentieth centuries, this new liberal education system has always amounted to more than just a curriculum program. Over time, university leaders came to see their chief aims as service, with students using their educational experience to aid the nation; research, with freedom of inquiry an ongoing pursuit of knowledge; and culture, with the making of character among the students.[4] AUB president Stephen Penrose wrote in 1950, the year the school acquired the Columbia Core Curriculum, "This education is essentially a training in true scholarship, a training which inspires men to think freely, to value truth in all phases of human experience, and to live by principle rather than by expediency."[5] Liberal education, in essence, is designed to teach students how to think, not how to absorb a prescribed canon of knowledge. Laboratories, electives, and seminar classes serve as the spaces where students learn the tools needed to critically analyze the data transmitted to them; only by learning how to do so, in an atmosphere unencumbered by ideological or religious constraints, can students use their educational experiences in productive means after graduation. A case study of the SPC/AUB illustrates how this American educational system could be successfully exported to the Middle East, by hewing to the foundations of the program but also by adapting to specific regional demands.

Liberal Education in America

The whole concept of teaching at American universities prior to the Civil War (1861–1865) had been premised on the view that knowledge was finite; organic connections holistically bound religion, science, the humanities, morality, and ethics in a contained box of knowledge, validated by Protestant denominational precepts. Leaders of old-line American universities—the Harvards, Yales, and Princetons—entered into the mid-nineteenth century with their belief in this so-called unity of truth largely intact. Students needed to show proficiency in Greek and Latin in order to be admitted and, once at school, spent most of their time reciting classical works of literature. Students had to abide by myriad rules governing their behavior, following a program of in loco parentis that severely curtailed their ability to initiate independent work and action. Professors and students sought to transmit and learn a knowledge that had already been codified and categorized, with no thought that their educational structures should lead to the production of new pieces of knowledge or that university work should train students for specific careers. Innovation happened outside university walls, not as a process generated by the educational experience taking place within them. Knowledge gatekeepers determined which new ideas and innovations fitted within the body of knowledge acceptable to religious precepts and the established canons of science and literature.

With the end of the Civil War and the rapid onslaught of industrialization, urbanization, and Western expansion, university leaders faced an acute crisis because they no longer provided the services their constituents demanded. When the US Congress passed the Morrill Land Grant Act of 1862, it established state-run public universities west of the Mississippi River, all of which focused first and foremost on running programs for teaching the technical skills the industrial economy craved. The American Protestant universities that had held educational monopolies for centuries now faced competition as they came to the realization that they were unprepared for the changing conditions. In this atmosphere, university leaders had to accept the fact that American society now influenced what and how they taught. On a procedural level, universities opened new schools of medicine, engineering, and commerce, tacitly accepting the fact that they could no longer teach esoteric topics disconnected from the real world existing outside their walls. The traditional informal networks for skills training, such as apprenticeships and guilds, could no longer train students in the skills needed for the industrial and national economy; only a modern university could do so. If the older American universities did not step into the breach, they would lose their leadership role to newer state-run institutions.

At the same time, university leaders faced conflicts over their reliance on the old unity of truth, given the plethora of new scientific innovations that came to light in the second half of the nineteenth century. Charles Darwin's work on evolution alone helped invalidate key elements making up the university liturgy until that point. His findings, along with new scientific research being produced all over the world, overturned established truths on an almost daily basis. No longer could university leaders legitimately tell students that they presented the only viable knowledge base; no longer could the knowledge gatekeepers keep up with the new research being produced all around them. With their unity of truth destroyed, professors and scholars had to find a new rationale for the existence of their universities. Their solution was to accept that "truth" no longer existed in a small, contained holistic box. Instead, university leaders sought to teach their students successful methods of critical analysis so that they could produce new knowledge for themselves. The fuel running this machine was freedom of inquiry, allowing professors and students an unfettered space in which to analyze information. Jon Roberts and James Turner report that "the recognition that knowledge itself was fallible and progressive cast doubt on the legitimacy of venerable doctrines" and "as higher education increasingly became identified with expanding the boundaries of verifiable knowledge, such knowledge became valorized in classrooms, seminar rooms, laboratories, and academic discourse." They explain further, "Colleges and universities became identified as institutions imbued with the faith that the only knowledge really worth having is obtainable through rational, 'scientific' inquiry." Losing out in this equation was the unity of truth, as "truth claims based on alternative epistemologies—tradition, divine inspiration, and subjective forms of religious experience—increasingly lost credibility within the academy." In this educational program, every intellectual endeavor, from history to sociology to chemistry, came under new analytical scrutiny. To teach the tools of critical inquiry, William Rainey Harper, the first president of the University of Chicago (1892–1929), eloquently identified the "birth-marks of a university" in his era as "self-government, freedom from ecclesiastical control, and the right of free utterance."[6]

In terms of the first and third elements of Harper's educational coda, Harvard University stood in the vanguard of the reform movement in the late nineteenth century, led by President Charles Eliot (1869–1909). He pioneered the elective system and abolished most elements of the in loco parentis program previously dominating student lives; he instituted a new emphasis on freedom of inquiry in his classrooms. At the opening of the American Museum of National History in 1878, Eliot identified what he felt were the most important characteristics of the human mind; namely, he imagined

> a searching, open, humble mind that, knowing that it cannot attain unto all truth, or even to much new truth, is yet patiently and enthusiastically devoted to the pursuit of such little new truth as is within its grasp, having no other end than to learn, prizing above all things accuracy, thoroughness, and candor in research, proud and happy not in its own single strength but in the might of that host of students whose past conquest made up the wondrous sum of present knowledge, whose sure future triumphed each humblest worker in imagination shares.[7]

As David Hollinger says of Eliot's speech, "The cultural hero Eliot outlined at the consecration of the American Museum of Natural History was not a possessor and user of knowledge; he was a searcher. This figure's virtue derived not so much from the goodness of knowledge as from the ethos of inquiry itself."[8] For a student to become a lifelong searcher for knowledge, Eliot said that "he has a right in these days to be free from the imposition of opinions, whether attempted by elders or associates, by one individual or a multitude. He has also a right to be free from all inducements to cant, hypocrisy, or conformity."[9] Eliot and his colleagues responded to all of these pressures by establishing laboratories so their professors and students could produce knowledge, particularly in practical sciences such as engineering and medicine. They gradually moved from a system of recitation of known facts to a seminar structure that encouraged differing opinions and new theoretical formulations. They broke up the "Collegiate Departments" into history, chemistry, and philosophy departments, acknowledging the fragmentation of knowledge and the differing skills required to analyze each discipline.

The second hallmark of William Harper's "birth-marks" of the American university was "freedom from ecclesiastical control"; in practice, this act finally and fatally destroyed the unity of truth. Prior to the American Civil War, Protestant denominational leaders and ministers served as leaders and professors at the oldest universities; the unity of truth demanded that all knowledge be verified by Protestant precepts. By the late nineteenth century, American university leaders, more frequently hailing from outside the clerical orders, sought to establish a new concept of freedom of inquiry where no religious constraints would be placed upon scholarship. In removing clerical supervision, however, these leaders did not want to secularize the educational experience. They still found validity in the moral maxims imparted by religion; these university leaders had traditionally seen themselves building good character among their students based on these tenets. By the late nineteenth century, university leaders sought to meld together the principles laid out by Protestantism with the new characteristics applying to liberal education. They believed that the character that would understand the limitations placed upon him by freedom of inquiry would be able to use these same skills and good sense in positions after graduation. For Charles Eliot, having the freedom to make mistakes improved a student's character, for "these are the habits that prove trustworthy in adult life. As in the outer world, so in the comparatively sheltered college world, freedom is dangerous for the infirm of purpose, and destructive for the vicious; but it is the only atmosphere in which the well-disposed and resolute can develop their strength."[10] That kind of person would be Eliot's lifelong searcher and a good future citizen of the nation.

As a result of this belief, the definition of the liberal education system being crafted in the late nineteenth century equated education not just with individual success but with success more broadly for the nation at large. When Woodrow Wilson served as president of Princeton University (1902–1910), he expressed the opinion that "the most pleasant thing to me about university life is that men are licked into something like the same shape in respect of the principles with which they go out into the world; the ideals of conduct, the ideal of truthful comradeship, the ideals of loyalty, the ideals of co-operation, the sense of *esprit de corps*, the feeling that they are men of a common country and put into it for a common service."[11] If character meant good citizenship and respect for others, then the universities had to devise ways that taught their students to acquire just such a character. To resolve this dilemma, university leaders did not throw out Protestantism along with its clerical leaders; instead, they sought the means to guide the students in their work without hampering the freedom of inquiry so essential to the whole liberal education project.

Their solution was to transform denominational Protestantism into a broad-based liberal Protestantism that emphasized the shared characteristics of all religious faiths and the best means for acquiring a moral and successful character. As George Marsden reports of American Protestant universities in the twentieth century, "By the early decades of the century, exclusivist elements of the heritage had been abandoned, and Christianity was defined more or less as a moral outlook. It promoted good character and democratic principles, aspects of the old Whig ideals that were potentially palatable to all Americans." Morality and ethics no longer stemmed solely from religious precepts, but could be acquired and learned from science, from practical experience in life, and from the intellectual interaction provided by liberal education. As Julie Reuben reports, "The emphasis on conduct over creed submerged religion into daily activity," and the university chapel services grew shorter and emphasized songs and simple prayers rather than the Protestant liturgy. In the new religious atmosphere spreading on university campuses, "Christianity, as presented in university chapels, became little more than appeals to clean living and good citizenship." Marsden has called this transformative process "a shift from a relatively narrowly defined Christianity to a broadly defined liberal Christianity that could be equated with civilization itself."[12] This liberal Protestantism thus provided the justification for the American liberal educational program to not only teach students professional skills but still aim for improving their characters as well. In this paradigm, no man could be truly modern without religious guidance; only a modernized and rational religion could successfully transform character.

While using liberal Protestantism as the guide for character building inside campus, university leaders looked outside the walls for signposts for how students could use their education as a means for national progress. The most famous enunciation of the integration of university education and societal improvement came in Woodrow Wilson's 1896 speech at Princeton, called "Princeton in the Nation's Service." He disdained the view that universities should remain aloof from the everyday concerns of the world. For him, "The object of education is not merely to draw out the powers of the individual mind: it is rather its right object to draw all minds to a proper adjustment to the physical and social world in which they are to have their life and their development: to enlighten, strengthen and make fit."[13] Going further, Wilson expressed this view:

> Of course, when all is said, it is not learning but the spirit of service that will give a college place in the public annals of the nation. It is indispensable, it seems to me, if it is to do its right service, that the air of affairs should be admitted to all its class rooms. I do not mean the air of party politics but the air of the world's transactions, the consciousness of the solidarity of the race, the sense of the duty of man towards man, of the presence of men in every problem, of the significance of truth for guidance as well as for knowledge, of the potency of ideas, of the promise and the hope that shine in the face of all knowledge.[14]

In this equation, liberal education imposed upon its adherents a duty to the larger community or, in the case of the United States, the nation itself.

William Rainey Harper of the University of Chicago articulated an even more activist connection between the work of the university and improving public life in America. For him, although his own university was private, having been founded by John D. Rockefeller, an organic connection existed between the university and the democratic workings of the American government. For Rainey, "On the one hand, the University is an institution of the government, the guide of the people, and an ally of humanity in its struggle for advancement; and on the other, Democracy is the highest ideal of human achievement, the only possibility of a true national life, the glorious and golden sun lighting up the dark places of all the world." Harper saw the university, as he put it, as the "prophet of Democracy," for "Democracy needs teachers who shall say, *Know thyself*; messengers who shall bring light to shine upon dark places." Because of the unique educational process now flourishing on American campuses, Harper felt that "the university, I maintain, is the prophetic interpreter of democracy; the prophet of her past, in all its vicissitudes; the prophet of her present, in all its complexity; the prophet of her future, in all its possibilities." In mimicking the words of Woodrow Wilson, Harper said that "the true university, the university of the future, is one the motto of which will be: Service for mankind wherever mankind is, whether within scholastic walls or without those walls and in the world at large."[15]

Progressivism, a political ideology dominant in America in the decades leading up to World War I, hewed to a view of government and citizenry that paralleled many elements of the character-building exercise university leaders were undertaking. Richard Hofstadter has said, "The key words of Progressivism were terms like *patriotism, citizen, democracy, law, character, conscience, soul, morals, service, duty, shame, disgrace, sin,* and *selfishness*—terms redolent of the sturdy Protestant Anglo-Saxon moral and intellectual roots of the Progressive uprising." In the new liberal education program, nation, morality, character, and citizen merged together as educational and national goals. Herbert Croly, an influential ideologue of the Progressive movement, identified education as the key factor in national development. In his view, "It is by education that the American is trained for such democracy as he possesses; and it is by better education that he proposes to better his democracy. Men are uplifted by education much more surely than they are by any tinkering with laws and institutions, because the work of education leavens the actual social substance." Fitting with Hofstadter's list of Progressive characteristics, Croly believed that "an individual's education consists primarily in the discipline which he undergoes to fit him both for fruitful association with its fellows and for his own special work." Under this philosophy, service to the nation became an integral element of the liberal education program. In essence, as Laurence Veysey states, university leaders wanted to "make each of its graduates into a force for civic virtue" and to "train a group of political leaders who would take a knightly plunge into 'real life' and clean it up."[16]

American liberal education thus contained within its umbrella by the early years of the twentieth century pedagogical elements enabling research into new scientific discoveries and training for careers in the industrial economy. It also called on students to be activists, activists in searching out new knowledge, activists in seeking out solutions to the nation's problems. Under the liberal education rubric, morality and service to the nation, religion, and democracy served interconnected goals. By facing the nineteenth-century crisis to the unity of truth with "a reordering of intellectual life," universities became dynamic centers for determining how to categorize and analyze not only new pieces of information but also the new problems arising throughout America.[17] Over the course of the twentieth century, this "liberal education" program came to be synonymous with "American education," whether within America's borders or beyond.

The brilliance of the American liberal education system is that it is designed to teach a person how to think, not to impart a set body of knowledge. Reforms can continue to take place without upsetting this basic framework. During the course of the twentieth century, this educational program has faced many changes, although its essential elements have not been altered. For example, university leaders had formulated liberal Protestantism precisely as a way to keep religion as part of the educational experience, even if clerical controls had to be eliminated. Inadvertently, they actually secularized the university sphere because the tenets of this new liberal Protestantism became so broad that students could no longer identify them as connected to a religion at all. Religion became just one more disciplinary field within the university, studied just as any other body of knowledge would be, without any connection to spiritual faith. Several Catholic and evangelical Protestant schools continued to teach within a specific religious framework, but the vast majority of American universities became zones of secularism where church and state were officially separate. When the religious umbrella disintegrated, so too did the goal of character building. By the mid-twentieth century, no secular university connected the educational experience so directly to building good character. Training for jobs after graduation, through the teaching of critical analysis and open debate, became far more important. As for serving the nation, that concept also evolved during the course of the century. The leaders of nineteenth-century university reform never specifically laid out the tangible signs of this connection, but given the Progressive influence on them, it often meant moving directly into government service after graduation or working for social welfare organizations like the urban settlement houses. Over time, this call for national improvement became more of an individual call, with the view that the nation could benefit overall from graduates succeeding in their chosen fields of endeavor. The reading of great books of Western civilization that had served as the foundation for classes like Columbia's Contemporary Civilization gave way by midcentury to classes designed to study world civilizations and literatures. The "West" no longer provided the sole focal point for knowledge; students now studied so-called area studies—the Middle East, East Asia, and Africa—alongside older fields.

Students, the consumers of liberal education, have also pushed for changes over the years; they did not remain passive as their educational options changed so dramatically. Student protests broke out repeatedly on American campuses over the course of the twentieth century, most frequently about the very definition of freedom the university leaders touted as the cornerstone of liberal education. University leaders generally hewed to the view that engaging in campus political action, based on any political ideology, infringed upon the rights of fellow students while also destroying a student's ability to assess a situation objectively and cautiously. Students, in turn, criticized university leaders for isolating themselves inside their gates, rejecting the whole concept of service to the nation enshrined in early liberal education debates. Students felt that only by interacting with political events outside of campus would they truly be trained for their lives after graduation; only then would they be able to think intelligently about the political, economic, and social conditions existing in their nation.

In America these complaints climaxed in the 1960s, when students came out in protest against their universities time and time again. In a rare study in the early 1960s of student academic freedom, E. G. Williamson and John L. Cowan found that broad agreement existed concerning the view that students could "talk all they want" while on campus.[18] However, administrators and students disagreed over students' rights to "act on their convictions," particularly in the form of political demonstrations and sit-ins. As one dean in the study stated, "Our students are restricted in social and political matters if *action* is involved." At the University of California, Berkeley, graduate student Mario Savio led the Free Speech Movement in 1964, demanding that students be allowed to bring the civil rights movement onto campus and to see campus, more generally, as a civic space where all political issues could be debated. By 1968 university campuses erupted all over the country, with students proclaiming their right to the same kind of political freedom. In the late 1960s, students also established so-called free universities, where they declared they would teach subjects truly relevant to their educational and political lives. They accused their universities of being too disconnected from the problems raging around the world. Even today, protests continue in American academia, as students deride the universities for not teaching them the skills they really need in their future jobs. In the past forty years, as university enrollments have skyrocketed, having a university degree does not give any special privileges in the American job market. Instead, students increasingly find they must go on to graduate work—in medicine, law, business, and the like—in order get that professional training.

In the end, these students did not force any major changes to the university structure; freedom of inquiry remained ensconced in the classroom, while political issues have remained primarily outside the gates. American university leaders have given in to some of these demands, namely, in terms of curriculum expansion, but have held to the claim that by teaching students a broad base of knowledge and the analytical skills to understand it, they give students the tools to go on to any kind of job or further graduate work. They continue to hold to the view that liberal education is designed to teach students how to think; what students do with this knowledge is their decision.

Liberal Education in Beirut

If American liberal education can be summarized as focusing on service, research, and culture, the type of program imported to the Middle East via the Syrian Protestant College and the American University of Beirut can be said to emphasize intellectual freedom, character, and service, in that order. While at no time did the school require that students embrace evangelical Protestantism as a prerequisite for their education, the school's founders hoped that their educational program would induce students to accept the Protestantism taught to them. When only a tiny minority did so, the school instead focused on establishing an educational program that would provide the skills students would need in a rapidly changing Middle Eastern arena.

Influenced by their own educational experiences back in America, the founders' successors gradually integrated elements of the new American liberal education program; the key for SPC/AUB was choosing the elements that would hold resonance with their Middle Eastern audience. Instead of breaking from ecclesiastical control, as their American colleagues were doing, they sought to break the pattern of rote memorization that controlled Middle Eastern educational systems up to that point. Instead of moving from denominational Protestantism to liberal Protestantism, SPC/AUB's leaders had to make the transition from missionary, evangelical Protestantism to the broad-based liberal Protestantism gaining currency on American campuses. Instead of primarily integrating students of different Christian denominations into their university community, they had to inaugurate freedom of inquiry amid a plethora of religious faiths and linguistic groups.[19] Instead of serving an already strong nation suffering a series of crises, they had to teach students to build nations from scratch. Out of this process emerged a liberal education program based in American precepts but suited for SPC/AUB and widely respected in the Middle East.

Daniel Bliss opened the Syrian Protestant College to sixteen students in December 1866; in his farewell address in 1902, he summed up the work he had sought to achieve among his students. For Daniel, "The great object of the college is to educate men so that they can understand the things that exist which we call Nature, and the relation between those things." In framing his talk around Paul's statement that man must "prove all things; hold fast that which is good," he felt that "the great value of education does not consist in the accepting this and that to be true but it consists in proving this and that to be true." Daniel believed of facts that "if you prove them to be true by reasoning from axioms or other truth, your mind, your intellect, the whole man is strengthened, and this strength will remain when the facts are forgotten and will give you power in the study, in the office, and in the church and in the state, and around the bed of the sick and the dying."[20] Despite enunciating a definition similar to liberal education's freedom of inquiry, in Daniel's day neither the classroom nor the chapel setting provided any real opportunity for independent thought. Rather, Daniel saw reason, will, and conscience as the tools necessary for understanding Protestantism and Jesus's message. As he declared, "In the Bible classes no attempt was made to combat error or false views, but we followed the method by which darkness is expelled from the room by turning on the light."[21] He hoped, per the mission of the school, that students would voluntarily embrace the faith, having seen the light, although at no time did he require that students do so as a prerequisite for matriculation or graduation.

Howard Bliss, his son and successor (1902–1920), made the first tentative steps toward the inauguration of the new liberal education program on campus. He established the first course electives and began the process of professionalizing the fields, by dividing disciplines into separate departments. More important, he introduced freedom of inquiry as the cornerstone of the educational program run by the school. His successors went further and institutionalized a research agenda on campus, but it would always be secondary to the undergraduate education the school's leaders saw as their duty to the region. In these classes, the school emphasized the element of freedom of inquiry that called on students to discuss and debate, with tolerance and respect, differing political, ideological, and religious views, all with the goal of finding solutions and compromises. As Howard wrote in his last article in 1920, "In all our classes, and especially in our Bible classes, there is a tradition of absolutely untrammeled inquiry; and woe be to the teacher who gives the impression that he is suppressing or fumbling question and answer, however blunt, embarrassing, or indiscreet the inquiry may seem to be."[22] Starting in the 1908–1909 course catalog, the school's leaders defined the method of instruction by saying:

> The primary aim of the college programme throughout all departments is to develop the reasoning faculties of the mind, to lay the foundations of a thorough intellectual training, to free the mind for independent thought. The permanent influence upon character exerted by the persistent requirement of thoroughness, seriousness, and diligence is more highly prized by the College than a brilliant show of a mechanical mastery of detailed information. In this sense, no course in the institution is considered to be an end in itself; it is rather the aim of all instruction to train the individual student to meet the highest requirements of his life in society.[23]

In this atmosphere, the knowledge, per se, was not as important as instilling the tools needed to critically analyze that information. SPC/AUB's leaders believed that only this definition of freedom of inquiry could produce students with the proper intellectual skills for improving their communities, of bringing progress to the Middle East.

Students, too, highlighted this aspect of the SPC/AUB experience as soon as they began publishing their own magazines and newspapers in 1899. In their articles, they consistently portray the educational program at the school as unique to the region and best fitted for training the minds of the region's future leaders. In the *Miltonian* on June 22, 1903, for example, a student described the importance of his education:

> It is very great the difference between the wise and the ignorant. The ignorant sees the things just as they seem to be, while the wise goes deep to the very original creation of them. The ignorant lives for the present only, while the wise not being contented with the present sees the tracks of the past and the results of the future. The ignorant lives for himself only, while the wise for all the world. The ignorant deceives himself when he feels as though he knows every thing, while the wise always feels the strong desire of something, and the more he learns the larger room he gives to learning.[24]

In June 1926, an article in the *Sub-freshman Star* described the unique education provided by AUB:

> It is not education that we seek; or fame, nor knowledge; No, it is the spirit of freedom that penetrates every heart and stays there forever. It is

the feeling of self-reliance and self-sacrifice. There we come to learn and to respect and not at all knowledge, fame and education. The America University of Beirut is the only school of its kind in the East and most probably in all Europe that teaches Freedom, Self-reliance and Self-Respect along with the best of education.[25]

For this student, his AUB education gave him the elements a successful life required. "Freedom is the life of a nation; Freedom is the life of men. Self respect and Self reliance also build up men, and the three of them together perfect a nation and the three of them together perfect a man." The *University* of December 21, 1927, reported that "our Alma Mater believes that by preparing broad-minded and open-minded men, men with world-wide ideals of service, she will render the most good to this land and to the world."[26]

As with their colleagues in America, SPC/AUB's leaders recognized that freedom of inquiry could be practiced only by those who understood their own limitations. The 1950–1951 course catalog, for example, stated that "in both the liberal and specialized phases of the program of the School of Arts and Sciences there is an attempt to develop a maturity of thinking, a basic understanding of fundamental research, and a sound appreciation of experimentation. Such aims, which are in fact the intellectual tools for independent and creative thought, are as alien to denationalization as they are to bigotry."[27] In this statement lies the second pillar of SPC/AUB's liberal education program, namely, the making of good character among the students. More frequently than not, the school's leaders articulated this element of the program as a duty to "make men" among their students. President Bayard Dodge (1923–1948) put particular stress on making this kind of man from among his students, focusing particularly on the role that religion could play in building up the necessary character. On his way to Beirut for his inauguration in 1923, Dodge detailed the most important attributes he felt the students needed to learn from the Americans at the school:

- The idea of the Brotherhood of Man.
- The great content of modern, scientific learning, which fits men for active life and professional service.
- A broad culture, which produces liberality of thought and a well-balanced judgment.
- A manly attitude towards work and play, which overcomes laziness, creates clean sport, and develops a well-rounded type of manhood.

- The fact that religion is not a matter of rites and names alone, but a matter of the spirit, which expresses itself in a practical way by noble character and good living.
- A devotion to the great moral principles of God and a consecration to the service of mankind, such as Jesus had.[28]

In so describing these American attributes, Dodge envisioned a society where upholding standards of honesty and hard work meant unlimited possibilities for economic and national growth in return. The most important elements he found in education were not the mysteries of mathematics or the beauty of Shakespeare's dramas, but the character traits all successful students acquire. As Dodge frequently quoted from American writer H. G. Wells, history is a "race between education and catastrophe."[29]

In essence, the school's leaders, like Dodge, called on the students to work on their character first, a new skill set later; with the proper character, a man could achieve anything, including scientific achievement and business success. Imbued with his new character, he would eschew his natural laziness by rolling up his sleeves, taking personal responsibility for his actions, and doing the hard work he once delegated to servants. Within the parameters of the new liberal educational curriculum, he had a breadth of knowledge in the humanities and social sciences and followed the precepts of freedom of inquiry and tolerance of difference in all interactions with colleagues. He recognized that spirituality did not mean blind recitation of elaborate religious rituals, but an acknowledgment that morality and ethics translated into good business tactics, better societal relations, and national strength. Given the tumultuous conflicts and divisions the Americans believed existed among the sectarian groups of the Middle East, they preached that religious tolerance alone would not be sufficient; it needed to be actively directed toward societal and national cooperation and brotherhood.[30]

In this way, personal energies would be siphoned only into productive, collective projects. In addition, freedom of speech and opinion—the cornerstone of the new liberal education system—could be enacted only as long as the practitioners understood that with freedoms came automatic limits. Freedom could not be exercised except by those who had proved themselves worthy of its responsibilities; only careful supervision and guidance could teach the students how to exercise that restraint.

In the early decades of the American University of Beirut's existence,

Dodge and his colleagues found in liberal Protestantism the keys to teaching this good character. They had by then rejected the earlier missionary goals of the founders, but they still wanted to use Protestantism as a guide for a moral and successful modern man. Here, too, freedom of inquiry came into play, as the whole university community was supposed to learn from each other. Professor James Stewart enunciated the religious policy at the school in a speech on March 28, 1927. In excerpts, he described the first element underpinning the policy:

> We believe that the first great essential for our experiment is Freedom. We grant the fullest freedom for the mind, for the conscience, and for individual growth. This means that there is genuine freedom to think differently from one another, on religion, and to develop on different lines.
>
> One further condition must be progressiveness met by each man after his appointment, be he Protestant, Catholic, Eastern Christian, Moslem or Jew. His career, through the unfolding years, must be such as to show that he is a growing man, growing in his understanding of right living, growing in his influence through right living. The man who has ceased to grow in character, has ceased to represent our type of freedom.[31]

Freedom of inquiry, as the basic source of liberal education, carried over into faith, as students were enjoined to maintain their beliefs while freely asking questions of those around them. This broad-based Christianity called on students to "rise up" and better themselves, to do as Jesus Christ had done, to sacrifice and struggle on behalf of the community. As Dodge said:

> Religion seems to be a consciousness of God; a life of the spirit, manifesting itself in the conduct of each day, and it is when we wish to make this fact intelligible to our students that we hold before them an ideal personality, whose actions were so supremely guided by submission to the divine will and whose sacrifice blazed forth as a beacon to mankind. God forbid that our University should carry on a new crusade in eastern lands, but we do long to make every student as loving, as pure, and as unselfish as Jesus was. The solution of problems of race hatred and sectarian strife must be brotherly love. The way of attaining social decency and honest business is by pure conduct. The only answer to the worldwide question of poverty and wealth is unselfishness.[32]

In Dodge's view, America needed to teach the Arab world how to create the Kingdom of God on earth. In more practical terms, he wanted to show the Arabs how, as the Americans were doing, they could maintain their faith by turning it into service to the community. As Dodge proclaimed, "Kindled by a fire from on high, may our men go forth into the sordid materialism of the world, to live for things which are eternal, and to die for those great moral principles, that alone can save mankind!"[33] For him, the best sign that he and AUB were succeeding was the fact that so many students chose to engage in voluntary social service activities.

> The finest influences of American life are being exemplified during vacations, by means of social service work. Members of the missionary organizations are encouraging young men and women to teach Sunday schools and vacation Bible schools. Conferences are held that bring the men and women teachers together to fit themselves for their work. It means a great deal for the educated men and women to share serious ideals with the poor children of the towns and villages. It awakens the peasant children and enables them to understand that there is something deeper in modern culture than extravagant amusement and intellectual cynicism.[34]

In Dodge's view, only America, shining its light on the Arab world, had the ability to spread such a practical form of spirituality, one designed to aid the community as a whole. Liberal education, as a whole, meant intellectual freedom for all involved, with students learning the tools of critical thinking just as they built up their characters sufficiently so they could aid their nations upon graduation.

Just as American universities adapted their educational programs to account for changing conditions within society throughout the twentieth century, so too has AUB. Liberal Protestantism failed in much the same way it did on American campuses inside the country's borders. In fact, many graduates point to their secular—and implicitly nonsectarian—education as a key reason for the school's success, with no mention of any kind of religious influence guiding their educational experiences. Character building disappeared from the school's statements in the middle of the twentieth century, after Bayard Dodge's presidency ended. When Professor Constantine Zurayq served as the acting president in the mid-1950s, he often spoke of the character-building elements he felt should be part of the educational experience but recognized that they were now old-fashioned ideals that few people followed.

Service to the nation remained a primary duty throughout the twentieth century, as seen in the continuing popularity of such programs as the Civic Welfare League and the many projects for teaching literacy and other skills in the neighborhood of the school. AUB in 2008 announced a new initiative to better integrate the campus and its activities with its neighborhood in Beirut, al-Hamra. All students must still complete a core curriculum, now called the Civilization Sequence Program, in their first two years, with the vast majority of students majoring in engineering, business, and medicine thereafter.

Like their counterparts in America, the school's students have been protesting against school policies since the era of the SPC. In the first such protest, in 1882, students criticized the administration for forcing Professor Edwin Lewis to resign after he gave a speech praising Charles Darwin's work. In 1909 Muslim and Jewish students walked out of obligatory Bible classes and chapel sessions because they did not feel the school had the right to impose religious beliefs upon them. In one exemplary opinion from the era, a student expressed in a *Lewa* article of January 24, 1909, "Now it is passing strange that our faculty have undertaken in forcing us to attend church and teaching us Christian doctrine inspite of us, in view of their pretense of religious liberty. It is contrary to reason and at variance with the regulation of all the schools of the world, among them those of America universally."[35] Throughout the early 1950s, students protested on behalf of Arab nationalist goals. The main complaint at that time was that university leaders would not allow political actions to take place on campus; students countered that they could never truly be educated without combining political action with their classroom studies, especially given how vital Arab nationalism was to Middle East politics and society. John Racy, 1951–1952 student council speaker and editor of *Outlook*, wrote in an editorial in May 1951, "The age when Education and Politics were completely separate things is past and gone. . . . No one can afford to turn a cold shoulder toward the political affairs of the day. The Administration of AUB seems to be unaware of this."[36] After the June 1967 war, the campus erupted continually, most often in support of Palestinian causes. In addition to pointing again to the limitations placed upon their freedom, students derided the school for not teaching them more "practical" subjects, ones that connected to their real-life concerns. To resolve this problem, students established a free university on campus in December 1970, and over the next few years faculty and students volunteered to teach courses as diverse as Revolutionary Philosophy, Politics and Economics of Israel, History of Palestine, The Guitar: A Counterculture

Workshop, and Analysis and Critique of AUB and the Forms of Education Present.[37]

With the outbreak of the Lebanese Civil War in 1975, faculty and students alike became far more involved in national events than those specific to campus. It is impossible to tell where these student protests might have led if war had not occurred. Instead, all members of the university body had to work together to keep the school open throughout the fifteen-year war; past differences evaporated. As the school rebuilds today, it has decided to maintain the same liberal education program announced at the end of the nineteenth century. In the 2003–2004 academic year, an AUB task force tracked the history of liberal education as part of the process of gaining accreditation with the American Middle States Association of Colleges and Schools.[38] In its final report, the task force voted to maintain this program on campus, despite pressure from some students to move to heavier emphasis on professional training.

Conclusion

The American liberal education system has proved so popular that not only the American University of Beirut but also the American University of Cairo, Roberts College of Istanbul, and myriad numbers of elementary and secondary schools based on the American system flourished throughout the twentieth century. In the twenty-first century, American universities opened in Kuwait and Sharjah; Georgetown University recently launched its School of Foreign Service in Qatar. Prince Alwaleed Bin Talal Bin Abdulaziz al-Saoud funded American studies programs at both the American University of Beirut and the American University of Cairo in 2003. The University of Tehran established the Institute for North American and European Studies, with a master's program, in 2005. These schools are trying to tap into what the *General Education in a Free Society* report of 1946 summarized as the holistic concept behind the American educational system. In the words of this report, "The objective of education is not just knowledge of values but commitment to them, the embodiment of the ideal in one's actions, feelings, and thoughts, no less than an intellectual grasp of the ideal. . . . For is not the purpose of educational institutions to train the mind and the mind only?"[39] The President's Commission on Higher Education for Democracy of 1947 summarized the consensus American education had reached by the mid-twentieth century, saying, in part, that "general education should give to the students the values, attitudes, knowledge, and skills that will equip him to live rightly and well in a free society. It should enable him to identify, interpret, select, and build into his own life those components of his cultural heritage that contribute richly to understanding and appreciation of the world in which he lives."[40]

Both of these statements aptly sum up the basic elements that make up the American liberal education system. Teaching students to think, and to think with an open mind and critical eye, gives them the potential to be the innovative searchers of knowledge that Charles Eliot described one hundred years ago. The system has evolved over the course of the twentieth century; proliferation of the American-style educational programs all over the world and the still high numbers of foreign students studying in American universities prove that this type of education resonates in a rapidly changing twenty-first-century world.

Notes

1. *Catalogue of the Syrian Protestant College, 32nd Year, 1897–1898* (Beirut: American University of Beirut/Library Archives, 1897), 2, 29.

2. Cited in Timothy P. Cross, *An Oasis of Order: The Core Curriculum at Columbia College* (New York: Columbia College, 1995), http://www.college .columbia.edu/core/oasis/.

3. *General Education in a Free Society: Report of the Harvard Committee* (Cambridge, MA: Harvard University Press, 1946), 65. In the introduction, James Bryant Conant explained that the purpose of the report was to have a committee of Faculty of Arts and Sciences professors inquire about the problems of general education in both school and college.

4. The list comes from Laurence R. Veysey, *The Emergence of the American University* (Chicago: University of Chicago Press, 1965), 12.

5. *American University of Beirut Including Intermediate Section of International College—Catalog, 1950–51* (Beirut: American University of Beirut/ Library Archives, 1951), 6.

6. Jon H. Roberts and James Turner, *The Sacred and the Secular University* (Princeton, NJ: Princeton University Press, 2000), 70–71; William Rainey Harper, *The Trend in Higher Education* (Chicago: University of Chicago Press, 1905), 4.

7. Cited in David A. Hollinger, "Inquiry and Uplift: Late Nineteenth-Century American Academics and the Moral Efficacy of Scientific Practice," in *The Authority of Experts: Studies in History and Theory*, edited by Thomas L. Haskell (Bloomington: Indiana University Press, 1984), 142.

8. Ibid., 150.

74 Betty S. Anderson

9. Charles William Eliot, *Academic Freedom: An Address Delivered before the New York Theta Chapter of the Phi Beta Kappa Society at Cornell University*, May 29, 1907 (Ithaca, NY: Press of Ithaca and Church, 1907), 17.

10. Ibid., 18.

11. Veysey, *Emergence of the American University*, 243.

12. George M. Marsden, "The Soul of the American University: A Historical Overview," in *The Secularization of the Academy*, edited by George M. Marsden and Bradley J. Longfield (New York: Oxford University Press, 1992), 27; Julie A. Reuben, *The Making of the Modern University: Intellectual Transformation and the Marginalization of Morality* (Chicago: University of Chicago Press, 1996), 125; George M. Marsden, *The Soul of the American University: From Protestant Establishment to Established Nonbelief* (New York: Oxford University Press, 1994), 5.

13. Woodrow Wilson, "Princeton in the Nation's Service," in vol. 10 of *The Papers of Woodrow Wilson*, edited by Arthur S. Link (Princeton, NJ: Princeton University Press, 1971), 22.

14. Ibid., 30.

15. Harper, *Trend in Higher Education*, 1, 13–14, 20, 27–28.

16. Richard Hofstadter, *The Age of Reform: From Bryan to F.D.R.* (New York: Alfred A. Knopf, 1955), 318 (emphasis in the original); Herbert Croly, *The Promise of American Life* (Indianapolis: Bobbs-Merrill, 1909), 400, 403; Veysey, *Emergence of the American University*, 72.

17. Thomas Bender, "The Erosion of Public Culture: Cities, Discourses, and Professional Disciplines," in *Authority of Experts*, edited by Haskell, 88.

18. E. G. Williamson and John L. Cowan, *The American Student's Freedom of Expression: A Research Appraisal* (Minneapolis: University of Minnesota Press, 1966), 88–89.

19. SPC/AUB has always attracted more students from Arab countries than from any other area, although students from all over the world have attended. During SPC's existence, Christians dominated the student ranks, but since the school became the AUB in 1920, Christians and Muslims have generally enrolled in roughly equal numbers. Just about every religious faith has been represented at the school since it opened in 1866.

20. Daniel Bliss, "Farewell Address," in *Voice of Daniel Bliss* (Beirut: American Press, 1956), 57, 67.

21. Daniel Bliss, *The Reminiscences of Daniel Bliss, Edited and Supplemented by His Eldest Son* (New York: Fleming H. Revell, 1920), 207.

22. Howard Bliss, "The Modern Missionary," *Atlantic Monthly*, May 1920, 667.

23. *Catalogue of the Syrian Protestant College, 43rd Year, 1908–1909* (Beirut: American University of Beirut/Library Archives, 1908), 17.

24. "The Twentieth Century," *Miltonian*, June 22, 1903 (American University of Beirut/Library Archives).

25. "The Most Valuable Thing in My College Life," *Sub-freshman Star*, June 1926 (American University of Beirut/Library Archives), 24.

26. Ibid.; "Opportunities for Self-Help in the S.P.C.," *University*, December 21, 1927 (American University of Beirut/Library Archives), 4.

27. *American University of Beirut Catalog, 1950–51* (Beirut: American University of Beirut/Library Archives, 1950), 14.

28. Bayard Dodge, "Article for al-Kulliyyah" [February 28, 1923], in *Articles, Speeches and Sermons*, vols. 3–4 (American University of Beirut/Library Archives). The articles and speeches collected in this series are the original typed versions. Dodge frequently made corrections to the typing with pencil and pen. I have quoted from the edited versions in all cases.

29. See Bayard Dodge, "America a Light to the Nations," in ibid., 3:424.

30. See Ussama Makdisi, *Artillery of Heaven: American Missionaries and the Failed Conversion of the Middle East* (Ithaca, NY: Cornell University Press, 2008), for a discussion of the tolerance present within Ottoman society and the ways by which the American missionaries misunderstood relations between the religious groups in the empire.

31. James Stewart Crawford, "The Religious Policy of the A.U.B.," *al-Kulliyyah*, no. 7 (May 1927): 192–193.

32. Bayard Dodge, "Inaugural Address," 130.

33. Ibid., 128.

34. Bayard Dodge, "American Education in the Near East" [September 1935], in *Articles, Speeches and Sermons*, 3:260–261.

35. "The Beirut College and Islam," *Lewa* (Egypt), January 24, 1909, translated by Dr. Porter from a local Beirut newspaper (American University of Beirut/Library Archives, Students 1900s/Box 1/File 12).

36. John Racy, "Degrees & Politics," *Outlook*, May 5, 1951, 2.

37. Free University Collective, "Sadeq al-Azm's Comeback: Free University Challenges AUB Educational Initiative," *Outlook*, January 19, 1971, 9.

38. *Institutional Self-Study: Commission on Higher Education, Middle States Association of Colleges and Schools* (Beirut: American University of Beirut), 146.

39. *General Education in a Free Society*, 72.

40. "The President's Commission on Higher Education for Democracy, 1947," in *American Higher Education: A Documentary History*, edited by Richard Hofstadter and Wilson Smith (Chicago: University of Chicago Press, 1961), 2:989.

CHAPTER 4

Shifting the Gorilla: The Failure of the American Unipolar in the Middle East

SCOTT LUCAS

Some years ago, when I began work on histories of American and British foreign policy in the Middle East, my mother offered the advice, "Why don't you write a nice novel like that John Grisham instead?" However, when I informed her in 2007 that I planned to publish a critique of the George W. Bush administration, she reflected a moment and then countered, "Why don't you write a nice history book instead?" Given that she is a devout Republican and supporter of President Bush, with "the sense of class and patriotism [that he] brought to the White House," my mother's change of heart may not have been entirely prompted by concern for my welfare. Still, it is pertinent to ask: Why did I choose to reinterpret Bush's foreign policy, particularly in the Middle East, even before he left office? And how does this critique connect with the growth of American studies programs in the Middle East?

In part, I was responding to sweeping classifications of the Bush administration. There were critiques of continuity, such as Michael Cox's claim that the "intellectual ground [for empire] was already shifting on the right" before the accession of George W. Bush to power.[1] There were numerous critiques of distinction, with labels from "neoconservative" to "neo-Wilsonian" to "democratic imperialist" to "democratic realist."[2] There were the interventions of historians rationalizing contemporary frameworks for policy making: John Lewis Gaddis's defense of preemption as the provision of security, Melvyn Leffler's depiction of an administration reacting out of fear rather than pursuing a pre-9/11 agenda.[3]

In part, I was spurred to comment because of the retrenchments of policy, undertaken when I first began the critique. Within the administration, foreign policy was repackaged—after the complications over its first-term objectives and actions—as a "Freedom Agenda" and then narrowed to the essential "will to win" of the 2007 surge in Iraq. As President Bush framed the objective in April 2008, "So long as I'm the President, my measure of success is victory and success."[4]

In large part, however, I was motivated to consider US foreign policy not because of the Bush administration but because of those who observed that policy, felt its effects, negotiated it, chose whether to respond to it. The center of attention was not necessarily in Washington but in the Middle East.

I think that decision put me at odds with US policy makers, whose approach was primarily "one-way," constructed with a disregard for and even an ignorance of the political, social, economic, religious, and cultural spheres into which they were intervening. (I recall the administration's use of the historian Bernard Lewis as the interpreter of "Islam" and George Bush's revelation, in a January 2003 meeting with Iraqi expatriates who supported US military action, that he did not know there were Sunni and Shia versions of that Islam.)

Yet I also think I was following a more productive development in the growth of "American studies" in the Middle East—not as a construction and interpretation of "America" delivered on tablets from the United States but as a sharpening and use of intellectual tools by those in the region in their negotiation of Washington's power. In the establishment of new teaching and research programs, in the growth of libraries and Internet resources, and in the creation of seminars and conferences to disseminate and debate ideas, scholars, students, and interested observers were making clear that they were more than pawns to be deployed either as supporters or opponents of US campaigns.

We are now years beyond the Bush administration and into the succession of President Obama, who promised in his inaugural speech, "We will extend a hand if you are willing to unclench your fist."[5] He followed this address with high-profile declarations in Ankara ("engagement based upon mutual interests and mutual respect")[6] and Cairo ("America and Islam are not exclusive, and need not be in competition. Instead, they overlap, and share common principles—principles of justice and progress; tolerance and the dignity of all human beings").[7] There were promises of new approaches to resolve the Israeli-Palestinian dispute, to break through US-Iranian animosity, and to remove the threat of nuclear weapons.

All this portrays a US government seeking dialogue with others rather than imposition of its wishes upon overseas communities. However, with little apparent movement toward productive resolutions from Ramallah to Damascus to Tehran, I wonder if the supposedly unclenched fist was accompanied by an unclenching of the grasp—or attempted grasp—on maintenance and extension of American power. That curiosity takes me back to a study of the grand mission of the Bush administration, not just to interrogate that specific pursuit of the "unipolar" but to consider how much of that pursuit is still pertinent today.

On the surface, retrenchments and realignments outside the Bush administration began well before Barack Obama stepped into the White House. In September 2006, the Princeton Project on National Security offered its blueprint "Forging a World of Liberty under Law."[8] The product of two years of discussions with more than four hundred participants, many of them officials in the Clinton administration or intellectuals who broke with Bush, the report proclaimed:

> A world of liberal democracies would be a safer and better world for Americans and all people to live in. It is thus in America's deepest interest to pursue such a world. But America must also pursue a values-based foreign policy to be true to itself—the cold calculations of realism, in its eternal quest for a balance of power, can never long satisfy the American people.[9]

However, the proposed strategy was not that distant from that of the Bush administration, apart from its pointed rejection of unilateralism.[10] Far from dismissing or even critiquing the use of military capabilities that distinguished American foreign policy since 2001, the Princeton participants argued that "US strategy must integrate our hard power with . . . our soft power, allowing us to use all of our assets in pursuit of our objectives." That "soft power," far from leading to a realignment of US objectives, was simply "our power to get what we want by attracting others to the same goals, rather than bending them to our will."[11]

New alignments of intellectuals and advisers emphasized modification rather than abandonment of the Bush approach. Robert Kagan, the "neoconservative" supporter of the Bush Doctrine, and Ivo Daalder, a member of President Clinton's National Security Council (NSC) staff, called for a "Concert of Democracies . . . to forge a renewed political consensus on the use of force."[12] Robert Kaplan, formerly a champion of American military unilateralism, embraced "a web of global arrangements and liberal institutions that will allow America to gradually retreat from its costly and risky position of overbearing dominance."[13] John McCain, the Republican candidate for president in 2008, set out the following: "We cannot build an enduring peace based on freedom by ourselves, and we do not want to. . . . We have to strengthen our global alliances as the core of a new global compact," to which the *Wall Street Journal* responded, "The truth is that, with a couple of exceptions, [Bush has] been the model of a modern multilateralist."[14] If, after September 11, "we were all Americans," now "we were all multilateralists," albeit multilateralists following an American-determined path.

Yet if US foreign policy since 2001 had been formulated with aspirations from the projection and extension of American power to the "spread of democracy," by 2008 it had to deal with the reality of setbacks, tensions, and complications from Afghanistan to Iraq to Israel-Palestine to Venezuela to North Korea to Somalia. Indeed, the distance between the political end point envisaged in presidential rhetoric or national security strategies (or both) and the existing situation in political, economic, and military arenas forced this question: how did we get here?

I believe three observations are essential. First, there was a Bushian "grand strategy" in 2001, even before the catalyst of 9/11 opened up the political space for the implementation of that strategy. This envisaged the American unipolar *for its own sake*—in other words, US power was to be sought not just as a means to particular political, economic, and military objectives but as an end in itself—anywhere and everywhere. This was the grand strategy first promoted in a 1992 Defense Planning Guidance, written by Zalmay Khalilzad and presented by Assistant Secretary of Defense Paul Wolfowitz to Secretary of Defense Dick Cheney, all of whom would have prominent roles a decade later in the George W. Bush administration:

> Our first objective is to prevent the re-emergence of a new rival. This is a dominant consideration underlying the new regional defense strategy and requires that we endeavor to prevent any hostile power from dominating a region whose resources would, under consolidated control, be sufficient to generate global power. These regions include Western Europe, East Asia, the territory of the former Soviet Union, and Southwest Asia.[15]

This preponderance required a demonstration—what use was the strategy if others did not know of and witness American superiority in practice? So, while the Bush administration could pursue the unipolar in capabilities such as missile defense, there had to be a place where capabilities were exercised. That location would be the part of "Southwest Asia" known as Iraq.

This strategy rested in turn on a second defining feature of the administration, the role of networks based not just on bureaucratic location but on personal connections and a shared vision of the American need and ability to reshape both Iraq and the Middle East. The presence of a relatively small group of officials, particularly in the civilian leadership of the Pentagon and the vice president's office, linked to vocal supporters outside government, skewed the process of intelligence, analysis, and policy making toward certain desired outcomes.

This organizational and cultural anomaly produced the third defining feature of the administration, one in which success ultimately and inevitably turned to failure. The Bushian grand strategy was not supported by a coherence in planning and implementation. The quest for a pro-American Iraq was not underpinned by preparations for reconstruction and development. This was more, however, than a tactical shortcoming in postliberation planning. Failure was inherent in the notion of the unipolar, for the extension and maintenance of American preponderance were predicated upon the "emptying"—through invasion and then dissolution of structures and institutions—of Iraqi political, economic, and cultural space. David Phillips, a senior adviser on the State Department's ill-fated Future of Iraq Project, summarized cogently: "It was clear from the beginning that empowering Iraqis was antithetical to the Pentagon's goal."[16]

But, of course, that space was never emptied. There remained individuals, groups, and communities with interests that might not correspond with those of the US government and its military and political representatives. In the conflict that ensued lay both the demise of the unipolar and the possibilities of new local, regional, and international configurations, in the Middle East and elsewhere, in which the United States might be not just an actor but the central, defining actor.

Regimes Aligned with US Interests

The Bushian grand strategy was first tabled only ten days into the new administration. On January 30, 2001, the first National Security Council meeting featured the opening topic "Regime Change in Iraq." The toppling of Saddam Hussein was not just a special self-contained case but part of a reevaluation of the US approach to the Middle East. As President Bush stated cogently, "We're going to correct the imbalances of the previous administration on the Mideast conflict. We're going to tilt it back to Israel." Two days later, in a follow-up meeting of the National Security Council principals, Secretary of Defense Donald Rumsfeld spelled out the wider conception: "Imagine what the region would look like without Saddam and with a regime that is aligned with US interests. It would change everything in the region and beyond. It would demonstrate what US policy is all about."

This dramatic statement did not reflect Rumsfeld's priorities. The secretary of defense was more concerned about military capabilities, specifically through the pursuit of a missile defense program and generally through a policy of "transformation," streamlining Pentagon bureaucracy and the military in favor of faster, more mobile military forces. Instead, Rumsfeld was bringing to the table the vision of his chief subordinates, namely, Undersecretary of Defense Paul Wolfowitz and Wolfowitz's assistants Douglas Feith and Harold Rohde, who in turn were working with key consultants such as Richard Perle.

Wolfowitz had been the primary bureaucratic sponsor of the 1992 Defense Planning Guidance, but while out of office over the next eight years, he commented only in general terms on foreign policy apart from specific attention to missile defense and Iraq. The Middle Eastern dimension was fleshed out instead by Perle, Feith, and David Wurmser, who would become Vice President Dick Cheney's adviser on foreign affairs. In 1996 the trio helped produce a blueprint, "A Clean Break: A New Strategy for Securing the Realm," for Israeli prime minister Benjamin Netanyahu. The document advocated "work[ing] closely with Turkey and Jordan to contain, destabilize, and roll-back some of [Israel's] most dangerous threats . . . [with a] clean break from the slogan, 'comprehensive peace' to a traditional concept of strategy based on balance of power." Israel would push every rival one step back, suspending the Oslo peace process until the Palestinian Liberation Organization met "minimum standards of compliance," establishing "hot pursuit into Palestinian-controlled areas," "striking Syrian military targets in Lebanon, and should that prove insufficient, *striking at select targets in Syria proper*," and cooperating with the United States on antimissile defense.[17]

Wurmser followed up "A Clean Break" two years later with intensive lobbying for support of the Iraqi National Congress, the opposition group based in Washington and London, from both the American and Israeli governments. He and Perle pressed Tel Aviv to diversify their challenge beyond the ayatollahs of Tehran: "One can only speculate what it might accomplish if it decided to focus its attention on Saddam Hussein."[18] As members of the Project for a New American Century, along with Rumsfeld, Wolfowitz, and several others who would later join the Bush administration, they wrote an open letter urging President Clinton "to turn [his] Administration's attention to implementing a strategy for removing Saddam's regime from power . . . [with a full complement of diplomatic, political and military efforts." It was the prelude to January 2001: taking up his post with Vice President Cheney, Wurmser emphasized that "America's and Israel's responses must be regional, not local" and proposed that Washington and Tel Aviv should "strike fully, not merely disarm, the centers of radicalism in the region—the regimes of Damascus, Baghdad, Tripoli, Tehran, and Gaza."[19]

This inner circle of activists would be checked in early 2001 with the initial National Security Council discussions failing to agree on an approved course of action. In part, this was because Wolfowitz and Feith were not confirmed in their posts until the spring. Without their day-to-day presence, Rumsfeld focused on transformation, almost to the point of obsession, and did not press the option of overthrowing Saddam. He commented, "I'm after the weapons of mass destruction [WMD]. Regime change isn't my prime concern."[20] In part, this was because of the opposition of key officials such as Secretary of State Colin Powell, and, in part, it was because Bush was reluctant to set out a defined course of action; as a White House official later reflected, "Faced with a dilemma, he has this favorite phrase he uses all the time: Protect my flexibility."[21]

The Iraq resolution also awaited the initial steps toward the unipolar, signaled during the campaign, through the development of capabilities and detachment from international agreements and bilateral negotiations. The emphasis on missile defense was supported by the administration's declaration that it would abrogate the 1972 Anti-Ballistic Missile Treaty and the suspension of the Clinton administration's talks on the North Korean nuclear program. Agreements on the environment, the International Criminal Court, and chemical and biological weapons were quickly rejected by Bush and his advisers.

Key officials thus hedged their bets on intervention in Iraq. At his confirmation hearings, Paul Wolfowitz professed his desire for the overthrow of Saddam Hussein but, when asked if there was a feasible plan to achieve this, admitted, "I haven't seen it yet."[22] Cheney said inspections of Iraqi facilities "may not be as crucial if you've got other measures in place."[23] At lower levels, however, the activists ensured that their plans were further developed, to the point that they constituted a de facto policy. Within hours of the initial NSC meetings, information leaked to the press that "the Bush administration has given Iraqi opposition groups permission to resume their activities inside Iraq with American funding," finally releasing the first tranche of four million dollars from the 1998 Iraq Liberation Act. Bush announced on February 6 that the United States would resume the funding of opposition efforts inside Iraq for the first time since 1996.[24] Ten days later, the moves for covert operations were complemented by the most extensive bombing of Iraqi positions—approved by members of the NSC, including Powell, and recommended to the president—since December 1998.[25]

Importantly, these plans and operations could always become part of the larger conception of the American unipolar in the Middle East, especially if they found a high-level advocate who could link government and the private sector. Cheney filled this role as he sought a redefinition of foreign policy linked to control of energy resources. A National Security Council directive of February 3 commanded NSC staff to cooperate with the Energy Task Force, led by the vice president, as it pursued the "melding" of "the review of operational policies towards rogue states" with "actions regarding the capture of new and existing oil and gas fields."[26] Industry executives and Cheney's staff pored over a map of Iraq, void of all features except the location of its main oil deposits, divided into nine exploration blocks.[27]

Still, with the administration occupied or constrained by crises such as the April 2001 clash with China over the downing of an American spy plane and an escalation of violence in Israel and Palestine, by "terrorism" (including consideration of action to undermine or topple the Taliban and break up al-Qaeda),[28] and by hostility to American policy in Europe and beyond, the focus had to remain on capabilities and the clearing of political and military space for unilateral action. Bush, often away from Washington, seemed detached from day-to-day discussions, let alone policy making.[29] Instead, it was Rumsfeld and Cheney who persisted with the broadest conception of the use of American power. The vice president spoke of "an organizing principle for US foreign policy that could be compared to the Cold War":

There are still regions of the world that are strategically vital to the
US. . . . And anything that would threaten their independence or their
relationships with the United States would be a threat to us. Also,
you've got to worry about North Korea. You've got to worry about
the Iraqis, what ultimately develops in Iran. . . . I think we have to be
more concerned than we ever have about so-called homeland defense,
the vulnerability of our system to different kinds of attacks. Some of
it homegrown, like Oklahoma City. Some inspired by terrorists external to the United States. . . . The threat of terrorist attack against the
US, eventually, potentially, with weapons of mass destruction—bugs or
gas or biological or chemical agents, potentially even someday nuclear
weapons.[30]

It was on September 11, 2001, that broad conception turned into the
reality of planning and implementation. Soon after al-Qaeda hijackers
struck the World Trade Center and Pentagon, national security adviser
Condoleezza Rice asked her staff, "How do you capitalize on these opportunities?" a sentiment repeated by President Bush to his closest advisers: "This is a great opportunity. We have to think of this as an opportunity."[31] Specifically, the Bush administration had the ideal pretext
to take up the demonstration case of Iraq. Rumsfeld commanded his
staff: "Best info fast. Judge whether good enough hit S. H. [Saddam
Hussein] at same time. Not only UBL [Osama bin Laden]. . . . Go mas-
sive, sweep it all up. Things related and not."[32] The president was in step
with his advisers, allegedly telling counterterrorism coordinator Richard Clarke, "I want you to find whether Iraq did this." While the National Security Council rejected the proposal, tabled by Wolfowitz, to
hit Iraq immediately, Bush confirmed to British prime minister Tony
Blair, "We must deal with this first. But when we have dealt with Afghanistan, we must come back to Iraq."[33]

Activists at working levels could now set up the pretext for overt as
well as covert operations. On September 18–19, Perle's Defense Planning Board met to discuss the topic of Saddam Hussein and regime
change. Their featured guest was Ahmad Chalabi, who assured the
gathering that Iraq was both an incubator for terrorists and a possessor
of weapons of mass destruction.[34] In October Douglas Feith set up the
Policy Counter-Terrorism Evaluation Group (PCEG) to convert such
assertions into the "intelligence" that would be presented as the casus
belli against Iraq.[35] (Francis Brooke, Chalabi's Washington aide, sum-

marized the process: "I sent out an all-points bulletin to our network, saying, 'Look, guys, get me a terrorist, or someone who works with terrorists. And, if you can get stuff on W. M. D., send it!'")[36] A few months later, the PCEG was supplemented by the Office of Special Plans, a war-planning unit under Wolfowitz and Feith's direction.[37] Bush gave the ad hoc units political cover; as he told a group of senators meeting with Rice, "Fuck Saddam. We're taking him out."[38]

The subsequent narrative of American intervention in Iraq is now generally known. On November 21, 2001, before the "liberation" of Afghanistan was completed, Bush asked Rumsfeld to draw up plans for the invasion of Iraq.[39] In early March 2002, as US forces were failing to capture Osama bin Laden in the Tora Bora Mountains, Cheney was traveling to the United Kingdom and Arab countries to announce the shift in attention from the Afghan theater to Baghdad.[40] When this initial attempt was checked by the skepticism of Arab leaders, the escalating crisis in Israel, and a lack of "intelligence" that could be presented as pretext for military operations, the Bush administration adjusted its timetable and rolled out the campaign for action in August, beginning with Cheney's speech at the Veterans of Foreign Wars (VFW) National Convention, warning of an imminent Iraqi nuclear weapons capability.[41]

Similarly, the devolution of "Mission Accomplished" into a protracted occupation of Iraq, with chaos rather than stability and a very untidy "freedom," is now being well documented. However, this ongoing story of Iraq still does not get to the heart of the Bush administration's strategy and, thus, the reasons for the failure of the "unipolar." The problem for the US government was that the invasion of Iraq was never pursued with attention to the specific conditions of Iraq but was conducted as the demonstration of a US preponderance of power, beyond Baghdad, "against everyone and against no one." The military assault could demonstrate American capabilities to all possible rivals. It could seek the extension of those capabilities with the acquisition and development of American influence over the Iraqi economy and resources. It could even be heralded as the catalyst of a regional transformation, demonstrating "freedom" while at the same time establishing an order supporting long-term American interests.

The unipolar was being projected against no one, its arena emptied of "local" political, economic, and cultural meaning. By definition, the unipolar could not recognize the possibility of alternative loci of power. Actors in Iraq, apart from Saddam and his henchmen, were reduced to the passive recipients of Bush's invocation in the 2000 campaign: "If we're a humble nation, but strong, they'll welcome us."[42] Instead, the "new" Iraqi political system would be brought in from outside by exiles, such as Ahmad Chalabi and the members of the Iraqi National Congress, supported by the civilian leadership in the Pentagon. This, in very large part, explained how the general aversion to "nation building" expressed in the 2000 presidential campaign became a specific avoidance of planning for postwar Iraq (and, before that, postwar Afghanistan).[43]

When the failure to address local structures and dynamics, including the rejection of elections throughout 2003, fed growing Iraqi dissatisfaction and then resistance, the Bush administration's rationale for the unipolar was turned against itself. Expressed in the president's West Point speech in June 2002, the American premise was that the display of military capability would prompt others—inside Iraq, throughout the Middle East, and throughout the world—to follow US political and economic agendas.[44] But as those agendas were exposed with social breakdown in Iraq, then the American demonstration of capabilities came under scrutiny. Instead of post-Saddam Iraq serving as a model for other countries that the United States wanted to transform, it provided the rationale for others in those countries who wished to challenge an American preponderance. Ironically, the architects of the 1996 "Clean Break" had been proved correct in their vision of a transformation across the Middle East; however, instead of enhancing US power, the "domino effect" was a regional and global increase in anti-Washington sentiment and an exacerbation of existing conflicts.

For a brief period at the start of 2005, there was a false dawn for the unipolar with the first Iraqi national elections and a wave of demonstrations and uprisings from the Ukraine to Georgia to Lebanon. Shifting from a security-based rationale ("We fight them over there so we don't have to fight them here") to one based on ideological projection, the Bush administration proclaimed a "freedom agenda" that would uphold the benevolent, transforming potential of American power. The president proclaimed in his 2005 State of the Union address, "We are all part of a great venture: To extend the promise of freedom in our country, to renew the values that sustain our liberty, and to spread the peace that freedom brings."[45]

The problem was that this American proclamation of "freedom" was just as abstracted, and just as detached from local political, economic, and cultural conditions, as the US military intervention that had preceded it. Elections in Iraq would not lead to stability. The demonstrations in Lebanon, as well as American pressure, might have accelerated a withdrawal of Syrian forces, but they did not produce either the welcoming of US influence or a lasting political accommodation. Even the less problematic cases such as Ukraine and Georgia would be complicated by internal political turmoil that fractured "pro-Western" governments, suspended parliaments, and led to the imposition of emergency rule.

And, inevitably, the American unipolar faced the tensions and even contradictions between its threat-based and ideology-based rationales. The June 2005 call of Condoleezza Rice, now secretary of state, in Cairo to stand with those "demanding freedom for themselves and democracy for their countries"[46] was soon overtaken by the Egyptian government's crackdown on dissent and political and religious opposition. Democracy in Palestine led to the popular election of Hamas in Gaza, a result that cut against the Bush administration's strategy for "security" and against "terrorism" in the area. And, somewhat ironically, the US government retreated from any call for liberation in North Korea because this would complicate efforts to deal with Pyongyang's possible capability in nuclear weapons. By 2006 the administration had effectively abandoned the "freedom agenda," apart from the set pieces of Bush's meetings with dissidents and a short-lived initiative at the G8 summit in Prague in June 2007.

In the current international context, it is easy to criticize a Bushian foreign policy, which, in the last months of the presidential tenure, was reduced to a desperate quest for some success heralding and extending American leadership. US power might remove a Saddam Hussein but offered little consideration of the political, economic, or cultural circumstances that followed regime change. Those who would either accept American preponderance or risk being on the receiving end of US capabilities were little more than an abstracted Other, a population that, despite signs of resistance and insurgency, supposedly had "flowers in their minds." In this construction of "us" and "them," failure lay not, as so-called neoconservatives claimed, in a negligence when establishing American hegemony but within the concept itself.

Recognition of this flaw, however, forces a more difficult task: to critique the pursuit of American preponderance, not by the Bush administration but by its would-be successors. A longtime supporter of the quest for the unipolar as Robert Kagan might persist with an assertion of American power that ignores any substantive consideration of the "recipients" of that power: "American predominance in the main categories of power persists as a key feature of the international system. The enormous and productive American economy remains at the center of the international economic system. American democratic principles are shared by over a hundred nations. The American military is not only the largest but the only one capable of projecting force into distant theaters."[47]

Yet Joseph Nye, even as he criticized the manner and approach of the Bush administration, did not question the notion of American hegemony; he merely searched for a kinder, gentler way of achieving it: "If I can get you to want to do what I want, then I do not have to force you to do what you do *not* want to do."

Unable to transcend the symbolism of 9/11 bifurcating the world between supporters of freedom and supporters of terrorism, those claiming to oppose the unipolar wound up as allies of those advocating the quest for that power. As Paul Berman ruefully lamented after his mission against Islamo-fascism ran aground in Iraq, "I'm not sure we're speaking the same language because I don't know how to judge the language of the neoconservatives."[48] Still, far from critiquing the fundamentals of such ambition and its demise, those advocating "liberal intervention" fashion a benevolent American imperium that—somehow—coexists with and even orchestrates the multipolar. Michael Ignatieff set out the rationalization just before the invasion of Iraq: "The choice is one between two evils, between containing and leaving a tyrant in place and the targeted use of force, which will kill people but free a nation from the tyrant's grip. . . . This is finally what makes an invasion of Iraq an imperial act: for it to succeed, it will have to build freedom."[49]

This advocacy of the benevolent hegemon, albeit with "soft power" rather than "hard power" as the favored method, spectacularly avoided the fundamental point about power, for it avoided those who perceive, receive, and negotiate that power. These non-Americans are far from an undifferentiated mass either welcoming their US-delivered freedom or—from ignorance, misguided anger, religious fanaticism, or self-hatred—pursuing "anti-Americanism." Indeed, in their consideration of political, economic, and cultural issues, they may not even wish to put "America" in the center.

At the state level, China pursues organizations such as the Shanghai Cooperation Organisation and establishes itself as the broker of US–North Korean talks, Iran builds up links not only with Middle Eastern groups but also with central Asian interests and India, and Venezuela positions itself as a possible rival to Washington in the political, economic, and cultural dynamics of a new Western Hemisphere alignment. Perhaps more important, at the level of the community or even the individual, decisions of identity, expression, and action are made that do not pivot around "What does America think of me?" or "What do I think of America?"

In one of the most arrogant post-9/11 statements, John Lewis Gaddis maintained: "Empire is as American as apple pie. . . . It seems to me on balance American imperial power in the 20th century has been a remarkable force for good, for democracy, for prosperity. What is striking is that great opposition has not arisen to the American empire."[50] The issue here is not whether America does or does not constitute an empire. Rather, it is that an interpreter like Gaddis—who, basing his analysis on his standing as a historian, claims to be beyond a political position such as "neoconservative"—can so easily conflate values and power and, by putting that conflation under an "American" umbrella, negate the values and power of others.

If Iraq exposed the folly of that simplistic formula, it is still the case that the wider constructions of power—for which Iraq was supposed to serve as the catalytic demonstration—will be pursued. The fact that this pursuit may be by those claiming benevolent "soft" leadership of the multipolar is not beside the point; indeed, it dangerously reaffirms it. Until the American gorilla is shifted from the center of our rooms, "liberation" will be no more than a political and ideological catchphrase.

That shifting of the gorilla need not be framed as an antagonistic response. Indeed, it should not be, as that merely plays into the agenda of those who use "anti-Americanism" as a pejorative cloak as well as those who frame international relations as conflict rather than dialogue seeking common advance.

American Studies in the Middle East

For me, "American studies" in the Middle East is part of the desired, perhaps essential, process. The productive is that American studies is not just about "America"; it is also about us, whether we are located in the Middle East, Asia, Latin America, Africa, or indeed in that "America" that is far more than a homogenous entity mobilized by the state. American studies is not a deference through reverence to US-based groups, any more than it is a presumed castigation of them. American studies, instead, interacts with our own aspirations that may include "America" but are not dependent upon it.

Pursuing that American studies, we invert the ambition of the US government's 1992 Defense Planning Guidance, the foundation of the Bush administration's approach: "Our first objective is to prevent the re-emergence of a new rival." We will not be prevented, we will emerge, and we—not anyone in a Washington office thousands of miles away—will set the terms of an examination rather than reduce it to rivalry.

Notes

1. Michael Cox, "Empire, Imperialism and the Bush Doctrine," *Review of International Studies* 30 (2004): 596–597.

2. Studies that characterize the Bush administration as "neoconservative" include James Mann, *The Rise of the Vulcans* (New York: Viking, 2004); Francis Fukuyama, "The Neoconservative Moment," *National Interest* (Summer 2004): 57–68; and Jacob Heilbrunn, *They Knew They Were Right: The Rise of the Neocons* (New York: Doubleday, 2008). "Neo-Wilsonianism" is invoked by academics such as James McCormick, "The Foreign Policy of the George W. Bush Administration," in *High Risk and Big Ambition: The Presidency of George W. Bush*, edited by Steven E. Schier (Pittsburgh: University of Pittsburgh Press, 2004), 189–223; and commentators such as Rich Lowry, "The 'To Hell with Them' Hawks," *National Review* (March 27, 2006), http://www.nationalreview.com/lowry/lowry200603200538.asp. "Democratic idealism" is the chosen label of Shadi Hamid, "The Vision Gap, Part 1," *American Prospect* (August 23, 2006), http://www.prospect.org/cs/articles?articleId=11913. The call for "democratic realism" can be found in Charles Krauthammer, "An American Foreign Policy for a Unipolar World," Irving Kristol Lecture, American Enterprise Institute, February 10, 2004, http://www.aei.org/publications/pubID.19912,filter.all/pub_detail.asp.

3. John Lewis Gaddis, *Surprise, Security, and the American Experience* (Cambridge, MA: Harvard University Press, 2005); Melvyn Leffler, "9/11 and American Foreign Policy," *Diplomatic History* 29, no. 3 (2005): 395–413.

4. George W. Bush, comments at joint press conference with British prime minister Gordon Brown, April 17, 2008, http://www.whitehouse.gov/news/releases/2008/04/20080417–4.html. A recent study that classified six doctrinal stages in Bush foreign policy, culminating with no strategy at all, is Jacob Weisberg, *The Bush Tragedy* (New York: Random House, 2008).

5. Barack Obama, inaugural speech, January 20, 2009, http://www.cnn.com/2009/POLITICS/01/20/obama.politics/index.html.

6. Barack Obama, speech, April 6, 2009, http://enduringamerica.com/2009/04/06/video-obama-speech-in-turkey/.

7. Barack Obama, speech, June 4, 2009, http://www.washingtonpost.com/wp-dyn/content/article/2009/06/04/AR2009060401117.html.

8. The Princeton Project on National Security, "Forging a World of Liberty

under Law," September 27, 2006, http://www.princeton.edu/~ppns/report/FinalReport.pdf.

9. Ibid., 58.

10. "By periodically using our status as the sole superpower to flex our military might, to disdain multilateral institutions, and particularly to try to unilaterally transform the domestic politics of other states, we have triggered a backlash that increases extreme anti-Americanism, discourages key actors from fully cooperating with us, and weakens our global authority" (ibid., 17).

11. Ibid.

12. Ivo Daalder and Robert Kagan, "The Next Intervention," *Washington Post*, August 6, 2007.

13. Robert Kaplan, "Equal Alliance, Unequal Roles," *New York Times*, March 27, 2008.

14. Larry Rohter, "McCain, in Foreign Policy Talk, Turns His Back on Unilateralism," *New York Times*, March 27, 2008; "Bush the Multilateralist," *Wall Street Journal*, March 28, 2008.

15. Public Broadcasting System, *Frontline: The War behind Closed Doors*, http://www.pbs.org/wgbh/pages/frontline/shows/iraq/etc/wolf.html.

16. David Phillips, *Losing Iraq: Inside the Postwar Reconstruction Fiasco* (New York: Basic Books, 2005), 8.

17. Institute for Advanced Strategic and Political Studies, *A Clean Break: A New Strategy for Securing the Realm*, June 1996, http://www.iasps.org/strat1.htm.

18. James Bamford, *A Pretext for War: 9/11, Iraq and the Abuse of America's Intelligence Agencies* (New York: Doubleday, 2004), 293–294.

19. Project for a New American Century, "Letter to President Clinton on Iraq," January 26, 1998, http://www.newamericancentury.org/iraqclintonletter.htm; David Wurmser, "Middle East 'War': How Did It Come to This?," *AEI on the Issues*, January 1, 2001, http://www.aei.org/publications/pubID.12266/pub_detail.asp.

20. Ron Suskind, *The Price of Loyalty* (New York: Simon and Schuster, 2004), 85.

21. David Rose et al., "The Path to War," *Vanity Fair*, May 2004, 106.

22. Stefan Halper and Jonathan Clarke, *America Alone: The Neoconservatives and the Global Order* (Cambridge: Cambridge University Press, 2005), 148; Andrew Bacevich, *American Empire: The Realities and Consequences of American Diplomacy* (Cambridge, MA: Harvard University Press, 2002), 207.

23. Quoted in John Prados, *Hoodwinked: The Documents That Reveal How Bush Sold Us a War* (New York: New Press, 2004), 4.

24. Nicholas Arons, "US Supported Iraqi Opposition," *Foreign Policy in Focus* (April 2001), http://www.fpif.org/briefs/vol6/v6n10iraq.html.

25. Bacevich, *American Empire*, 207–208; Inter Press Service, "Is There a Strategy?," February 20, 2001, http://www.highbeam.com/doc/1P1-42047216.html; Alan Sipress and Dan Balz, "Bush Signals Escalation in Response to Hussein," *Washington Post*, February 17, 2001; Bob Woodward, *State of Denial* (New York: Simon and Schuster, 2006), 22.

26. Jane Mayer, "Contract Sport: What Did the Vice-President Do for Halliburton?," *New Yorker*, February 16, 2004, http://www.newyorker.com/archive/2004/02/16/040216fa_fact.

27. Mark Levine, "Waist Deep in Big Oil," *Nation*, December 12, 2005, http://www.thenation.com/docprem.mhtml?i=20051212&s=levine.

28. Lewis Solomon, *Paul Wolfowitz: Visionary Intellectual, Policymaker, and Strategist* (Westport, CT: Praeger, 2007), 71–73; Mann, *Rise of the Vulcans*, 298–299; Michael Meacher, "This War on Terrorism Is Bogus," *Guardian* (London), September 6, 2003; Bob Woodward, *Bush at War* (New York: Simon and Schuster, 2003), 35.

29. See Katharine Seelye, "President Is on Vacation, Mostly Not Taking It Easy," *New York Times*, August 7, 2001.

30. Cited in Nicholas Lemann, "The Quiet Man," *New Yorker*, May 7, 2001, http://web.archive.org/web/20040918102730/http://www.newyorker.com/archive/content/?040906fr_archive06.

31. Rice cited in Nicholas Lemann, "The Next World Order," *New Yorker*, April 1, 2002, http://www.newyorker.com/archive/2002/04/01/020401fa_FACT1?currentPage=2; Woodward, *Bush at War*, 26–32.

32. "Plans for Iraq Attack Began on 9/11," *CBS News*, September 4, 2002, http://www.cbsnews.com/stories/2002/09/04/september11/main520830.shtml.

33. Rose et al., "The Path to War," 108, 110.

34. Bamford, *Pretext for War*, 287; Rose et al., "The Path to War," 108.

35. Bamford, *Pretext for War*, 289–291.

36. Jane Mayer, "The Manipulator," *New Yorker*, June 7, 2004, http://www.newyorker.com/archive/2004/06/07/040607fa_fact1.

37. Robert Dreyfuss and Jason Vest, "The Lie Factory," *Mother Jones*, January–February 2004, http://www.motherjones.com/news/feature/2004/01/12_405.html.

38. Daniel Eisenberg, "We're Taking Him Out," *Time*, May 13, 2002.

39. Woodward, *State of Denial*, 81–82.

40. Michael Gordon and Bernard Trainor, *Cobra II* (London: Atlantic, 2006), 40–43; Steve Richards and Rupert Cornwell, "United They Stand. But Will Tony Follow George All the Way to Baghdad?," *Independent* (London), March 10, 2002; Toby Harnden, "Cheney Begins Mission to Win Arab Minds," *Daily Telegraph* (London), March 13, 2002.

41. "Vice President Speaks at VFW 103rd National Convention," August 26, 2002, http://www.whitehouse.gov/news/releases/2002/08/20020826.html.

42. Bush-Gore presidential debate, October 11, 2000, http://www.debates.org/pages/trans2000b.html.

43. On Afghanistan, see Ivo Daalder and James M. Lindsay, *America Unbound: The Bush Revolution in Foreign Policy* (Hoboken, NJ: Wiley, 2005), 112, 115.

44. "President Bush Delivers Graduation Speech at West Point," June 1, 2002, http://www.whitehouse.gov/news/releases/2002/06/20020601-3.html.

45. George W. Bush, State of the Union address, February 2, 2005, http://www.whitehouse.gov/news/releases/2005/02/20050202-11.html.

46. Rice, remarks at the American University in Cairo, June 20, 2005, http://www.state.gov/secretary/rm/2005/48328.htm.

47. Robert Kagan, "End of Dreams, Return of History," *Policy Review* (August–September 2007), http://www.hoover.org/publications/policyreview /8552512.html.

48. Quoted in George Packer, *The Assassins' Gate: America in Iraq* (New York: Farrar, Strauss, and Giroux, 2006), 59.

49. Michael Ignatieff, "The Burden," *New York Times Magazine*, January 5, 2003.

50. John Gaddis and Paul Kennedy, "Kill the Empire! (Or Not)," *New York Times*, July 25, 2004.

CHAPTER 5

Discourse, Palestine, and the Authoritative News Media

LUKE PETERSON

The Palestinian-Israeli situation pervades the atmosphere in the Middle East. Students in American studies, reading accounts of events from both Middle Eastern and Western media, soon become aware of the discrepancies in reporting the same event. "How to read the media" becomes an important part of their experiences. They strive to understand how the West, particularly the United States, perceives the Palestinian situation.

This chapter attempts to elucidate the process by which "we" in the United States think about, discuss, comprehend, and evaluate Palestine, the Palestinians, and the Palestinian-Israeli conflict. The fuel that propels these thoughts is language: what is said about Palestine, and how it is said. For the purposes of this study, the source location of this language as it is actively used is the contemporary news media, the standard-bearers of information about events in the world and the vehicles for its distribution. Using examples from news media coverage during the violent summer of 2006, this chapter seeks to explain the manner in which public knowledge about Palestine is formed and to demonstrate the ways in which that public knowledge is structured, maintained, and dispersed by authoritative print news media in the construction of a discourse on Palestine in the contemporary United States.

The theoretical approach that guides this investigation is the tradition of critical discourse analysis (also called critical linguistics). Despite the important role of the news media in discourse formation, an analysis of news media representations alone does not constitute a comprehensive examination of contemporary discourse. Instead, what is offered here is a consideration of authoritative statements constituting a crucial and indivisible part of the complete discourse on Palestine in the

United States. I offer this framework not as a singular authoritative volume on the state of contemporary discourse, but rather as an active and functional approach for considering how we, as consumers of the news media in the United States, conceive of Palestine and the Palestinian.

The extent of the impact of the contemporary, authoritative news media upon the creation of the discourse on Palestine in the United States is difficult to overstate. According to University of Texas at Austin journalism professor Robert Jensen, the press is considered an important part of free society in the United States and, even when openly criticized, is generally trusted to present accurate information. As an institution of discourse production, the news media are responsible for a vast amount of public education on an incredible array of topics, from the distant and experientially unknowable to the local and intimately familiar. The information received by the consuming public is generally trusted because of the structures of verifiability applied in the production of the news. The public assumes that the information being reported is authentic and reliable.[1]

The construction and reconstruction of events by the news media come from multiple and ostensibly independent sources. But when many authoritative news sources construct and distribute similar versions of the same story, the discourse becomes substantially narrowed. The knowledge subsequently constructed based upon the information related by the popular news media begins to conform among the consumers of the news.

Alternative presentations that do not conform to the standard authoritative narrative create a cognitive dissonance and therefore appear spurious and illegitimate. This imbues the information generated by the authoritative media with a substantial amount of weight when compared with independent or otherwise marginal news sources. The authority bestowed upon the popular news media and the assumed veracity of the information they present renders the authoritative news media as a discursive elite. Discourse analyst Teun Van Dijk describes discursive elites as "members of dominant groups and organizations [that] have a special role in planning, decision-making and control over the relations and processes of the enactment of power. . . . [S]uch elites also have special access to discourse: they are literally the ones who have most to say. . . . [W]e define elites precisely in terms of their . . . power . . . as measured by the extent of their discursive and communicative scope and resources."[2] This position of the "discursive elite" is one of expansive ability to structure the parameters of a given discourse. Discursive elites control the construction of frames of knowledge and social representations. The authoritative news media in the United States can be a "discursive elite" in the ongoing discourse on Palestine, given that it serves to provide a substantial and authoritative contribution to the discourse on Palestine. As Van Dijk shows, the news media have the most to say about Palestine and the most authoritative and institutional power with which to say it.

According to other theories of discourse construction, however, the relationship of power between the popular news media and the general public is not unidirectional. In these conceptions, the individual actor can accept or reject the offerings of the discursive elite and can reform, redistribute, or reify the structure of the discourse presented to him or her.[3] Three primary factors combine to reduce individual agency in the contemporary discourse on Palestine in the United States, however. First, Palestine is too distant (both experientially and cognitively) for most individuals to feel capable of questioning the structure of discourse. Few in the media-consuming public have firsthand knowledge that can challenge or otherwise contradict mass-produced and popular media representations. Second, the degree of homogeneity of perspective that exists within the news media, even across diverse media outlets, significantly reduces a reader's, listener's, or viewer's access to broader views of the issues. Relying regularly upon the news media to relay information about Palestine, a news media consumer may not be aware that important components of the discourse are either missing from popular representations or that information on Palestine is deterministically or reductively represented by the news media. Finally, the active pursuit of alternative media sources either domestically or internationally, whether in the discourse on Palestine or in general, has not been encouraged in the contemporary United States,[4] even though technology offers outlets for such searches.

For these reasons, the news media have "a powerful role in the final definition of the situation."[5] With regard to Palestine and to the Palestinian-Israeli conflict, this final definition "sets [the] boundaries around thinking on Palestinian-Israeli issues." According to analyst Kathleen Christison, the news media definition of the conflict "is for the most part Israel-centered, approaching the conflict generally from an Israeli perspective and seldom recognizing the existence or the legitimacy of a Palestinian perspective."[6] This Israel-centered perspective in the news media effectively structures reality about Palestine-Israel for the news consumer. In interpreting Palestine-Israel, therefore, individuals are isolated from the formation of alternative, non-"Israel-centered" frames of knowledge and are therefore hindered in their practical construction of political and social realities. Crucially, given that "social realities form the cement with which we construct our conception of what is real and what is not, what is important and what is not,"[7] the reality of what are Palestine-Israel and the Palestinian-Israeli conflict is substantially determined by the composition of contemporary discourse, itself heavily informed by news media representations. Students in American studies suspect this, and a growing number of readers and viewers in the United States do as well. But an analysis of one incident can show how this skewing of the news is accomplished. Knowing this can aid the media consumer to read with a more assured critical stance. A classic example of such media skewing lies in the story of Gilad Shalit.

From "Captured" to "Kidnapped": Palestine, 2006

The pattern of discourse construction described above was effectively maintained within news media representations in the United States during the summer months of 2006. On Sunday, June 25, 2006, a group of Palestinians crossed the border between the Gaza Strip and Israel and staged an attack on an Israeli military position. The Israeli soldiers, part of the permanent Israeli military presence occupying Palestine since June 1967, sustained a number of casualties. Additionally, this maneuver resulted in the capture of an Israeli soldier. He was removed from the battlefield and taken to an unknown location somewhere within the Gaza Strip.[8] This event received immediate and intense news coverage around the world, especially in the United States. The events surrounding this attack and capture soon resulted in widespread violence in Palestine and, shortly thereafter, in Lebanon too. There, two weeks after the capture of the Israeli soldier near Gaza, Hezbollah fighters[9] surprised Israeli soldiers in positions along the border between those two nations, far to the north of the earlier cross-border maneuver in Gaza. These Hezbollah members, acting independently from Palestinian groups based in Gaza, attacked Israeli positions, inflicted a number of casualties, and captured two Israeli soldiers, subsequently removing them from the battlefield to a location in southern Lebanon.[10]

The two events served as catalysts for expansive Israeli military action in both Lebanon and Gaza. A campaign of aerial bombardment widely criticized by regional and international human rights groups resulted in more than a thousand civilian deaths throughout Lebanon. A concomitant artillery assault in Gaza, one of the most densely populated areas in the world, cost more than a hundred civilian lives there. But even before the outbreak of open war in the region, the import of the capture of an Israeli soldier in Gaza, and the subsequent capture of two additional Israeli soldiers by Hezbollah in southern Lebanon, was evident. The impending elevation of tensions and the potential for war quickly materialized. As such, a number of prominent newspapers and newsmagazines in the United States ran the story of the capture of the Israeli soldier in Gaza in the days following the event. Similar headlines and media attention followed the capture of the two Israeli soldiers on the Israel-Lebanon border. Although limited space allows for a consideration of only a small number of these articles, the stories that ran in the days subsequent to the event were notable for their homogeneity of journalistic perspective.

A typical example of the consideration of the aforementioned events appeared in the *Los Angeles Times* on June 26, 2006, in an article titled "2 Israeli Troops Killed in Attack," subtitled "One Soldier Is Believed Captured as Palestinians Stage Raid into Israel, Which Warns of Reprisal." The article headlined the World News section, indicating the importance of this international event to the reader. As is customary in newspaper reports, the opening paragraph (or lead) provided readers with all pertinent details of the event: "The Israeli government Sunday threatened drastic consequences after a rare cross-border raid by Palestinian militants that left two Israeli soldiers dead and another missing. . . . The *capture* of an Israeli soldier . . . sent shock waves through Israel."[11]

The leading paragraph in this type of news story has significant impact upon the manner in which the reader will comprehend and process the information presented in the remainder of the story. This paragraph provides the factual foundation upon which subsequent commentary and elaboration will be built. While all news stories ostensibly report facts throughout, the most basic information, that is, the synopsis of recent events, is typically located at the beginning of the text. Because this initial paragraph is so crucial to the interpretation and cognition of the reader, it bears closer analysis.

From the structure, order, lexical choice, and semantic device of this paragraph, the reader understands paramount action, primary actors, cause(s), and effect(s). In this particular news story, the paramount action (the journalistic "what" in question) is clearly stated, "raid by Palestinian militants." In this same phrase, a primary actor is identified as "Palestinian militants." While this is not a precise identification, it satisfies the question of "who" essential to all basic news reporting. Other important actors are similarly identified by their membership in a group participating in these events, "Israeli soldiers."

The identifying characteristics "Palestinian militants" and "Israeli soldiers" are far from neutral nomenclatures. This point can perhaps best be shown by considering possible alternative identifiers for the two main actors in this news item. For instance, the Israeli soldiers are not called "Israeli occupiers," which would emphasize their status as participants in what is internationally recognized as an illegal occupation of Palestinian territory in violation of the UN Charter, the United Nations Universal Declaration of Human Rights, and the Fourth Geneva Convention.[12] Nor are the Palestinian actors referred to as "freedom fighters" or "resisters." Instead, the reader comes to understand the Palestinians as "militants" and the Israelis as "soldiers." Although these terms may seem like obvious choices for a discussion about this particular event, or about Palestine-Israel generally, they nevertheless convey substantial meaning to the reader and contribute to the formation of frames of knowledge and subsequent cognition regarding the event and the circumstances related to it.

The identifying terms used impart character and intention and, ultimately, structure morality in the primary action being described. In this particular retelling, an "Israeli soldier" is "captured" by "Palestinian militants." Explicit in the use of the word "soldier" is the idea of legitimacy. The individual so identified is performing a military function for a recognized state or national group. Order is implied. Soldiers exist within a political and bureaucratic structure. They follow directives; they are sober and restrained precisely because the limits of their behavior are mandated by political and judicial structures that impart penalties for deviance from regulated action. The word "soldier" connotes a state structure and administrative procedures. In soldiery, there is rule of law.

But the reader is informed that "militants" captured a soldier. The slight difference that exists between the characterizations "soldier" and "militant" is roughly equivalent to the difference between "regular" and "irregular." Militants organize, arm, and direct themselves, whereas soldiers are organized, armed, and directed by state institutions. Militants are not bound by rigid bureaucratic structures—quite the opposite; their actions are unguided and unpredictable. Whereas soldiers act on behalf of states, militants, by definition, act outside of the state structure and therefore outside of established practices of policy construction, decision making, and traditional political parameters by which militaries and their constituent components, soldiers, behave. Soldiering is a legitimate profession. Militancy is illegitimate and is therefore constituted as the opposite of soldiery in every meaningful cognitive way.

These distinctions are important in processing the crucial action that took place on June 25, 2006: the "capture" of an Israeli soldier. While it has been established that "militant" is far from the lexical or cognitive equivalent of "soldier," the action that connects them, the "capture," nevertheless imparts a sense of approximate equality between the two actors. "Capture" suggests a difficult act, one that requires a combination of guile and strength. In common usage, only those things that are difficult to obtain are "captured" or caught through effort or through deception. In a broader sense, the term "capture" suggests a contest between equals, or, if not equals, between two parties that can fend for themselves and in the process either harm, frustrate, or exhaust one another. This lexical choice seems appropriate in an interaction between militants and soldiers. Both actors are armed, each with the potential to inflict deadly harm.

Consumers of media in the United States structured their understanding of this crucial event during the summer of 2006 based upon these key lexical choices, "militant," "soldier," and "capture." This format was not to remain fixed, however. In the days that followed the initial reporting of this event in the United States, a related story in the *Washington Post* commented upon details of two Israeli engagements: the capture of an Israeli soldier on the border of Gaza and the capture of two Israeli soldiers on the border of Lebanon. The article threatens the escalation of tensions in the region and suggests the possibility of a broad reoccupation of the Gaza Strip by significant numbers of Israeli forces: "Israel's government . . . signaled it was preparing to act on its own to try to rescue Cpl. Gilad Shalit, *kidnapped* a day earlier during an attack on an army post at the Gaza Strip's southeastern edge. . . . The corporal is the first Israeli soldier to be *kidnapped* by a Palestinian armed group since 1994."[13] Originally reported as a soldier "captured" in June 2006, one of the most publicized events in the Middle East during this long and violent summer metamorphosed from a "capture" into a "kidnapping" in newspapers around the United States. This alteration of the verb that elucidates the nature of the interaction between

Palestinian and Israeli fighters during the event in question favors terminology aligned with the Israeli perception and description of the event. This practice within the news media of the United States is, in fact, as commonplace as it is influential: "Many in the American media are guilty of the practice of accepting terminology coined by the Israelis. This is a highly effective device for influencing opinions."[14] In this specific case, within weeks of the initial coverage, the term "capture" was all but eradicated from media discourse surrounding this event.

The relationship between actors in this circumstance changes dramatically with this lexical shift. In the original context provided, the capture of the soldier indicates that he did not go willingly and that his resistance or, rather, his own strength, power, or ability in the paramount action resulted in exertion, trial, or difficulty experienced by his captors. A new perception results with the adoption of the term "kidnapping" to describe this event. The terms of engagement, the distribution of power, and the rule of law must be reinterpreted in order to account for this new term. The new lexical choice obliterates the roughly comparable power dynamic implied by "capture" and establishes a new one in its place. No longer are the two parties possessed of similar capabilities within the context of this action. "Kidnapping" automatically establishes victimization and, consequently, offense. The "kidnappers" are relegated to this status of offenders in the new moral structure, while the "kidnapped" is rendered as the ultimate innocent victim. As the most common venue for the application of this term typically involves the abduction of children, the subsequent effect that the term creates applied outside of the normal realm of discourse is similarly evocative, indicating a criminal perpetrator and a defenseless, innocent victim.

This shift in lexical choice and the accompanying restructuring of public perception about the event in question did not occur on a small scale or in select media markets. Rather, the newly rendered "kidnapping" appeared as a known and accepted occurrence in all major publications around the United States. In the weeks following the original reportage of the events, the *New York Times* conformed to the new standard for reporting the incident: "[Palestinian prime minister Ismail] Haniya's government . . . agreed to a historic compromise with Fatah and . . . [Palestinian] President Mahmoud Abbas. . . . But this breakthrough was quickly overshadowed by Israel's offensive into Gaza in retaliation for the *kidnapping* of an Israeli soldier, Cpl. Gilad Shalit, by Palestinian militants." A week after the event, the *Seattle Times* reported: "Analysts say the *kidnapping* of an Israeli soldier last Sunday by Hamas-led militants and the subsequent Israeli retaliation have laid bare the rift . . . [with] Palestinian Authority Prime Minister Ismail Haniyeh." And a month after the event, the *Los Angeles Times* informed: "Palestinian Authority Prime Minister Ismail Haniyeh . . . said the Israeli military offensives in the Gaza Strip and Lebanon were an attempt to establish regional dominance under the pretext of rescuing *kidnapped* soldiers, and he called for unity among the armed Palestinian factions."[15] The change in the representation of these events was ubiquitous, the effect of this alteration on contemporary discourse profound. The armed, trained, and capable Israeli soldier is remade as the powerless victim. The militant Palestinian now has an exaggerated role in terms of both power and intent. He is no longer simply aggressive; he is criminal. With the application of an alternative and powerfully evocative lexical item to describe this event, a new moral universe is created. The new altered discussion unequivocally establishes guilty Palestinian and innocent Israeli. Further, as a result of the inherent victimhood of the Israeli soldier created by the application of the term "kidnapping" in the retelling of these events, wide-scale Israeli military action in Gaza (and in Lebanon) subsequent to this event was mitigated. The new structure of the discussion asserts Israeli military action as retaliation for Palestinian instigation. Much like the opening paragraph of a leading news item, the structure of this discussion, the opening event in a summer of widespread violence in the Middle East, substantially informed public comprehension of each of the events that were to follow.

Israel in News Media Discourse: Kfar Giladi

In the discourse on Palestine in the contemporary United States, Israel receives focus as a dialectic and logical opposite to Palestine. Israel is cognitively constructed in contrast to Palestine; an understanding of one structures as well as depends upon an understanding of the other. Within contemporary discourse in the United States, both Palestine and Israel are constructed restrictively within delineated parameters. Both constructions are affected using various strategies previously mentioned: lexical choice, association or disassociation, alliance structuring and "othering" (the creation of a collective enemy), and omission of relevant historical or contextual information. Media consumers interpret these representations and subsequently conceive of Israel and the discursive counterpart to Israel, Palestine.

In an example of this reductive construction taken from the news media, a specific village in northern Israel is discussed during the 2006 Israeli engagement with Hezbollah, the de facto social, political, and military authority of southern Lebanon. The village is described in some detail and is contextualized historically, especially given its history of stalwart defense in the face of overwhelming odds: "Kfar Giladi, which sits on a small hill overlooking the valley . . . was known as the home of Joseph Trumpeldor, a legendary pioneer who helped organize an armed unit to defend Jewish farming communities in the 1920s. . . . According to Israeli legend, Trumpeldor's last words after being mortally wounded defending the community were: 'Never mind, it is good to die for our country.'"[16]

Several overtly patriotic themes are at work in this presentation. The first of them is an idealization of the rural and the pastoral. In his work on representations of the Palestinian-Israeli conflict, *Image and Reality of the Israel-Palestine Conflict*, Norman G. Finkelstein describes the importance of representations of the rural in narratives of state building. In a comparison of narrative state building that included examples from the founding of the United States as well as examples of more recent descriptions from writers in Israel, the rural landscape is constructed as beautiful, unspoiled, pastoral, and virginal.[17] It is in the narrative of the rural that the spirit of place is constructed and idealized; a state's identity develops substance through these romantic pastoral representations. The brief but important description of a settlement set upon "a small hill overlooking the valley" effectively establishes the character of the community in question, evoking an association with domestic purity and historical righteousness.

The village is alternatively referenced as a "kibbutz" at other points in the article, a term that describes isolated and independent Israeli farm communities. In fact, the term "kibbutz" evokes more than pastoralism, but actually references the foundation of the Israeli state, which involved processes of land acquisition and the establishment of communal farm projects centered on the kibbutzim along with simultaneous military conquest. The designation "kibbutz" therefore grounds the village of Kfar Giladi in the historical beginnings of the Israeli state itself and substantially reifies it as a pioneer settlement, both foundational and sacred within the mythos of modern and historic Israel.

Conceptions of the rugged, the pioneering, and the stalwart Israeli village abound in this passage characterizing both the village and its residents. The founding father of the village is also named as a "pioneer," a term that reminds the reader of the founding of the state of

Israel and further establishes the pastoral, robust nature of this discursively constructed local legend. In this sense, "pioneer" acts as a synonym for "hero" or "champion," someone who overcomes great odds to accomplish a difficult task, as well as one who innovates, invents, breaks through, or stands out. Furthermore, the descriptive connection between the modern town and the historic village serves to laud the modern residents for their stalwart determination and sets up an analogy between the legendary founders of the village and the contemporary residents. Both are constructed as peace loving, simple, and humble. Yet in the face of hostile enemies, which are subtly yet pointedly created by this same discourse, they are defensive, righteous, and ultimately victorious (both historically and contemporarily). In this brief presentation, readers understand this village to be scenic, strong, rural, and idyllic, while its inhabitants are noble, driven, and heroic in the past and today.

Self-defense and self-sacrifice are present in this narrative as well. The death of the founding father of Kfar Giladi in defense of "Jewish farming communities" calls forth the most esteemed and laudable qualities within the contemporary United States: selflessness, honor, and patriotism. The legendary founding father becomes complete as he is bestowed with perhaps the highest honor of them all, death in defense of the state. Years later, the village remembers this hero and idolizes him. The text provides the reader with the obvious analogy between the historical village with its roots as a noble town of patriots and the contemporary village as a besieged bastion of purity during recent conflict. By extension, this pure and wholesome yet besieged village is constructed as a representation of Israel itself as the cognitive frames of the reader and news consumer are formed and re-formed through news media discourse.

The adherence to duty in the face of danger, a staple of the evocative past of the village, is a quality preserved by today's Kfar Giladi soldiers: "While members of the kibbutz said they urged those [soldiers] resting near the cemetery to seek shelter . . . such concerns usually matter little to soldiers. 'We've been there for a week, and if we went to seek shelter every time there was an alarm we wouldn't be able to do our job as soldiers,' [one soldier] said from his hospital bed."[18] In this case, the comments of the wounded Israeli soldier are revealing. In this narrative of the Palestinian-Israeli conflict, only one side is given a voice in the retelling. Testimonies from the Lebanese or Palestinians wounded by Israeli action are not presented here and, as mentioned, represent perspectives that are conspicuously absent in the US news media: "The Palestinians have always to a great degree been politically invisible." This absence of perspective contributes to the one-sided nature of news media considerations of events in Palestine-Israel given that "the frame of reference that defines the limits of discourse on the Palestinian-Israeli issue is not a matter solely of terminology . . . but of knowledge withheld."[19] In the article under consideration, this assertion is true. The retelling of these events includes a single perspective only; this perspective constitutes the entire story for the reader. As with the general description of the village itself, in this abbreviated context the wounded Israeli soldier, like Joseph Trumpeldor, represents all Israelis: dutiful, moral, and noble. Because of the implied dichotomy at work in this and other news items, duty, nobility, and honor rest only with the Israeli side. Israel is represented not as hostile but rather as reluctant to hostile actions and strictly defensive as the reader hears the monologue of the Israeli soldier: "Sadly, for us, there is no happy end to this story."[20] As Palestine-Israel is understood in the contemporary United States as almost exclusively associated with violent conflict, representations of Israel in the United States contribute to an understanding of the representations of Palestine, Israel's counterpart.

A number of linguistic and conceptual elements present in this discussion are discursive staples. Israel is portrayed as the perpetual defender, even to the extent of evoking examples of historical defense or foundational legend. The discourse constructed maintains Israel's character as defensive beginning from the period of modern Jewish settlement of Palestine and continuing forward through to the most recent regional conflict. The strategy of omission is also applied within this article. Relevant historical context, including the history of Israel's occupation of Palestine, the deleterious effects of Israel's founding on Palestinian society, and the long history of violent conflict between Israel and Lebanon, is removed from the discussion of contemporary political phenomena. Although deliberately brief and direct, general news items might still bring pertinent histories to bear when describing modern circumstance (the description of the founding of Kfar Giladi, for instance, upholds this assertion). The absence of important historical content about Palestine is a regular feature of this discourse in the United States and is an important strategy responsible for the discursive narrowing and cognitive reduction that categorizes the US interpretation of Palestine.

Contemporary representations of Palestine, in fact, deliberately omit such information.[21] Provided with some measure of historical context, including the establishment of the state of Israel in 1948, the resulting flight of some seven hundred thousand Palestinian refugees, and the implementation of complete Israeli military and civil control over all areas of historic Palestine beginning in 1967, the vast majority of Palestinian action in the ongoing regional conflict could logically be framed as retaliation.[22] The consequence of this omission is the refashioning of the political and social realities of the region within the dominant discourse. As such, the historical reality of occupation, the contemporary reality of occupation, indeed all references to occupation are removed from the representations of Palestine.[23] In this new reality, Palestine threatens baselessly; Israel defends heroically.

Palestinian Guilt and Israeli Innocence: Structuring the Moral Universe

In one highly publicized incident, Israeli soldiers killed seven Palestinians picnicking on the Gaza beach in June 2006 using long-range artillery from an undisclosed location. In reporting the incident, the *Washington Post* suggested Israeli responsibility for the civilian deaths, but only in uncertain terms. More important, the article simultaneously presents the context of ever-present Palestinian militancy that might serve as motive for the Israeli military to carry out civilian killings. In doing so, this particular media report unravels the already timidly asserted argument for Israeli culpability. The text casts aspersions on any element of Israeli guilt, insinuating that Palestinian violence and an unrelenting threat to Israeli soldiers served as motive for the bombing of a civilian area. This structure presents two distinct yet discernible strategies with regard to the violence that exists in Palestine and Israel. In the first, the media provide a moral structure in which Israeli action is restrained, necessary, and even when brutal and violent justifiable. In the second, Palestinian action is simplistic, aggressive, and wholly unjustified.

The article in question begins with a neutral tone: "Israeli artillery fire targeting the northern Gaza Strip on Friday killed at least seven Palestinian civilians and wounded 30 others, Palestinian hospital officials and witnesses said."[24] In this presentation, however, there are no culpable actors for the civilian casualties save the "artillery fire" itself. The emphasis is the object, the artillery, and the reader is presented with only an implied subject. By omitting reference to the Israeli soldiers who fired the shells, or to the commanders who gave the order to fire, the article fails to impart blame on any Israeli, either an individual, a group, or an institution, responsible for the civilian deaths. The presence or absence of a named subject formulates immediate cognitive frames regarding the incident being described and serves to contribute effectively to the formation of a moral universe. Actors who can be named are guilty of action; those without names cannot be blamed.[25]

The article then shifts from a discussion of the seven dead and thirty wounded Palestinians to a consideration of other events that serve to demonstrate Israeli victimhood as a result of Palestinian violence: "The Israeli city of Sderot . . . has been hit [by rockets] several times this week. Although no Israelis have been killed in rocket fire since Israel evacuated its settlements and military bases in Gaza last year, the homemade projectiles have proved fatal in the past. At least one Israeli woman in Sderot was wounded by shrapnel this week after a rocket crashed into a house."[26] The scope of the story changes, leading the reader to a different story, the presentation of which relies upon a number of effective discursive strategies. First, it is important to consider why the above information would be presented in an article titled "Israeli Fire Kills 7 Beachgoers in Gaza." This information has no practical bearing on the death of seven Palestinians or the injury to thirty others on a Gaza beach. The purpose of this information within this particular news item is left for the reader to supply within the context of established moral frames and narrowed popular discourse. According to the structure of the issues as presented in this article, rockets fired upon Israel from positions in Palestine may very well provide reason for Israeli targeting of the Palestinian civilian population. The text goes a long way toward explaining Israeli actions and complicating social and political circumstances for Israel. Similar effort is not made to explicate Palestinian rocket fire into Israel, however. Significant context and a depth of understanding accompany the discussion of Israeli action. Discussions of Palestinian actions are reductive and simplistic. This practice establishes and reifies a moral universe in which Palestine is accused while Israel is acquitted.

The analysis above demonstrates the media's routine categorization of Israeli actions as restrained and justifiable and Palestinian actions as militant or aggressive. These categorizations speak about not only the actions themselves but the actors behind them as well. Violent Palestinian actions impugn Palestine with a violent character within discourse and subsequent public knowledge; justifiable Israeli actions impugn Israel with a passive and restrained quality. In describing events, the news media imply these characteristics and structure guilt and innocence in the process. These categorizations also take less subtle forms, however, when the media intentionally and overtly portray Palestinians as violent and Israelis as benevolent. These simplistic descriptions distort regional histories as well as contemporary realities. This process further contributes to the formation and maintenance of a restricted moral universe in the discourse on Palestine in the contemporary United States within the cognitive frames of consumers of popular news media.

Conclusion

According to UN resolutions passed during the fighting, Israeli action during the summer of 2006 constituted the invasion and occupation of another sovereign nation (Lebanon) and the simultaneous perpetuation and reification of the illegal occupation of Palestine. Nevertheless, through the news media strategies analyzed here, frames of reference including Palestinian violence and Israeli restraint, Palestinian usurpation and Israeli historical context, and Palestinian guilt and Israeli innocence all became part and parcel of the authoritative media's retelling of events in the region. Narration and contextualization mitigated Israeli action while explaining, qualifying, and justifying the results of these acts. Either overt or menacing (or both), or alternatively vaguely described or assumed (or both), Palestinian threats present the justification for broad Israeli military activity. Israel was cast as the defensive party; Palestine was the aggressor. The results of Israeli actions in terms of both human costs and damage to regional infrastructure, while devastating, went either unmentioned or underemphasized, further lessening the cognitive impact of Israeli aggression.

What ran in the *Washington Post* as a story about Israeli aggression, for instance, in fact functions as a story of Palestinian culpability. The narrative structure of the article "Israeli Fire Kills 7 Beachgoers in Gaza" leads the reader back to aggressive action and violent motive on the part of the named Palestinian actors in this narrative. The unnamed Israeli actor is alleviated of blame and re-created as just and rational. The clear threat in the article comes from the Palestinian, even though the news piece ostensibly reports about Palestinian civilian deaths as a result of Israeli aggression. This news item restructures action, causality, motive, and justification in both the story told and the broader conflict between the two parties. This moral positioning has a significant impact upon social cognition as the discourse on Palestine is interpreted through the information provided by the media coverage of these events. As such, the news media as a discursive institution go beyond the recapitulation of facts by actually imparting judgments of parties involved. These judgments conform to the broader discourse that limits the frames of knowledge of both Palestine and its discursive counterpart, Israel, through linguistic restrictions, contextual omissions, as well as value-laden characterizations consistently describing Israeli innocence while impugning guilt onto Palestine and the Palestinians.

Effectively, the authoritative news media coverage described here is part and parcel of contemporary American Orientalism, a cognitive and representative approach to the object (East) by the agent (West), which simplifies, stereotypes, and essentializes the Asian, Eastern, Oriental "other." First articulated by Edward Said in his foundational work of the same name, Orientalism was a concept that primarily described a European phenomenon characterizing the conceptual objectification of an entire region by scholars, researchers, and pundits alike. These individuals saw only the base, the backward, and the bizarre while studying the Middle East. Contemporary scholars (both American and European) have adapted this theoretical approach in order to take into account the vastly expanded political and cultural influence of the United States in the region over the course of the last century. No longer seen as an exclusively European phenomenon, Said's Orientalism has been revised in consideration of American hyperpower and is now used to describe the contemporary political and cultural approach of the United States toward the Middle East: "Orientalism is a certain type of lens; through it, Europeans *and* Americans have 'seen' an Orient that is the stuff of children's books and popular movies: a world of harems and magic lamps, mystery and decadence, irrationality and backwardness. Said's *Orientalism* provided a detailed analysis of the history of such images, as well as a language for understanding how the cognitive mapping of spaces (East versus West) and the stereotyping of peoples are both intimately connected with the processes of economics, politics, and state power."[27] The news media, while an important part of this ongoing perceptual phenomenon, are by no means the only source of Orientalist cultural products in the United States. Still, as has been elucidated herein, the news media's consideration of Palestine-Israel fits easily within the theoretical realm of a uniquely American kind of Orientalism, the pervasive "tendency to underestimate the peoples of the [Middle East] and to overestimate America's ability to make a bad situation better." Reinforced by numerous other media products, American Orientalism has arguably reached its zenith within the past decade and finds within the Palestinian-Israeli conflict a wellspring of source material from which to draw continued momentum: "Having been fed a steady diet of books, films, and news reports depicting Arabs as demonic anti-Western others and Israelis as heroic pro-Western partners . . . the American public understandably fears Osama bin Laden and cheers Aladdin."[28]

As I have argued, this manner of representation finds fertile ground for expression in the printed news media in the contemporary United States. Acknowledging that these representations are commonplace, however, "it is simply inaccurate to say that *all* American representations of the Middle East demonized Arabs and/or Islam." Nevertheless, "such demonization [is] never entirely absent" from news media presentations of events in Palestine-Israel and therefore forms an integral and irrevocable component of popular American conceptions about Arabs, Islam, and the constructed East.[29]

Within the discourse on Palestine in the United States, and decidedly so during the years of the growth of American studies programs in the Middle East (1998–2008), identities have been structured and maintained, alliances formed, and threats identified both overtly and subtly through comparisons and associations. This discourse provides substantial cognitive evidence for "othering" the Palestinian while simultaneously reinforcing the military-political alliance between Israel and the United States within popular social cognition. Likewise, significant effort has been made to equate Israeli and American positions, whereas Palestinian perspectives are grouped with other radical, violent, or terrorist motives. Frames of knowledge generated by these repetitive discursive strategies reinforce reductive constructions of complex and multifaceted political, historical, and cultural entities.

These associations and categorizations are meaningful in the development of cognition about Palestine among members of the news media–consuming public. These processes of discourse formation continue to structure and inform the American knowledge of Palestine today. As the dominant and authoritative discourse eliminates rival discourses, these frames of knowledge remain pervasive in contemporary American society; authoritative representations repeat complimentary tropes and serve as mutually reinforcing agents within the authoritative discourse. These bounded parameters of knowledge about Palestine have significant consequences for the way consumers of news media within the contemporary United States conceive of "Palestine." Cognitive frames about Palestine, Israel, and the Palestinian-Israeli conflict perpetuate accordingly.

Notes

1. Robert Jensen, "Characteristics of Journalism in the Contemporary United States."
2. Teun Van Dijk, "Principles of Critical Discourse Analysis," 255.
3. Michel Foucault, *Power/Knowledge: Selected Interviews and Other Writings, 1972–1977,* 77.
4. Jensen, "Characteristics of Journalism."
5. Teun Van Dijk, *Racism and the Press,* 42.
6. Kathleen Christison, *Perceptions of Palestine: Their Influence on US Middle East Policy,* 2.
7. Nachman Ben-Yehuda, *Sacrificing Truth: Archaeology and the Myth of Masada,* 189.
8. In August 2011 this soldier, Gilad Shalit, was released to his family.
9. These individuals are members of the political party, social aid agency, and paramilitary organization founded during the 1982 Israeli invasion of Lebanon as part of the indigenous Lebanese defense system. Tensions between Hezbollah and Israel have remained high since the bloody fighting that occurred during the original Israeli incursion. In Lebanon, as in Palestine, a state of war gave way to a state of occupation. Israel retained possession of significant portions of autonomous Lebanese territory. In 2000 the majority of this territory was vacated by the occupying Israeli army save a fertile section of territory known as the Shebaa Farms located in southwestern Lebanon. With these Occupied Territories as a source of contention, the history between Israel and Hezbollah, the acknowledged political, social, and military authority in southern Lebanon, has been volatile.
10. The dead bodies of these two soldiers (identified as Ehud Goldwasser and Eldad Regev) were returned to Israeli officials in July 2008 in exchange for Palestinian prisoner and convicted murderer Samir Kuntar, four members of Hezbollah, and roughly two hundred other Palestinian and Lebanese prisoners of Israel.
11. Laura King and Ken Ellingwood, "2 Israeli Troops Killed in Attack; One Soldier Is Believed Captured as Palestinians Stage Raid into Israel, Which Warns of Reprisal," *Los Angeles Times,* June 26, 2006, A1 (emphasis added).
12. Israeli military control of the West Bank and Gaza Strip was deemed "acquisition of territory by force" in United Nations Security Council Resolution 242. Subsequent Israeli policies inside these Occupied Territories have been deemed illegal as well, including the permanent settlement of Israeli

citizens within the borders of Occupied Territory, acts of collective punishment including the demolition of Palestinian homes, and, most recently, the construction of a separation wall that allows for the de facto Israeli annexation of significant portions of what is internationally recognized as Palestinian territory.

13. Scott Wilson, "Captors of Israeli Soldier Issue Demand: Olmert Warns of Strike," *Washington Post*, June 27, 2006, A16 (emphasis added).

14. Edmund Ghareeb, ed., *Split Vision: Arab Portrayal in the American Media*, 15.

15. Scott Attran, "Is Hamas Ready to Deal?," *New York Times*, August 17, 2006, 25 (emphasis added); Dion Nissenbaum, "Gaza Crisis Reveals Hamas Rulers' Rift with Leaders in Syria," *Seattle Times*, July 1, 2006, A10 (emphasis added); Ashraf Khalil, "Palestinian Chief Says Israel Seeks Regional Dominance," *Los Angeles Times*, July 22, 2006, A10 (emphasis added).

16. Dion Nissenbaum, "Rocket Attack 'Like Nothing You Can Imagine,'" *Seattle Times*, August 7, 2006, A12.

17. Norman Finkelstein, *Image and Reality of the Israel-Palestine Conflict*, 101.

18. Nissenbaum, "Rocket Attack," A12.

19. Christison, *Perceptions of Palestine*, 8.

20. Nissenbaum, "Rocket Attack," A12.

21. Robert Jensen in the film *Peace, Propaganda, and the Promised Land*, directed by Bathsheba Ratzkoff.

22. Rashid Khalidi, *The Iron Cage: The Story of the Palestinian Struggle for Statehood*, xxxiii–xxxiv.

23. Jensen in *Peace, Propaganda, and the Promised Land*, directed by Ratzkoff.

24. Scott Wilson, "Israeli Fire Kills 7 Beachgoers in Gaza; Military Suspends Anti-rocket Assault to Conduct Probe," *Washington Post*, June 9, 2006, A12.

25. Norman Fairclough, *Media Discourse*, 49.

26. Wilson, "Israeli Fire Kills 7 Beachgoers," A12.

27. Melani McAlister, *Epic Encounters: Culture, Media, and US Interests in the Middle East, 1945–2000*, 8–9 (emphasis added).

28. Douglas Little, *American Orientalism: The United States and the Middle East since 1945*, 314.

29. McAlister, *Epic Encounters*, 270 (emphasis added).

References

Ben-Yehuda, Nachman. *Sacrificing Truth: Archaeology and the Myth of Masada*. Amherst, NY: Humanity Books, 2002.

Christison, Kathleen. *Perceptions of Palestine: Their Influence on US Middle East Policy*. Berkeley: University of California Press, 1999.

Fairclough, Norman. *Media Discourse*. London: Edward Arnold, 1995.

Finkelstein, Norman. *Image and Reality of the Israel-Palestine Conflict.* London: Verso, 1995.

Foucault, Michel. *Power/Knowledge: Selected Interviews and Other Writings, 1972–1977.* New York: Pantheon, 1977.

Ghareeb, Edmund, ed. *Split Vision: Arab Portrayal in the American Media.* Washington, DC: Institute of Middle Eastern and African Affairs, 1977.

Jensen, Robert. "Characteristics of Journalism in the Contemporary United States." Media in the Middle East, RTF 342/MES 322 K, University of Texas at Austin, April 23, 2007.

Khalidi, Rashid. *The Iron Cage: The Story of the Palestinian Struggle for Statehood.* Boston: Beacon Press, 2006.

Little, Douglas. *American Orientalism in the United States and the Middle East since 1945.* Chapel Hill: University of North Carolina Press, 2002.

McAlister, Melani. *Epic Encounters: Culture, Media, and US Interests in the Middle East, 1945–2000.* Berkeley: University of California Press, 2001.

Ratzkoff, Bathsheba, dir. *Peace, Propaganda, and the Promised Land* [film]. Boston: Media Education Foundation, 2004.

Said, Edward. *Orientalism.* New York: Vintage, 1979.

Van Dijk, Teun. "Principles of Critical Discourse Analysis." *Discourse & Society* 4, no. 2 (1993): 249–283.

———. *Racism and the Press.* London: Routledge, 1991.

PART III

CULTURAL ENCOUNTERS

CHAPTER 6

Arabic Poetry in America

HANI ISMAIL ELAYYAN

The beginning of the twentieth century witnessed the immigration of many Lebanese and Syrian poets to America.[1] Those émigré poets, most of whom left for economic reasons, practiced different professions but also edited Arabic-speaking journals and wrote poetry in Arabic. Some of them, such as Jibran and Mikhail Noaimy, did gain a reputation in America. But many others were not noticed by American cultural circles, especially if they wrote only in Arabic. On the other hand, they are studied and admired in the Arab world and are labeled as *al-Mahjar* poets (the émigré poets). However, most of the studies dedicated to them focus on their homesickness. To Arab critics, émigré poets are Arabs who live away from home, always long for it, and are obsessed with it in their writing (Azeez Abaza 1955, 12). Although such nostalgic feelings were common, they were hardly the poets' main concern. What is ignored in such accounts is the émigrés' poetry about America.

This article examines the poetry of three émigré poets who have received recognition in the Arab world. They are Lebanese poets Illya Abu Madi and Riziq Hadad and Egyptian poet Ahmad Zaki Abushady. Abu Madi, who was born in 1891, left for Egypt in 1902 and then moved to the United States in 1911 (*Complete Works* n.d., 20). He lived in Cincinnati until 1916 and then moved to New York, where he established an Arabic journal called *as-Samir* (Companion). He is now considered one of the most famous émigré poets. Hadad, on the other hand, was a minor poet. But like Abushady, he was a medical doctor who played an important role in the Syrian community's affairs. His collection of poems was published posthumously in New York in 1945. No date of birth is mentioned in his book, but the first poem in the collection is dated 1896 in Beirut (5). His poems cover many occasions but also address some of the aspects of the immigration experience and the promotion of America. Ahmad Zaki Abushady is different in two ways: he was a Muslim Egyptian, and he immigrated to America late in his life. Born in 1892, he was trained as a medical doctor. Upon earning his degree from the University of London, he went back home only to immigrate to New York in 1946. He passed away in 1955. Abushady is credited in the Arab world for introducing free verse into Arabic poetry.

Those three poets wrote many poems about their homelands and the political predicaments of the region. However, they also wrote a lot about America. A close reading of the poetry of those important figures will demonstrate the ways in which they contributed to the discourse of acculturation and assimilation. They played a key role in the process of transforming the Arab immigrants into American citizens by creating an identity for them that would suit their new milieu. As Werner Sollors explains, "Works of ethnic literature . . . may thus be read not only as expressions of mediation between cultures but also as handbooks of socialization into the codes of Americanness" (1986, 7). The paper studies examples of such codes that were explained in émigré poetry.

The first step in that transformational process was to offer a public discussion of immigration. By voicing their feelings about leaving home, Arab poets helped other immigrants to come to grips with such a major move. The most problematic emotions that accompanied immigration and had to be dealt with included the feelings of guilt about leaving their home and families and anxiety about the new country. By pointing out the reasons for leaving home, those poets made immigration sound rational and acceptable. But entering the new country was not, of course, the end of all trouble. Immigrants needed to develop a sense of belonging to their new country and their new identity in order to get the acceptance of a white Anglo-Saxon America. During that transitional stage, those poets interfered to help in identity formation by creating an emotional unity with the American nation, a unity that is achieved through writing about incidents and events that had a significant position in the collective consciousness of the nation. Ahmad Abushady wrote, for example, about Pearl Harbor and Abu Madi about the *Titanic*, and they both did so with great empathy. They wrote about such events using the traditional genres of Arabic poetry that were usually dedicated to serious topics such as war and tragedies. Thus, they helped evoke the feelings of anger and sadness about those events in America among the Arab immigrants.

Educating immigrants about landmarks in American history would enable them to enter, to use Benedict Anderson's phrase, "the imagined community" of Americans. Such a community requires that as an

American, one shares in the making of that history or, at least, acknowledges it as his or hers and feels proud of it. However, such education was simply not enough. The immigrants needed to familiarize themselves with the cultural heritage of the country and its ethics. They needed to learn the ropes in order to survive and carve a niche for themselves in the American mosaic. That knowledge included the ways and mores of American society and its ethics. It also related to the geographical, cultural, and natural scenes in America. This is why our poets did not write only about landmarks in American history, but also wrote about religious occasions, holidays, and even everyday events. They wrote about Christmas, the beginning of spring, and everyday life. New York City is the topic of many poems, which is understandable since it was usually the first place Middle Eastern immigrants came to in America. Such poems helped create an affinity with the American natural and cultural landscapes and made the immigrant feel at home in America.

Through a close reading of the poetry of these three poets, this chapter focuses on America. The following sections will address the ways through which those poets helped to prepare Syrian immigrants to become Americans. One important step was starting the discussion of immigration and then facilitating some social, cultural, and psychological transformations in their compatriots' lifestyle.

Debating Immigration in the Poetry of Abu Madi, Hadad, and Abushady

Lebanese and Syrian immigrants left Syria, as mentioned above, for economic, religious, and social reasons. Many went to Egypt first, because it was better off and away from the direct control of the Ottoman Empire. As an Arab country, Egypt was not alien in its culture. It was, however, the first stop, a point from which immigrants left for the Americas. Immigrants would leave from Alexandria to New York, which would be their first destination. Some chose to stay in New York (like Abushady), while others went to other places but ultimately came back to New York (Abu Madi lived in Ohio but moved back to New York).

The émigré poets discussed immigration even before arriving in America. Abu Madi (n.d.g.), in one of his earliest poems, "Farewell and Complaint," addresses the steamship that he took to America:

To New York, oh daughter of Steam, take us!
For the West might help us forget the East

> A Home we wanted to elevate high,
> But it wanted nothing of that[2] (n.d.g., lines 49–52)

The speaker finds emigration to be the best way out for wise people who are rejected and fought in their homeland. He blames this unwelcoming environment on the governments that are led by despotic leaders and the illiteracy of the people who do not believe in science but instead believe in myths and talismans (515). The poet chooses to leave because he has not gotten the recognition he deserves. So it is not the speaker's fault that he is leaving.

One should not conclude from the poem above, however, that the poet disowned his homeland. In the poems that Abu Madi read at public celebrations for the community, he tended to be nostalgic about Lebanon. The fluctuations in his feelings about home probably reflected his personal feelings and also audience expectations. At Syrian functions, people expected to hear nostalgic poems that idealized the homeland. But even in such poems, the poet makes the case of the immigrants against those who condemn them for leaving their country. Not only people but even the ghost of Lebanon blame the Lebanese for leaving, and in one poem the ghost says to them:

> You are a loan to America, and should be paid
> Isn't it sarcastic for the rich to take a loan from the poor?
> Come back, for money will not make it up for me or you (n.d.j.,
>   lines 28–30)

The speaker answers Lebanon that those Lebanese people have left their country not because they hated it, but because they have inherited the love of travel and adventure from their Phoenician ancestors. It is Lebanon's influence on them to make them people who never settle for less than the best that the world could offer. The speaker then turns to his compatriots and says:

> What Lebanon said has saddened me,
> But seeing you made me happy again
> Lebanon is in you, whether you are in China or India. (lines 31–32)

The immigrants are not, as the lines show, ungrateful or disloyal. Lebanon is inside their hearts and heads. They take it with them everywhere, and thus they never actually leave it. They are not outside Lebanon for merely materialistic reasons but are trying to live up to the image of the Lebanese as entrepreneurs who always seek adventure and renewal. Lebanon in this poem is a ghost; the pressing physical presence is gone, and only a phantom remains.

Like Abu Madi, Hadad, too, glorified the immigration of Syrians in his poetry and speeches. In 1908 he delivered a speech to the Syrian Ladies' Charitable organization in which he praised Syrian immigrants to the States. His speech was entitled "New Syria," a term he used to refer to the United States. He concluded the speech with these verses:

> We overcame obstacles,
> We sought the highest places and got them,
> In spite of all our enemies
>
> Uncle Sam will know,
> We've been the protectors of magnanimity since Sam. (1945a, lines 23–24, 29–30)

The efforts of those pioneers, the poet argued, will ultimately pay off. To demonstrate the good influence of immigration on Lebanese immigrants, he told an anecdote of a visit he had paid to a little Lebanese village. There, he witnessed the death of a lady who was more than 110 years old. Despite all the years this lady lived, she had never visited a close-by castle. He used that example to remind the immigrants of the advantage they had over such people. Being in New York, he affirmed, gave the immigrants the opportunity to be witness to the emergence of one of the greatest metropolitan centers in the world. As a result of their immigration, they became richer in experience, knowledge, and culture.

Just like Abu Madi's, Abushady's poems about immigration started before he arrived in America. His first poem, "Welcoming America," is very enthusiastic about the new home:

> Peace, happy home, for I have buried death and fear
> Yesterday was a sad day for leaving my family
> And today is a feast to be free with you. (1949c, lines 1–3)

The poem, dated April 28, 1946, shows that he arrived in America with the intention of staying there. He calls it home, even before becoming an American. That initial response does not change later on. In "My

Forum," the poet comments on the eighth anniversary of his emigration from Egypt:

No place or time limit my existence
No night or day
Wherever I am, like an eagle I will be
Or like a lion (2001, lines 12–13)

In "I Will Not Go Back," he answers those who ask him to go back to Egypt. He says that Egypt never gave him the recognition that he deserved, whereas in America he gained what he dreamed of:

How should I desert a land that honored my art, and elevated me for
    no return?
I won't go back; I have a home in my exile, but from my birthplace
    I am exiled (1983g, lines 8–10)

Egypt, in the poem, is relegated to a birthplace, while America becomes home. Such a country then, he implies, should be celebrated and loved. Not only this, but one should also establish official ties with America. In a poem, "Uncle Sam," that was read at a party celebrating the naturalization of a Syrian friend, a poet named Isa Khalil Sabbagh, on December 17, 1954, Abushady says:

Good News! For uncle Isa has become Uncle Sam
Look at his beard; it has grown thicker and straighter
He was a wise old man and now is a proud young lad
Who can compete with him, when skyscrapers are built for him?
    (2000p, lines 1–3)

Naturalization, then, is a happy incident for anyone. It is a magical sea change, a total transformation that is felt at all levels, physical, emotional, and financial. This is quite a shift from the time when Syrian immigrants did not care about their official status in the States. However, the quota system established in 1924 alerted them to the importance of gaining naturalization papers to avoid trouble and potential deportations. But gaining American citizenship was not an end in itself for many Syrians. They actually sought to become Americans through belonging to America and adopting its myths as their own. The poets catered to such interests by teaching immigrants about issues that they thought mattered for Americans. They also succeeded in increasing immigrants' attachment to American institutions. The following section contains some of the lessons the poets taught the immigrants about America.

The Education of Immigrants: History Lessons

Abu Madi sought to create an emotional unity with America. By discussing great events that had a large impact on the nation, he wanted the immigrant to feel and understand those incidents. Furthermore, it was an indirect way to say that he was an American, emotionally and culturally. In one poem, "1931," he comments on the tragedy of the *Titanic*, which sent shock waves across America and touched many people immensely.

> I could never forget the perishing of the Titanic,
> Or our shock when the news flew to us
> Many nights we spent enjoying no sleep,
> And finding no pleasure (n.d.b, lines 45–47)

The speaker significantly uses "we" instead of "I" to show that he is part of a group that is touched by that tragedy. He ascribes what happened to the *Titanic* to fate that has hit the East hard and now wants to hit the West. The moral lesson he draws is that one should leave behind a good reputation (57). This idea of a good name still appeals to Arabs in general. It is usually the motive for good deeds.

Fate, however, is not to blame for other tragedies such as the atrocities of World War II, according to Hadad. In a call to Arabs, he urges them to cooperate with the Americans against Hitler, the real cause of the war. This leader, he argues, "has ranked the Arabs among the backward people in the world. And Mussolini has never pitied them. America, however, wants nothing but the good of the Arabs, and they have to work with it because it will never be defeated in the war, as he and other immigrants could see and observe" (246). In several poems, Hadad keeps reminding the immigrants of America's might. But he stresses the point that such a powerful country uses its power for the good of humanity, unlike Germany, which is an arrogant power, as evidenced by Nietzsche's idea of the superman. His descriptions of American military forces, such as in "Salute to the American Fleet," are very poetic: "Look at the fleet, many ships in a single formation / Smoothly gliding over water, like white pigeons" (1945g, lines 1–2). This fleet is so huge that even whales fear it. However, it is a force of good, not evil. With the American flags flying over it, it inspires feelings of awe in the hearts of all who see it. This fleet, the poet keeps reminding his readers, could be used for the good of Syria. In another poem, "Farewell Day," he addresses an American soldier of Syrian origin who enlisted in 1918:

Attack the army of devils, for the sake of Syria and Lebanon

Go fight and be the best fighter under that flag
For its stars tear injustice apart,
And its stripes liberate countries (1945f, lines 1, 2–4)

Liberation is not always a military act, Dr. Hadad emphasized. He also praised American attempts to liberate people from ignorance. In "A Ceremony in Honor of Dr. Howard Bliss, the President of the Syrian Protestant College" (now the American University of Beirut), he praises that group of Americans who helped establish the college and addresses the college saying,

The Bride of Syria,
All its hopes are in you concentrated
You will grow more and more beautiful everywhere
As long as that flag is flying over your buildings
Everybody saluting it, in many tongues
America is the hope of all nations small and large
America is the paradise of the universe (1945c, lines 8–13)

The lines above imply that to help Syria, Syrian immigrants should love America and be loyal to it because Americans will appreciate that and support Syria in return.

Loving one's country constitutes hating its enemy. This is why Abushady wages a strong attack against the Japanese in "The Disaster of Pearl Harbor" (1983c). In the introduction to the poem, he explains the historical background in strong terms: "In the evening of Sunday, December 1941, the telephone awoke an old American man who was taking a vacation in the countryside to tell him the news of a Japanese attack against Pearl Harbor while their delegation was negotiating peace. They caused great destruction, and harmed America with that barbaric, malicious attack. That man was shocked by that attack which was unprovoked and unjustifiable, according to any moral or civilized criteria" (263).

That old man was Harry Truman. The poet then addresses those who died in the attack and draws a comparison between the civilized and just Americans, on the one hand, and the "barbaric" Japanese, on the other. The noticeable thing is that the poem does not mention the use of the nuclear bomb against Japan. This could be some type of self-censorship, or it could indicate that he is probably buying into the American official version of the war.

Abushady also celebrated American national holidays and helped immigrants grasp their significance for Americans. In "Flag Day," marking the June 14 holiday, he salutes the American flag as a symbol of liberty and sacrifice and calls on the immigrants to appreciate what they have in America. Another poem, entitled "June's Holidays," celebrates the establishment of the Egyptian Republic in 1953 and connects it to the Fifteenth Amendment of 1868. Both occasions, he argues, were great watersheds in the quest for liberty in the world. A previous landmark is American independence, which is described in "Independence Day Holiday": "No rule today, but what the people choose / Or it will collapse if people don't want it" (1983e, line 8).

Abushady teaches his compatriots not only about historical episodes but also about the founding fathers. In "George Washington," he praises this leader for establishing the best country in the world (2000g). In "Lincoln," he praises Lincoln's humble origins and quotes him: "You defended those among us who were enslaved and shamed / And you declared, 'there will be no government, unless all are free'" (2000k, lines 8–9). Notice that the speaker equates slavery with shame, which is a term that resonates with Arabic speakers. The speaker then proceeds to analyze the reasons for the Civil War:

> You reached the highest office, and made it more honorable
> But prejudiced stupid leaders in the South
> Would not settle for less than an unjust war
>
> You made the abolition of slavery a policy,
> And the union a redline (lines 12–15, 73–74)

The lines above give the official story of the Civil War and put it in clearly ethical terms. In a poem dated 1951, "Gettysburg Address," the poet gives an analysis of the Civil War and then concludes by saying:

Be proud Gettysburg of what you have gained
The heritage of a people, a most prominent place
The sanctuary of any refugee (1983d, lines 17–19)

During the Cold War, Abushady wrote poems to make the case against communism. In "There May Be a Life That Even Pigeons Flee," he comments on an incident that took place in 1954 and involved a pigeon that was found in Algeria with a bracelet identifying its origin in Moscow. The poet saw in that pigeon a symbol of the lack of freedom in the Soviet Union. It was a country that did not appreciate individualism, unlike America, which supported free enterprise and individuality (2000o). The poets felt it was important for the immigrants to understand the free-market economy in America and appreciate the work ethic in order to succeed in the world of business. Our three poets explain these aspects of American culture in their poems.

The Work Ethic and Individualism

Abu Madi usually published translations of English poems that illustrated some aspects of American culture. One of these poems, "The Best among All Men," explains the characteristics of life in America that make it unique:

Gone is the time when a man would boast of his origins
When your heritage will do or undo you
So work, work hard, for you are not where you come from
You are not what you wear, but what you do
If you hail from a backward country and still win
Son, then you are the best among all men (n.d.c, lines 1–9, 562)

The lines above call upon the Syrians to accept the American myth of hard work as the only path to success. But they also contain a defense of immigrants' rights. Anyone who works hard, including Syrians, should be accepted by society. He or she is even better than those who are born in America because although the Syrians' country of origin is a big liability, they still manage to make it in the New World.

The reasons that Syrians were good candidates to succeed in America were tackled by many journalists at the time. Syrians were cited as being hardworking, God-fearing, family-oriented people. They also had independent spirits and great spirituality because of their closeness to the Holy Land and their roots in history (Naff 1985). However, Abu Madi realized that Syrians needed to be educated because years of Ottoman rule had diminished the educational opportunities they had.

Abu Madi urged his people to learn from Americans and be like them, especially in relation to the work ethic and good social customs. For example, in "An Intrusive Guest," he describes a night when while writing some poetry, he suddenly hears knocking at the door. It turns out that a priest wants to ask the poet for a favor. The poet explains that such practice is very rude and unacceptable (n.d.l, 481). On the other hand, good behavior, such as charity and entrepreneurship, is praised. The poet attended many events run by community members and read poems in public about them. For example, in the inaugural ceremony for a hospital in Detroit, Michigan, the poet read a poem that praised that state-of-the-art hospital, which was built through donations by Lebanese people. In "Tal Shiha Hospital," he says he has come to Detroit not for Henry Ford's money but to witness the beginning of the project and thank those who contributed to its success (n.d.t, lines 747–748). The fact that the poet was invited to attend the ceremony testifies to the function such poets played as publicists and promoters of Lebanese institutions.

Hadad, in like manner, analyzed some of the achievements and ills of the community, especially after the riots that took place in New York in 1905. Apparently, some disputes between a newspaper editor and a merchant developed into riots in the streets. Those incidents warranted coverage by the *New York Times*. A news item in the October 24, 1905, issue read, "Syrians Riot in Streets, and Many Are Hurt." Hadad was bothered by what happened. He ascribed it to sharp-tongued people who backbite and insult others. Those tongues are like fangs in snakes' mouths. He wonders in the poem "Sharp Tongues":

What caused all those fights among us
And caused them to spread like an epidemic?
Nothing but a little organ, very harmful, truly corrupting (1945h,
    lines 25–28)

He warns that all other Americans shun Syrians because of such practices. This comment demonstrates his attempt to create a sense of community by making Syrians feel responsible for the deeds of their compatriots. This is not quite the individualism that America supported. But, after all, immigrants indeed were seen as Italians, Syrians, Jews, and so forth and not as individuals. It seems the individualism stage followed assimilation.

Hadad even uses a derogatory term for non-Arabs, "A'ajim," which typically used to refer in Arabic to those who could not speak Arabic and thus were thought to be less civilized. This distinction between Arabs and non-Arabs is something that the Syrian immigrants brought with them, but probably was further fueled by frictions among the many nationalities they had to coexist with in America. The pressure on one to identify his or her national origin was stronger in a society that was too aware of race. After all, it was the habit of American newspapers to cite the national origins of criminals who were reported.

Prejudice, then, was a fact about America that Hadad understood. That awareness made him less complacent about life there. A poem entitled "The Crescent and the Dollar in New York" complains of the rampant materialism in America. He addresses the poem to a woman called Salma who lived in Syria and who was probably an imaginary character, as was the habit in old Arabic poetry:

> Do not wonder if, Salma, I told you I am a machine
> Running to work without a will of my own
> Those are the people I am mixing with, and making me like them
> A country where people from all over the world are gathered
>
> The weak fall down, and the strong survive
>
> Electricity is the goddess of the West, the protector of all countries.
>   (1945d, lines 21–23, 26, 30)

The above lines show the speaker's unease with the materialism of the country and people's obsession with work. But he recognizes that there is no way but to keep working. It is fine to blow off steam by writing poems, but he knows he has to go back to work. This is not quite the middle-class attitude that glorifies work, but he also recognizes that hard work is the best way to survive and make money. He is sick of vehicles and trains, but Americans cannot do without them.

Abushady's poetry is more upbeat about advantages of life in America. He focuses in many poems on the opportunities available to anyone who seeks to have them and works hard. In "Labor Day," a poem dated September 1954, he praises American values of hard work:

We are a nation who never accepts injustice
Opportunities are equal for all, and unemployment does not exist
The best values are equality, and fruitful labor (2000j, lines 10–13)

The portrait of America above is very idealistic. The competition field is level, so if anybody fails to achieve his or her goals, it must be a result of an individual mistake or shortcoming. America offers its citizens everything; they have to take advantage of that. In "Thanksgiving Holiday," he gives the historical background of the holiday and then voices his thanks to God for America and all that it offers:

Giving Thanks is a holiday,
To renew the happiness of our forefathers
A heritage full of glory but never too proud (1983j, lines 1–2)

America's glory, Abushady and other poets felt, was rooted in its idealistic past and its steady march toward a modern lifestyle, very unlike the regimes that controlled their countries of origin. For them, America was on the cutting edge of technology and modernity. The poets admired and celebrated modernity in their poems. They sought to teach their compatriots to enjoy new technologies and modern relations between the state and its subjects.

Modernity

Abu Madi saw a big clash between the Ottoman Empire and the West. He urged Arabs to become more scientific, more like the West. If one draws a comparison between the conditions in Syria and the West, one will notice a big gap, as reflected in his poem "1914":

They fly up in balloons, like ships in the sea
Miracles never worked even by prophets
And never dreamt of by people of yore
Westerners have flown above the skies
And we are still crying over ruins (n.d.a, lines 30–38)

The last line is a direct reference to the traditional opening of an Arabic poem, which usually starts by addressing the ruins of the beloved's house. Abu Madi had special admiration for scientific inventions. For example, he wrote poems entitled "Flight" and "On the Train" that expressed his admiration for those means of transportation. His fascination with trains and planes is understandable because at the time many of the immigrants left Syria, such methods of transportation were extremely limited. That was also true in relation to means of communication. Many immigrants were unfamiliar with such inventions, so much so that the Arabic daily *Mirror of the West* commissioned Hadad to write a poem describing the telegraph. In that poem, he praised Marconi for his genius. Science and technology were one aspect of the multifaceted Western culture. The poets sought to teach the immigrants not only about inventors but also the cultural heritage, including famous writers, works of art, and so on.

Western Cultural Heritage

Abu Madi believed in educating his compatriots about Western culture to empower them and enable them to cope with life around them. For example, he familiarized his Arab readers with the names of some famous poets. In a poem entitled "The Blind," he argues that blind poets are more inspired and have better vision than those who see with eyes that only glance at the surface of life. He mentions Milton, Homer, and the Arab poet Bashar Bin Burd. Such comparisons focus on a humanistic and universal understanding of culture that sees no major differences between Arab and Western poets. In "Hamlet," he reviews a performance of the play by a Syrian group in Canton, Ohio. He praises the young people for such an endeavor:

> It is of you, and civilized people like you
> That both scholars and commoners feel proud
> You resurrected Hamlet from his grave,
> And he is now with you in the crowd (n.d.k, lines 9–12)

After praising the group, the speaker proceeds to explain some of the lessons one can learn from *Hamlet*. Among them are the inevitability of the defeat of evil, that there will always be winners and losers, and that right will always win at the end. Therefore, Syrians should work hard and have to trust that the East will regain its past glory. Such positive moral lessons are coupled with a less flattering comment about women. The speaker finds *Hamlet* to teach that women do not keep a promise.

Abushady, too, introduced his readers to high culture. For example, "Inspiration of Beethoven" describes the double pleasure of listening to Beethoven's first symphony in an open-air performance in Central Park (1983f, 151). Abushady usually promoted Western culture upon his own initiative, through the encouragement of Syrian intellectuals, and sometimes upon the request of American cultural institutions. One example is his translation of a poem requested by the Department of Education in New Haven, Connecticut. He translated it to be displayed during the United Nations week in 1947 and then to be kept in the educational museum of that department. The poem, "My Confidence in the Fate of Humanity: A Constitution for World Unity" (1949c), explains the things that humans have in common. It also stresses rationalism. Such propaganda for the United Nations is, indirectly, a promotion of the microcosm that is America. Accepting diversity is the first step to be acculturated to life in America (Abushady 1949, 106). Syrian immigrants needed to accept their minority status and the great diversity in this new country. However, the spirit of tolerance and acceptance was not always the strongest among them. Sometimes the competition among minorities created prejudices. Abu Madi's poetry contained such examples of prejudice against African Americans.

In a poem dedicated to the beauty of Florida, Abu Madi describes the state and then turns to African Americans and expresses a racist attitude toward them:

> I was asked what I liked about it,
> "all what I could see and couldn't see," I said
> All what I saw in it was gorgeous,
> And especially its people
> All but those with black skin,
> Oh, even paradise has flies? (n.d.i, lines 25–26)

The poem does not contain any explanation for such a harsh attitude toward blacks, which is characteristic of racism, which is based on no rational reason. But then he tells himself to ignore such blemishes in the beauty of this land because there are many good things that balance out. Night always tries to suppress the light of the stars but never succeeds. And then there are Syrians in Florida who make it beautiful: "And there my people, of the best elements / Whose good natures resemble its daisies" (lines 30–31). The color symbolism is clear in the line, as he equates whiteness with beauty (both internal and external) and blackness with ugliness. He does not even need to deal with African Americans to hate them. Seeing them is enough for him, for "[it] grieves my soul to see them with the same eyes I saw the beautiful women with" (810).

Abu Madi, however, translated an English poem in which the speaker is a slave who complains about his predicament. The choice of such a poem shows sympathy for slaves. The speaker in "A Slave" complains that he cannot enjoy many things around him, just because he is a slave:

> The white rooster in the farm
> Is as beautiful as Joseph
> And I wish to hunt it but I cannot
> Because I am a slave (n.d.q, lines 4–16)

Racism and antislavery, however, are not strange bedfellows, as it might seem. Such an attitude was shared by many Americans who regretted the period of slavery in American history but could not imagine African Americans to be their equals. Many Syrians, unfortunately, shared the same racist attitude toward blacks. It is hard to judge whether it was an attitude they brought along with them or something they acquired in America. Evidence with other groups, though, shows that new immigrant groups quickly realized that dehumanizing blacks was the best way for them to be accepted in American society. In a very color-conscious culture, Syrians wanted to make sure everybody understood they were white, not colored people. That technique goes back to the time the Irish used riots against blacks to be included in America, as Noel Ignatiev argues in his excellent book *How the Irish Became White*.

The Place of Women

Although our three poets did not support total liberation of women, they were not misogynistic. They supported women's rights but called for more traditional roles for them in society. They especially talked about the injustices back in the Middle East such as arranging marriages and depriving women of education. Abu Madi's "Complaint of a Girl" is spoken by a woman who has been forced by her father to marry an older man. She says:

> The ghoul of a father threatened me
> Oh, how could I flee the ghoul of fate

They married me to a dull man who knows no pleasure
He colors his hair, but can one ever miss
The accent of someone learning Arabic? (n.d.f, lines 14–18)

The lines above acknowledge a woman's right to choose a match. Marriage not only is a duty but also involves having pleasure. Such an attitude is very different from a religious view that sees marriage as necessary for one's duty to procreate and to protect man from sin. In another poem, "The Story of Our Situation" (540), he says:

People who do not honor their women will always be low
If women are not allowed to be the suns, then our days will be
    long nights (n.d.r, lines 41–43)

Although Abu Madi mentioned beauty a lot, it was not the only criterion for love. In "The Woman and the Mirror," he asserts that physical beauty is transient and that only the beauty of the soul and morals would last (547).

Hadad, too, supported women and condemned the notion among Syrian immigrants that it was better to have boys rather than girls. This matter is discussed in his poem "Doctors and Medicine" about his practice during the Great Depression in which he points out in a comic style his suffering dealing with patients who keep complaining and blame the doctors for everything:

If the baby is a girl, they turn blue in the face, and won't have a bite
But if the baby dies, they say we killed her, and they believe it is right
    (1945e, lines 15–16)

Dr. Hadad was one of the staunch defenders of women, as the many speeches he delivered to women's organizations show. However, his message was conservative. In "Address to Syrian Women's Society," he urges Syrian women not to seek high political positions or to rebel against men. For him, women are the source of beauty in the universe. It is a romantic image but probably falls short of affirming rights for women. Having delivered his speech, Hadad read a poem in which he praised the ladies for their beautiful faces and slim bodies.

Abushady's poetry about women was along the same lines of Hadad and Abu Madi. He usually talked about a lover's suffering at the hands of a beautiful woman who would not reciprocate his love, as in "Beauty's Selfishness" (1949a, 83). Women in his poetry are the incarnation of romantic notions about love, but we do not see them as real people. A similar romantic idealization could be observed in the poetry about the countryside and nature.

The Natural and Cultural American Scene

Most of the immigrants, as mentioned in the introduction, settled in big cities, since such environments guaranteed them jobs. However, people needed to familiarize themselves with the rest of the country to get a sense of its geographical immensity. The three poets traveled to a lot of places in America, and they wrote poems about such places. These poems introduce other immigrants to major cities and natural resorts. Abu Madi, for instance, introduces his readers to different places in the United States in such poems as "Los Angeles" (n.d.m, 434), "Boston's Nights" (n.d.e, 490), "Miami, Florida" (n.d.n, 724), and "Florida" (n.d.i, 809), as well as to Canton, Ohio. He tends to focus on the natural beauty of such cities. Thus, he usually complains about New York but praises Central Park.

Hadad, too, admired Central Park. In "The Captive Lion in the Land of Freedom," he describes a visit to the zoo in New York where we see a lion trying to escape from its cage but to no avail. The poet pities it and finds it unfair of humans to restrict a wild animal's freedom, especially in such a nice place as Central Park. He moves on to describe the park's beautiful trees, animals, and ladies. He says of New York:

> God granted you all beauties, like a unique necklace
> I look around and see unique things, of old and new
> Oh, bride of time, be proud
> The mother of lights you are, and may you stay so (1945b,
>   lines 9–10)

The poem above shows the kinds of leisure activities people could have in the city. It also introduces the topic of animal rights.

Abushady wrote a lot of poems about the cultural and natural scene of America. Places, especially the countryside, were the subject of many poems. In "Take It Easy, Train," he addresses the train and asks it to go slowly so that he could enjoy the beauty of the countryside on his way back to New York (2000, 89). But the city has its beauty as well. In "Island of Lights," he praises New York (2000h, 66). Other poems he wrote had titles such as "Farewell to New York" (2000e, 197) and "Cherries Bloom in D.C." (2000b, 231).

Although he was a Muslim, Abushady dedicated several poems to Christian religious holidays. After all, these were part of American culture. Addressing the Christmas tree in Rockefeller Plaza, he wonders: "For whom the stars are dancing over trees and bushes / Like warm kisses and dreams that last long?" ("Christmas in New York," 1). Then he answers the question: "These are only part of the heart of the world / Showing its love for him who brought us the Bible" (1983, 20).

Abushady saw a potential unity, not rivalry, between Islam and Christianity, as his celebration of Christian holidays shows. In "Jesus: The Giver of Love and Beauty," he says of Jesus: "A real Muslim would not fail to express his love for you / And you are a hero, a real one" (1949b, 11).

He also wrote in *Unknown Poetic Works* "The Resurrection of Jesus" (2000m, 70), "Ash Wednesday" (2000a, 68), "Easter" (2000c, 239), and "Salute to Christmas" (1983i, 41) as well as about Islamic holidays. Such poems are important in helping the immigrant to avoid alienation from the majority of Americans who celebrate Christmas. Even Muslims, Abushady seems to argue, should not find this occasion irrelevant. It celebrates the birth of an important figure for them as well. His message concerns all people, since it is the message of love and peace. A similar idea is found in a poem that is significantly titled "The Birth of Liberty," which celebrates the birth of the Prophet Muhammad (1983a, 207). He asks: "Who liberated the mind when most people, like dumb animals, worshipped idols?" (line 16). Then he adds: "Who shaped dreams for people, and his inspiration was to make them the superman?" (line 22). The word "superman" shows the conflation of German philosophy with religious belief to create a system of thought that is rooted in both faith and rationalism. The connection between Islam and Christianity is clear in a poem entitled "The Prince of Peace." In that poem, he refers to Christmas 1954, when many countries gave trees to be planted on Peace Avenue in Washington, DC, as a symbol of peace. The government of Pakistan donated a model of a mosque instead, arguing that it was the symbol of peace for Muslims. The poem praises Pakistan and points out the multiplicity of symbols that stand for the idea of peace: "Allah is many notes and hues in love / Allah is many flowers and scents in peace" (1983h). Such connection makes it easier for immigrants to accept their place in the new society. It also teaches them to appreciate diversity in America and accept secularism as a general framework for governing citizens but acknowledging, at the same time, their right to practice their religions.

Reception of *Mahjar* Poetry in the Arab World

The responses to Arabic poetry in America have been mixed. Some figures such as Illya Abu Madi have become popular in Arabic textbooks, and some of their poems were set to music. Critics, however, vary in their appreciation of the style and topics in *Mahjar* poetry. Azeez Abaza, for example, contends that *Mahjar* poets did not explore new horizons. They haven't crystallized into a unified school and haven't had an influence on Arabic poetry or introduced novel ideas that were not heard of in Lebanon (18).

Antoun Karam, on the other hand, argues that *Mahjar* poets marked a "sweeping turning point and a revolt the like of which our Arab heritage has not witnessed since the third century A.H." (Naimy 1985, 12). Between these two extreme positions, one could find a wide array of responses that express appreciation for the innovations in their poetry but lament their rebelliousness and breaking the frame of language (Abbas and Najem 1955, 256).

Regarding responses to the poets' political and social influence, many critics argued that the freedom they saw in the West made the poets aware of the importance of democracy and individualism. However, some argued that the context of America was distinctly different from that of Syria, and so attempts to introduce American-style individualism would contradict the traditions of the Middle East.

Conclusion

For many immigrants who came to America too old for formal schooling, émigré poets helped fill the gaps in their education and taught them about their new homeland in a form that they could react to and understand easily. An advantage that Arabic poetry has is its songlike quality, which makes it easy to learn by heart. This is no mean feat, bearing in mind that the majority of immigrants were illiterate. Even they, however, enjoyed listening to poems and usually learned them by heart.

The call for acculturation and adoption of the new home had significant influence on the community. Alixa Naff (1985) argues that because the Arabic press (which was the forum for such poets) was pro-Americanization, it led to the community's "assimilating itself out of existence" by World War II. Sarah M. A. Gualtieri, however, disagrees with this view and argues that we should not take the claims of assimilation at face value. Arab American intellectuals, including those who wrote in English, were in between America and the Middle East. They were participating not in assimilation but in "ethnicization" (2009, 156).

Gualtieri's argument is very helpful in explaining the mixture in topics in the poetry of the three poets. Longing for the homeland is mediated through a reconstructed vision based on the reality of life in America. And, as Gualtieri convincingly argues, the "in-betweenness" of Arab Americans before World War II could explain the continuing alienation of post–World War II Arab immigrants to the United States. For Naff, the second wave of immigrants was very distinct from the previous one. Mostly Muslim Arabs from Palestine, Syria, and Egypt, the second wave was educated and lived through the tide of Arab nationalism, which explains their alienation from America. But according to Gualtieri, even the first wave of Christian Lebanese immigrants was positioned between America and the Arab world. We can see that distinction, for example, in Gibran's celebration of the spiritualism of the East and the freedom of the West. Even when the three Arab poets were promoting acculturation, they were very aware and proud of the potential contribution of Eastern culture to America. Thus, being not quite white or not totally American set the community up for more exclusion when the second wave arrived after World War II.

Viewing Arabs as a racial and religious other has existed since American newspapers noted their strange costumes and habits when they first lived and worked on Washington Street, in downtown Manhattan. This view of Syrians and Arabs as alien and new to America has ironically continued in the controversy over the planned Islamic Center near Ground Zero, not very far from the historical location of Washington Street.

Because of their role in the creation of an Arab American identity, those poets deserve more recognition and study as examples of the literature produced in America, for America, and by Americans. Seeing them merely as immigrant poets would not explain many images and emotions in their poetry. They are a good example of the intellectual elite who occupied a liminal space between the American culture and Arabic culture. The ease with which they moved from Arabic to American topics gives us hope that there might be some room for understanding and offers us an antidote to monolithic views of identity.

However, despite their popularity in the Arab world, those poets would not probably enjoy the same popularity if they were translated into English for the didactic nature of their poems. In a nation that values indirection and impersonality, the heritage of modernist poets, such poetry would sound like sermons. However, the popularity of Gibran shows that at least some Americans might enjoy this type of poetry.

Notes

1. Until the independence of Lebanon on September 1, 1926, "Syrian" was the term used to refer to Greater Syria, which included the countries now known as Syria, Lebanon, Palestine, and Jordan. In this paper, the terms "Syrian" and "Lebanese" will be used interchangeably.

2. All translations are mine. They attempt to capture the style of the original as much as possible. Line references refer to the original Arabic.

References

Abaza, Azeez. 1955. Introduction to *Al-Shi'r al-Arabi fi al-Mahjar*. Edited by Mohammad Abdul Ghani Hasan. Cairo: Maktabat al-Khanji.

Abbas, Ihsan, and Mohammad Yousef Najem. 1955. *Al-Shi'r al-Arabi fi al-Mahjar: Amreeka al-Shamalieh*. Beirut: Dar Saed.

Abu Madi. n.d. *The Complete Works of Abu Madi*. Beirut: al-Awda Press.

———. n.d.a. "1914." In *The Complete Works of Abu Madi*, 325–329.

———. n.d.b. "1931." In *The Complete Works of Abu Madi*, 176–180.

———. n.d.c. "The Best Among All Men." In *The Complete Works of Abu Madi*, 562.

———. n.d.d. "The Blind." In *The Complete Works of Abu Madi*, 754–756.

———. n.d.e. "Boston's Nights." In *The Complete Works of Abu Madi*, 490–491.

———. n.d.f. "Complaint of a Girl." In *The Complete Works of Abu Madi*, 140–141.

———. n.d.g. "Farewell and Complaint." In *The Complete Works of Abu Madi*, 510–517.

———. n.d.h. "Flight." In *The Complete Works of Abu Madi*, 115–117.

———. n.d.i. "Florida." In *The Complete Works of Abu Madi*, 809–810.

———. n.d.j. "Ghost." In *The Complete Works of Abu Madi*, 726–728.

———. n.d.k. "Hamlet." In *The Complete Works of Abu Madi*, 554–555.

———. n.d.l. "An Intrusive Guest." In *The Complete Works of Abu Madi*, 481–482.

———. n.d.m. "Los Angeles." In *The Complete Works of Abu Madi*, 434–436.

———. n.d.n. "Miami, Florida." In *The Complete Works of Abu Madi*, 724–725.

———. n.d.o. "Milford." In *The Complete Works of Abu Madi*, 384–391.

———. n.d.p. "On the Train." In *The Complete Works of Abu Madi*, 418–419.

———. n.d.q. "A Slave." In *The Complete Works of Abu Madi*, 589.

———. n.d.r. "The Story of Our Situation." In *The Complete Works of Abu Madi*, 540–543.

———. n.d.s. "Tal Shiha Hospital." In *The Complete Works of Abu Madi*, 747–748.

———. n.d.t. "The Woman and the Mirror." In *The Complete Works of Abu Madi*, 547.

Abushady, Ahmad Zaky. 1949. *From the Heavens: Collected Poems*. New York: al-Huda Press.

———. 1949a. "Beauty's Selfishness." In *From the Heavens*, 83–84.

———. 1949b. "Jesus: The Giver of Love and Beauty." In *From the Heavens*, 155–156.

———. 1949c. "My Confidence in the Fate of Humanity: A Constitution for World Unity." In *From the Heavens*, 106.

———. 1949d. "Welcoming America." In *From the Heavens*, 99.

———. 1983. *The New Man, and Other Poems*. Edited by Wadi' Falastin. Beirut: al-Mustakbal Press.

———. 1983a. "The Birth of Liberty." In *The New Man, and Other Poems*, 207–208.

———. 1983b. "Christmas in New York." In *The New Man, and Other Poems*, 266–269.

———. 1983c. "The Disaster of Pearl Harbor." In *The New Man, and Other Poems*, 263–265.

———. 1983d. "Gettysburg Address." In *The New Man, and Other Poems*, 248–257.

———. 1983e. "Independence Day Holiday." In *The New Man, and Other Poems*, 173–175.

———. 1983f. "Inspiration of Beethoven." In *The New Man, and Other Poems*, 151–154.

———. 1983g. "I Will Not Go Back." In *The New Man, and Other Poems*, 322–323.

———. 1983h. "The Prince of Peace." In *The New Man, and Other Poems*, 219–220.

———. 1983i. "Salute to Christmas." In *The New Man, and Other Poems*, 41–42.

———. 1983j. "Thanksgiving Holiday." In *The New Man, and Other Poems*, 258–262.

———. 2000. *Ahmad Zaky Abushady: The Unknown Poetic Works*. Edited by Wadi' Falastin. Beirut: Dar al-Jadid.

———. 2000a. "Ash Wednesday." In *The Unknown Poetic Works*, 68–69.

———. 2000b. "Cherries Bloom in Washington D.C." In *The Unknown Poetic Works*. 231–232.

———. 2000c. "Easter." In *The Unknown Poetic Works*, 238–239.

————. 2000d. "Eid el Fitr." In *The Unknown Poetic Works*, 173–174.

————. 2000e. "Farewell to New York." In *The Unknown Poetic Works*, 197–198.

————. 2000f. "Flag Day." In *The Unknown Poetic Works*, 176–177.

————. 2000g. "George Washington." In *The Unknown Poetic Works*, 78–79.

————. 2000h. "Island of Lights." In *The Unknown Poetic Works*, 66–67.

————. 2000i. "June's Holidays." In *The Unknown Poetic Works*, 180–181.

————. 2000j. "Labor Day." In *The Unknown Poetic Works*, 195–196.

————. 2000k. "Lincoln." In *The Unknown Poetic Works*, 73–74.

————. 2000l. "My Forum." In *The Unknown Poetic Works*, 169–170.

————. 2000m. "The Resurrection of Jesus." In *The Unknown Poetic Works*, 70–72.

————. 2000n. "Take It Easy, Train." In *The Unknown Poetic Works*, 89–90.

————. 2000o. "There May Be a Life That Even Pigeons Flee." In *The Unknown Poetic Works*, 141.

————. 2000p. "Uncle Sam." In *The Unknown Poetic Works*, 217–218.

Anderson, Benedict. 1983. *Imagined Communities: Reflections on the Origin and Spread of Nationalism*. Rev. ed. London: Verso.

Gualtieri, Sarah M. A. 2009. *Between Arab and White: Race and Ethnicity in Early Syrian American Diaspora*. Berkeley: University of California Press.

Hadad, Riziq. 1945. *Scent of Gardens: Poems and Speeches of Dr. Riziq Hadad* [in Arabic]. New York: Mirror of the West Press.

————. 1945a. "Address to Syrian Women's Society." In *Scent of Gardens*, 327–330.

————. 1945b. "The Captive Lion in the Land of Freedom." In *Scent of Gardens*, 69–75.

————. 1945c. "A Ceremony in Honor of Dr. Howard Bliss, the President of the Syrian Protestant College." In *Scent of Gardens*, 266–273.

————. 1945d. "The Crescent and the Dollar in New York." In *Scent of Gardens*, 163–168.

————. 1945e. "Doctors and Medicine." In *Scent of Gardens*, 169–171.

————. 1945f. "Farewell Day." In *Scent of Gardens*, 177–179.

————. 1945g. "Salute to the American Fleet." In *Scent of Gardens*, 22–26.

————. 1945h. "Sharp Tongues." In *Scent of Gardens*, 130–132.

————. 1945i. "The Telegraph." In *Scent of Gardens*, 81–85.

Ignatiev, Noel. 1995. *How the Irish Became White*. New York: Routledge.

Naff, Alixa. 1985. *Becoming American: The Early Arab Immigrant Experience*. Carbondale: Southern Illinois University Press.

Naimy, Nadeem. 1985. *The Lebanese Prophets of New York*. Beirut: American University of Beirut.

Sollors, Werner. 1986. *Beyond Ethnicity: Consent and Descent in American Culture*. New York: Oxford University Press.

"Syrians Riot in Streets, and Many Are Hurt." 1905. *New York Times*, October 24, 5.

CHAPTER 7

The Stones We Throw Are Rhymes:
Imagining America in Palestinian Hip-Hop

DAVID A. MCDONALD

"This is where our music comes from," Tamer Nafar says to me, pointing over his shoulder at the tenement building and parking lot adjacent to his family's home in the Palestinian quarters of Lyd, Israel. Bullet holes, graffiti, and piles of garbage mark the sides of this derelict low-income apartment complex. Nearby, we notice drugs freely bought and sold through slots carved into the neighborhood's concrete walls.[1] Lights strewn over the slots, called ATMs, mark whether a certain drop-off point is open for business. Passersby clandestinely stop for a moment, push their money through the opening of these ATMs, and retrieve an envelope or plastic bag of illicit narcotics: cocaine, crystal meth, and others. As we walk to the nearest bus stop, Nafar carefully points out areas of routine violence, drug activity, and clashes with Israeli police. "This is the Israeli ghetto, and we are in a war for our survival, every day. Our rhymes are about what it is like . . . to see the crime and the violence and the suffering." My informal tour of this neglected Israeli neighborhood was clearly intentional. Walking these troubled streets, Nafar insisted I take an inside look into the environment from which his music emerges.

Tamer Nafar's anger and frustration at the dire situation in Lyd are what originally inspired him to speak out against the racism and ethnic discrimination he feels as a Palestinian citizen of Israel. His voice, carrying words like weapons, has now come to dominate the burgeoning Palestinian hip-hop movement currently taking hold among disenfranchised and dispossessed Arab youth throughout the Middle East. As spokesman for this movement, Nafar has assumed a prominent place in the international mediascape. CNN, BBC, the Associated Press, Reuters, *Rolling Stone*, and hosts of foreign journalists, filmmakers, and other researchers have flocked to these streets for the chance to inter-view the unquestioned champion of Palestinian hip-hop. His story has been told in various forums, including two documentaries, *Channels of Rage* (2003) and the highly anticipated *Slingshot Hip-Hop* (2008). However, despite international notoriety as front men of the first Pales-tinian hip-hop crew, DAM, Tamer Nafar, Suheil Nafar, and Mahmoud Jariri remain rooted in this Lyd neighborhood.[2] For them, Lyd remains a crucial site of inspiration. It is both home and a cause, a dominant marker of their identity as Palestinians as well as motivation to fight for ethnic equality as Israeli citizens.

Without question, the primary reason DAM has caught the attention of the international media is its fluid use of a distinctly African Ameri-can popular music as their medium for social protest. In an environment where Arab and Muslim cultures are typically portrayed in conflict with Western or cosmopolitan aesthetics and values, DAM offers a unique al-ternative. In performance, these young men confound essentialist de-pictions of "angry intolerant Arabs," seeking to destroy the "free" and "civilized" West. Rather, in DAM's music American-derived discourses of race, ethnicity, and civil rights are reframed to argue for Palestinian self-determination and racial equality. Through hip-hop DAM reveals how cosmopolitan aesthetics and values may be appropriated and re-fashioned into an ideological weapon against American and Israeli oc-cupation. To a cosmopolitan audience, DAM's music is immediately fa-miliar, drawing upon a shared canon of musical sounds, beats, images, and ideas commonly associated with American ethnic strife, youth cul-ture, and social protest. Reframed within the Israeli-Palestinian con-flict, DAM facilitates new imaginings of America and Israel-Palestine as equally determined by long histories of ethnic discrimination, ur-ban blight, and racism. Through shared repertories of popular culture, hip-hop, and rap, DAM offers audiences an aesthetic space where Pal-estinian self-determination may be seen in concert with African Ameri-can struggles against poverty and ethnic discrimination. To a Palestin-ian audience, hip-hop offers an aesthetic space where America may be imagined not simply as a monolithic global power but as a diverse col-lection of ethnic communities engaged in a struggle for civil rights and equal opportunity.

Palestinian Israelis, colloquially called '48s for their presence in Is-rael at the time of its founding, are often caught within the interstices of two competing national discourses. To Israeli Jews, Palestinian Is-raelis are a feared internal other, a potential fifth column able to destabilize Jewish hegemony through political enfranchisement and demographic expansion. To Palestinians living under occupation in the West Bank and Gaza Strip, Palestinian Israelis are often portrayed as collaborators or traitors for being *bityûḥid* (Judaized) or *bitâmrak* (Americanized), carrying Israeli passports, speaking fluent Hebrew, and participating in Israeli politics and society. The difficulties of being both yet neither Israeli nor Palestinian require a constant attention to code switching in language, manners, dress, behavior, values, and so forth. Within the minutiae of everyday life, Palestinian Israelis must negotiate between two sides of an intractable "dual society model" that rarely permits cultural interaction or dialogue between Arab and Jewish communities.[3] The constant struggle to reconcile these competing ideational forces has compelled many Palestinian Israelis to seek alternative means of identification cognizant of cultural hybridity, interaction, and exchange.[4] Coupled with the very real consequences of racial discrimination, poverty, and urban blight, Palestinian Israelis are often left with few options to be recognized as full members of Israeli or Palestinian society.

What is especially fascinating, however, are the many ways in which DAM's music transcends the rigid nationalist structures that have dominated both Israeli and Palestinian cultural narratives. Their music reveals how the established discourses of ethnonational purity (in the case of Israel) and direct linkages to the land and a particular peasant ethos (in the case of Palestine) are both betrayed by social heterogeneity and new forms of media and communication. In performance DAM explicitly confounds the nationalist history of Israel based on Jewish homogeneity, throwing into relief a long history of interaction and indoctrination with and within the Arab world. Likewise, through the performance of an explicitly transnational African American popular music, these young rappers create spaces where traditional conceptions of Palestinian nation and resistance are reconfigured to include media, aesthetics, and technologies from the cosmopolitan mediascape. Through rap DAM seeks to decenter stereotypical representations of Palestinians in the mainstream Israeli media as well as to open new spaces for public discourse on Palestinian ethnic rights. Unlike the long history of resistance music produced and consumed by Palestinians under occupation or in diaspora, this new form of hip-hop seeks to engage Israeli society from within, as a voice for equal rights and opportunity as Israeli citizens.[5]

Sitting together in their family's apartment, Tamer Nafar explained the connection he feels to rap, and by extension the African American experience, in communicating his message of protest and resistance.

> It is a *spiritual* connection. It is the things they say, the things they describe, it is the things I see. When [rappers] describe something in hip-hop, I don't close my eyes and try to imagine a movie . . . I see pictures that I have seen in my life. . . . When [rappers] say that it is a white man's world, this is what I see here. . . . This is the connection to hip-hop. [African Americans] have this four hundred years of slavery; we have our occupation. They have the speeches of Malcolm X . . . who got killed, and we have Naji Al-Ali, who got assassinated. It is the big picture, and *we just need this spot that you can see it. And get connected to this spot, and then you can open your eyes and see the whole picture.*[6]

For Nafar, hip-hop speaks to him in ways no other music possibly could. Drawing from an American discourse of civil rights, Nafar feels a spiritual connection to the African American experience, a connection that transcends boundaries of the nation-state. Embedded in a shared urban experience of ethnic discrimination and resistance, hip-hop culture, practices, and values do not signify a foreign cultural experience. Rather, for Nafar, hip-hop represents a distinctly Palestinian subjectivity in Israel perceived through shared associations of slavery and occupation, resistance and martyrdom.

But most important, Nafar speaks of the need to find a "spot" where one may see, feel, and experience the spiritual connections between subaltern communities. Nafar believes that from this spot, "you can open your eyes and see the whole picture," the interconnections and dialogues of shared experiences, histories, and values between Palestinians and African Americans. I interpret these comments to mean that from such a position, cultural barriers such as nationality, language, religion, class, and politics may be overcome, allowing a truly relational dialogue to begin between African American and Palestinian cultural narratives. This "spot" might allow for unencumbered dialogue to take place cognizant of the relational, interconnected histories of people around the world fighting a similar cause within similar frames of meaning. What may seemingly be an innocuous passing comment is, I believe, a powerful statement on the need to transcend the dominant paradigms of difference that govern how people come to know themselves and others around the world.

Nafar's insistence on using music and popular culture as a means for fashioning such a dialogue is extremely informative and worthy of further reflection. Hip-hop, and popular culture more generally, provides a discursive space, a "spot," where imaginings of "America" and the "Middle East" interact outside traditional discourses of modernity and the nation-state. In this chapter I seek to expound on the necessity for understanding popular culture as an important means for approaching larger issues of power and politics. In studying the development of hip-hop in Israel-Palestine, we may come to better understand the capacities of popular culture to model new ways of imagining "America" in the Middle East. Such a conceptual move will, as Nafar concludes, allow us to "get connected" and "open our eyes to see the big picture," the shared dialogues and interrelations of culture and practice at the heart of American and Middle Eastern studies.

Imagining America in the Middle East

In this chapter I seek a better understanding of the various ways "America" is imagined and articulated among Palestinians living in Israel, Jordan, and the Occupied Territories. In particular, this chapter argues for the necessity of incorporating popular culture and media (music, dance, poetry, cinema, graphic design, television, and so forth) into scholarly work in both American and Middle Eastern studies. As centers for American studies have now begun to spread throughout the Arab world, it is worth reassessing traditional paradigms for understanding and representing "America" inclusive of myriad international and transnational perspectives. The internationalization of American studies programs compels a new paradigm for approaching America's profound influence around the world. With this expansion it is clear that American studies must move beyond the deep-seated tradition of self-reflexive inquiry. This literature was once founded upon the work of cultural "insiders" interested specifically in the deconstruction of "America" in relation to specifically US interests. However, as the US government exerts unprecedented political, economic, and military power with increasing arrogance, and as American cultural products, media, and institutions now circulate with ever-increasing speed throughout the world, it has become imperative to reassess traditional models for research. What has become apparent is the need for a "new American studies" cognizant of and responsive to the various ways "America" is defined, imagined, and articulated by all those subjected to its far-reaching influence.

Such a paradigm must first recognize the relational, interconnected histories of American influence within a wide spectrum of cultural practices and perspectives. In pushing toward the "new American studies," where "America" is interrogated as a relational construct, it may be necessary to rethink many of these ideas. As the discipline of American studies becomes an international endeavor, the means by which we define "America" should be reconsidered cognizant of its histories of interaction and influence with various cultures around the world. By examining the ways America is imagined through Palestinian hip-hop, this chapter investigates many of the dominant social and political issues facing Palestinian rappers as they negotiate their identities amid a long history of protracted national struggle. In doing so, this chapter engages issues of power and politics and argues for the utility of music and popular culture in resolving central questions of individual subjectivity and collective identity formation.

Popular Culture, Power, and Politics

The fundamental goal of this chapter, however, is to argue for the inclusion of popular culture and media into this "new American studies." Historically, the fields of American and Middle Eastern studies have been determined by the interdisciplinary study of society, culture, and history within the territorially bounded nation-state. However, as anthropological understandings of culture and identity have shifted toward recognizing diversity, difference, and hybridity, so too have scholars of American and Middle Eastern studies emphasized varying and competing cultural formations of class, gender, race, and so forth. Where once was culture, now we see cultural formations made up of shared habits of thought and action negotiated across various strata of society. With this, scholars have begun to rethink relations of power and knowledge while focusing on new objects of study and analysis.[7] Critical theory, queer theory, and poststructural theory advocate assuming a decolonizing posture in research, moving beyond traditional paradigms for thinking about power and politics. In such literature power is not conceptualized as a singular monolithic force exerted by the state or the ruling classes upon an unwilling and passive peasantry.[8] Rather, power, following Antonio Gramsci, Stuart Hall, and many others, is the result of shifting transactional relations between competing groups.[9] Simply put, power is a negotiated and unstable consensus of leadership actively pursued across various economic, social, and cultural domains.[10] Various competing forces actively seek to accumulate and exert their influence through an ongoing struggle carried out across various institutions and practices.

Broadening this discussion, researchers are now seeking to better understand issues of power and politics through a careful consideration of cultural practices, performances, and media. Such literature reveals that music, dance, poetry, cinema, literature, and other performative media are equally important for understanding issues of identity, power, and politics. In particular, recent ethnomusicological studies argue persuasively that popular culture and media do more than simply reflect the societies from which they emerge. Rather, popular culture and media have the capacity to generate cultural understandings of society, providing the terrain through which commonsense interpretations of the self and the world are formed and articulated.[11] Applied to the "new American studies," this conceptualization of power and politics changes traditional modes of understanding America's dominant position in the world. Contrary to traditional paradigms, the United States does not exert its profound influence upon the passive, helpless, dominated third and fourth worlds. To the contrary, "America" is a negotiated construct, a terrain of often unpredictable consent, conflict, and influence articulated across myriad sites of engagement. To study America beyond its conventional borders begs an approach to power and politics more aligned with understanding these various sites of engagement, sites where consent and influence are freely negotiated.

Unfortunately, traditional scholarship in American and Middle Eastern studies often ignores the influence of popular culture, giving the impression that such media are best left to the margins or peripheries of "serious" academic discussion. For scholars of the "hard sciences," popular culture is often omitted so as to save space for more meaningful discussions of politics, economics, and other societal issues. Given the severity of the ongoing conflict between the United States and the Arab world, imagined through the lens of protracted occupation (both American and Israeli), destabilized local governments, collapsing economies, and the constant threat of attack, it would seem natural that issues of popular culture might seem unimportant. Yet in this chapter I argue that traditional assumptions of the insignificance of popular culture and media must be reconsidered. Based on a substantial literature in cultural studies and ethnomusicology, it has been widely shown that popular culture offers a progressive means of circumventing the conceptual and methodological limitations of traditional scholarship in American and Middle Eastern studies.[12] Music, movies, fashion, literature, drama, graffiti, blogs, television, and many other forms of popular culture are powerful sites of engagement in the negotiation of American hegemony throughout the world. Popular culture must be taken seriously in the fields of American and Middle Eastern studies, for it broadens our understanding of the ways in which power and the politics of identity are performed in everyday life.

Hip-Hop in Israel-Palestine

The idea to form a rap group came to Tamer Nafar in 1999. With the help of his younger brother Suheil and a close friend, Mahmoud, Tamer decided to create a new hip-hop sound that reflected the hybridity the three felt as teenage Palestinians growing up in Israel. Filtered through the lenses of African American popular music and movies, these young men began to explore an emergent sense of dispossession and discrimination in their daily lives. Growing up in one of Israel's most dangerous neighborhoods, amid glaring signs of urban neglect and racial disempowerment, Nafar found common ground in African American popular music and movies. Spike Lee, Tupac Shakur, Public Enemy, Malcolm X, and many others were especially influential in drawing out the similarities between America's legacies of racial injustice and Palestinian experiences in Israel. In particular, Tupac Shakur's immense talent for capturing the essences of racial discrimination, ethnic inequality, and minority empowerment resonated with these young Palestinians living under similar circumstances. In an interview with fellow rappers on an Internet blog, Tamer Nafar writes of his awakening to African American popular culture and media:

> Up until the age of 17 I was writing all kinds of love songs, until I met Pac's [Tupac Shakur's] music. Then I studied crime knowledge [criminology] and noticed that there is a reason for crime, like poverty, unemployment . . . basically political reasons. But still I chose to ignore politics because I wanted to succeed. I was a coward until . . . one of my closest friends died from a drive by so I . . . began my lyrical war, began to be real . . . and what threw more gas on to my fire was that same month, when the second Intifada began, Black October, that got me . . . back to my Palestinian roots, and I noticed that all my life (TV,

books, school, environment) was created by Israel only to make me un-
connected to my roots. So I started writing songs for the young Arabs
to shorten their process of getting them to their roots in a way that I
didn't have.[13]

The above passage was quoted at length in order to reveal the process
by which Nafar internalized rap to such an extent that it was the most
natural and most appropriate means for communicating his messages of
resistance to the culture of drugs and crime that had gripped his community. More important, in this statement Nafar very clearly cites popular culture as a fundamental means through which he came to understand himself and his surroundings. Through popular culture Nafar
began to formulate a very complex cultural understanding of the political situation he faced. Popular culture did not simply reflect the difficulties he encountered living as a Palestinian-Israeli during the beginning
of the al-Aqsa Intifada. Rather, television, books, music, and movies
were powerful means of generating Nafar's interpretation of the tragic
events of October 2000. Through his interaction with popular culture,
Nafar came to understand the history and politics of living as a Palestinian in Israel and was inspired to speak out against the structures of
Israeli discrimination separating him from his "Palestinian roots."

However, what is especially interesting about this quote is Nafar's
usage of American hip-hop to reclaim his "Palestinian roots." "America," as it was portrayed in hip-hop, was a powerful tool for uncovering
a missing element in Nafar's life. A culturally determined imagining of
urban America presented in countless hip-hop songs motivated Nafar to
seek out and explore his Palestinian ancestry. Simply put, in listening to
American rap, Nafar came to *feel* more Palestinian. Yet given the long
history of Palestinian "roots" music and dance and the dominance of
hard-core Palestinian nationalists in the mainstream media, how could
African American music possibly be associated with Palestinian roots?

Many nationalist artists familiar with Nafar's music were quick to
criticize his work as lacking an authentic Palestinian identity. As one
such singer declared, "[He has] surrendered his Palestinian identity to
imitate America." "How can he say he wants to be Palestinian when he
only sings American music?"

Others questioned his motivations for wanting to develop a rap audience when indigenous Palestinian arts and practices continually face ex-
tinction under Israeli occupation. Palestinian folklorists and other researchers have for decades worked tirelessly to preserve the treasured

cultural history of Palestine. Several of these folklorists related to me their fear that the coming of hip-hop would ultimately deter and confuse young Palestinians from learning about the history and music of their forefathers. I raised this issue to Tamer Nafar in one of our interviews. With exasperation he responded: "What are you talking about *sha'bi* [Palestinian indigenous music]? . . . So for me to be Palestinian I have to sing wedding songs about olive trees or farming or goats? What does that have to do with my life here and now? Look out my window. Do you see any olive trees? Or goats? My music is about where I am, and who I am."[14]

For Tamer Nafar, hip-hop speaks directly to a contemporary Palestinian experience in ways indigenous song and dance cannot. It reflects a condition of subaltern conflict, hybridity, and ethnic empowerment "here and now," cognizant of the dynamics of cosmopolitan youth culture. Looking out Nafar's bedroom window it is difficult to see the pastoral life idealized in Palestinian indigenous song and dance. Such imagery (rolling hills, olive groves, mountains, and the like) cannot be found amid the decaying city streets of Lyd. Sprawling open spaces and centuries-old olive and citrus groves have long since given way to urban expansion, settlement, and seemingly endless networks of railway tracks and industrial factories. Nafar's life "here and now" is surprisingly best imagined through the lenses of African American hip-hop. In hip-hop Nafar has found a voice that resonates with his experiences of racial and ethnic strife. It is what initially motivated him to begin singing out against what he perceived to be gross inequalities between Jewish and non-Jewish citizens of Israel.

In similar fashion DAM cohort Mahmoud Jariri spoke to me at length about the power of American hip-hop to energize Palestinian issues. Speaking before a performance in Bethlehem, Jariri stated, "Rap is the language of protest and challenge. . . . [I]t is the language of [the] youth that expresses their feelings and thoughts." In my many conversations with these young performers, it became quite clear that from the beginning, rap was never seen as a foreign art form. Rather, rap was imagined as a space where youth regardless of nationality might freely express their frustrations and experiences of social marginalization. In popular culture these rappers find fields of interaction stretching beyond national borders. Within this performative space both "Palestine" and "America" may be imagined not as diametrically opposed national constructs but rather as a shared cultural experience of ethnic marginality and minority empowerment.

October 2000 and the Outbreak of the al-Aqsa Intifada

The immediate events of September 28, 2000, and its aftermath, when then Likud party leader Ariel Sharon forcefully visited the Temple Mount (Harâm al-Sharîf), igniting the al-Aqsa Intifada, have been well detailed. In particular, this literature has focused primarily on the lasting effects and impact these events have had on the Palestinian resistance in the Occupied Territories and in the near diaspora. However, Sharon's incitement had an incredibly powerful effect on Palestinians living in Israel as well. As violence spread through the streets of East Jerusalem, Gaza, and the West Bank, so too did Palestinians in Israel gather in the streets of Nazareth, Umm al-Fahm, Haifa, and several smaller villages in the Galilee to protest the violence. Watching the fighting on television, where Israeli police confronted stone-throwing demonstrators with armored vehicles, Apache helicopters, and live ammunition, Palestinian Israelis were understandably outraged. Palestinian deputy Mohammad Kanaan of the Israeli Knesset stated, "We are an integral part of the Palestinian-Arab people and we cannot remain motionless when faced with the deaths of children and other horrors that are taking place in the occupied territories."[15]

Many Palestinian Israelis took to the streets in solidarity with friends and family suffering under occupation. Internal demonstrations broke out across Israel, revealing a growing frustration on the part of Palestinian Israelis. Such protests were indicative of a severe political and ethnic crisis. Sharon's visit to the Harâm al-Sharîf and the televised murder of young Palestinian Mohammad al-Durra were only the flash points for a political crisis that had been brewing for many years. Widespread concerns of gross disparities in employment, living conditions, social programs, and education served only to exacerbate feelings of political and social dispossession among the Palestinian minority. Deputy Mohammad Kanaan went on to say, "Our demonstrations also express the frustration of the one million Israeli Arabs faced with the striking inequality with Jews."[16] It was clear that the protests and demonstrations taking place within Israel's Palestinian communities were a product of sympathy for the intifada as well as the dire social and economic situation in Israel.

Within the first four days of the rioting, thirteen Palestinian Israelis were killed and more than two hundred injured by Israeli police. The deaths of these thirteen Israelis sparked outrage throughout the country among Palestinians as well as Jews, for it marked the first time in nearly thirty years that Israeli citizens were killed in demonstrations against the state. Funerals held in each of the victims' villages quickly turned to stone throwing, burning tires, and mass vandalism. Roads leading to and from Palestinian areas in the Galilee were blocked, and hordes of riot police were called in to quell the disturbances. What was perhaps most damaging, however, was the way in which several of these demonstrators were killed. Eyewitnesses at the scene in Arabeh described to the media how they watched seventeen-year-old Asil Asleh beaten by soldiers and then shot in the neck.[17] Others were shot by long-range snipers positioned on rooftops as they stood in crowds of people, including women and children. And one victim reportedly died from stab wounds by police forces. The brutality of the police reaction, as well as widespread outrage across the political spectrum, brought to the fore an ethnic conflict that had been ignored for many years. Despite forming a special inquiry into the government response to the riots, little action was taken to assuage the fears of the Palestinian community or against the police responsible for the deaths.[18]

At the heart of the issue, however, was a crisis of identity: Palestinian Israelis who had lived for more than a generation at peace with their Jewish neighbors were suddenly confronted with Israeli brutality against their friends and extended family members. Living as a minority within greater Jewish society, Palestinian Israelis have developed collective identities as Israeli citizens. Yet despite this Palestinian Israelis are often excluded from the national discourse. Among Jews they are Arab; among Palestinians they are Israeli. In either case, they have been told that they are neither true Israelis nor true Palestinians. As the violence erupted in Jerusalem, and the Israeli military mobilized its response to the rioting, Palestinians in Israel were confronted with powerful images of national affiliation with the demonstrators. However, in taking to the streets the Israeli police treated the protesters of Nazareth, Arabeh, Sakhnin, and Jat as if they were those in Gaza or Ramallah. The social disconnect came in seeing their state apparatuses engage internal protests as if they were facing an external adversary. All of the signs of loyalty to the Israeli state put forth by Palestinian Israelis, the willingness to speak Hebrew, hold jobs, and participate in social and political life, seemed irrelevant given the Israeli army's deadly response to their demonstrations. Ironically, similar demonstrations by Israeli Jews protesting against government brutality were met with a very different response. In Jewish demonstrations police were instructed to use only batons and other nonlethal methods to break up the disturbances. The apparent double standard by which the state chose to engage civil disobedience prompted Tamer Nafar to write in his song "Innocent Criminals":

> The minority is opening its mouth,
> You say the Arabs are primitive,
> You say the Arabs are aggressive,
> You say we are criminals and barbarians, we aren't.
> But just in case we are, this is what the government has done to us.
>
> Jews demonstrate, the police take clubs in hand,
> The Arabs demonstrate, the police take their lives.

The horrible events of "Black October" made a significant impression on the direction of DAM's music. If experiencing firsthand the effects of social neglect had drawn DAM to speak out against drugs and crime in their earlier work, watching "Black October" unfold only solidified their resolve to sing against the occupation as well. As the violence escalated, the ethnonational binary of Israeli-Palestinian widened, pulling many Palestinian Israelis in two directions. Tamer's difficulty in articulating his dissected loyalties speaks to this crisis of identity. In each case the established national imaginary had failed to account for these margins. In effect, the "dual society model" could not account for the growing sense of hybridity, interaction, and exchange.

To memorialize the thirteen victims of "Black October," Tamer Nafar wrote their names into a verse of the song "Gharbi fî Balâdî" (Stranger in my own country). Through a play of meanings, Nafar was able to fold the name of each victim into the structure of the verse. In Arabic it is common for proper names to have specific meanings or roots describing characteristics, qualities, or actions. Here, Nafar fashioned a coherently powerful verse of Palestinian resistance poetry using the meanings of each of the thirteen names. For ease of reading, the translation of the verse is provided, marking each of the names in capital letters together with their meaning.

> 13 Martyrs, death is close when the stones are in the hand.
> 13 Martyrs the ALA [elevated status] of our land, and the EMAD [foundation].
> Black October proved that EYAD [support/strength] is in our blood.
> Everyone of them was WALID [born] under occupation,
> But still RAMY [throwing] himself like a sharp stone,

Fighting the disease of those who think our blood is worthless.
Killing the MUSLEH [the righteous] voices with live ammunition.
And the mother shouts, I am ASSIL [falling down],
On Christ's and MOHAMMAD's cheek.
We are like a mountain that won't be shaken by any wind or any storm.
We will remain RAMEZ [the image] of the nation, and the WISSAM
   [the badge] of freedom.
The light of our great grandparents will never fade away.
I'm a stranger in my own country, but I AHMAD [praise] God,
That I'm still attached to my culture.
All of you can call us renegades or the inner Arabs or the Arabs of '48.
Whatever, we'll remain the roots of Palestine until the OMAR [the end
   of time].[19]

In prose, metaphor, and meaning, this passage reveals a close relationship with the established archetype of Palestinian resistance song from the 1970s and 1980s. The common stock of icons and indexes of the Palestinian nationalist narrative is all included. Most notable of these are references to stones, to the land, and to the unwavering loyalty of a united Palestinian nation. In addition, Nafar brings in all-important allusions to birth and motherhood. The plight of the mother of the martyred (*umm al-shahîd*) is played out within a combined reference to Christianity and Islam, establishing the connections between Christian and Muslim Palestinians. The people are "like a mountain" facing a wind and storm (of Zionism). And through this engagement the people are an emblem of the nation and of freedom, proclaiming strength from generations (great-grandparents) of attachment to the land.

However, it is in the final two lines of this verse that Nafar breaks from the traditional rhetoric of resistance poetry and confronts a slightly different internal audience. In the lines "All of you can call us renegades or the inner Arabs or the Arabs of '48. / Whatever, we'll remain the roots of Palestine until the end of time," there is a momentary yet significant shift. "All of you" can be interpreted to mean both Israeli Jews who commonly use the term "Arabs" to deny a Palestinian national identity as well as Arabs in general who position '48 Palestinians outside of their national struggle. The particular usage of the word "renegade" (*khawân*) is significant in that it is employed in several other DAM songs to mean Palestinians in collaboration with Israel. From the Arabic root *khûn* (to be disloyal, faithless, to betray), *khayân/khawân* is a powerful epithet calling forth a betrayal of faith and treachery against the nation. To be called *khawân* in this context implies that someone is a traitor to his or her Palestinian ancestry and complicit in Israel's occupation of Palestinian lands. In the ensuing verse sung by Suheil Nafar, he uses the term "renegade" similarly:

Raised in poverty, and poverty is the only thing in our minds,
But our hearts are still beating and our Arabian roots are still strong,
But still our Arabian brothers are calling us renegades! NOOOOO!
We never sold our country, the occupation wrote our destiny,
Which is, that the whole world until today treats us as Israeli,
and Israel until tomorrow will treat us as Palestinians.
I'm a stranger in my own country.

The word "renegade" in this song signifies a dual object. In each case the artists are defending themselves from being labeled traitors from an outside force. However, in the first example, it is ambiguous who constitutes that force, Israeli Jews or Palestinians. The line can be interpreted both ways. The second example is much more specific, lashing out at "our Arabian brothers . . . calling us [Palestinian Israelis] renegades." Taken together, the two verses signal a shift in object within a continuity of language. In talking with the artists about this particular passage, they were unfazed by my inquiry. "We are called renegades by both sides [Israel and Palestine]," Suheil Nafar reminded me. "That is why we are strangers in our own country/homeland." They are strangers twice over in that they feel dispossessed by both their state (Israel) and their nation (Palestine).

The deaths of these thirteen demonstrators constituted the linchpin for drawing DAM into this struggle on two fronts. In both seeking socioethnic reform internally as well as ending the Israeli occupation, DAM is making an important assertion of identity toward both Israeli and Palestinian national narratives and identity constructs. As Nafar admits, he doesn't "know exactly where he fits in" all of this. The failure of the "dual society model" to account for hybridic, fragmented, and otherwise disconnected segments of the national imaginary is perhaps the reason.

"Born Here"

As an example of DAM's ethnic engagement with the Israeli mainstream through American hip-hop, there is perhaps no greater statement than their highly influential song "Hûn Anwalîdat" (Born here).

Coupled with a large-scale music video produced and directed by Guliano Mer-Hamis, "Born Here" has circulated widely among both Jewish and Palestinian hip-hop communities. The production of the song and video was sponsored by the Israeli nonprofit organization Shatil, whose mission is to raise awareness regarding civil rights violations and discrimination against Palestinian Israelis. Support for this project was derived from the belief that music is a powerful means of social protest and that DAM has a particularly unique talent for engaging both Jewish and Palestinian communities through rap. With this in mind, DAM recorded the song in two versions, one Hebrew and the other Arabic. Since its original production, "Born Here" has been freely downloaded more than two hundred thousand times across the Middle East.

The video begins with the all too common moment in which Israeli police demand to see the identity cards of three Palestinian youths. Filmed to resemble documentary footage, one of the officers looks into the camera and demands that it be turned off. Slowly, as Tamer Nafar steps out of the vehicle and reaches for his wallet, the camera pivots to reveal trepidation and fear on the face of the young rapper. Ominous synthesized descending fifths narrate the introductory moments when Nafar is about to be searched by police. Then, as the main beat track begins, the camera quickly flashes in on the young rapper to indicate a break with reality and the beginning of a fantasy montage where Nafar's true rage and anger at the situation may be fulfilled. Nafar then begins his first verse, posturing and gesturing angrily in the faces of the police officers. Scenes of police control and surveillance are then juxtaposed with images of the rappers leading angry crowds through the streets of Lyd. Rapping in perfect Hebrew, Nafar sings out:

> This is hunting season, the prey is one more home.
> Of a dove trying to survive under the hawk's regime,
> (*page ripped*) lets try something more optimistic:
> Each day I wake up and see 1000 cops.
> Maybe they came to arrest a dealer . . . (he's here, he's there, oh no,
>   they came to destroy his neighbor's home)
> What is happening here?
> A hate bubble surrounding the ghetto.
> Why is it hard for him? And who's going to answer him?
> Everywhere I go, excuses greet me.
> I broke the law? No, no the law broke me!
> Enough, enough gentlemen.

I was born here, my grandparents were also born here.
You will not sever me from my roots.
Understand, even if I have faith in this "imaginary" regime.
You still haven't allowed me to build a porch to stand on and express it

In speaking directly to an Israeli Jewish audience, Nafar draws upon common Hebrew vernacular phrases, slang, and references idiomatic to Israeli Jewish cultural frames. "A dove trying to survive under the hawk's regime" is an overt reference to former Israeli prime minister Ariel Sharon's iron-fisted policies of home demolition in Israel and the West Bank. Pointing out the ever-present police who demolish homes built without government approval but do little to combat rampant drugs and crime reveals an apparent hypocrisy in the way Palestinians are subjected to Israeli law and raises awareness of an important though often neglected social issue. Nafar's claim that "he didn't break the law, the law broke him" is also a reference to African American empowerment, especially visible in the work of Tupac Shakur and others.[20] Confronting his target audience directly, Nafar calls out, "I was born here, my grandparents were born here. You will not sever me from my roots." The constructs of birthplace, roots, and ancestry are perhaps the most powerful indexes of Israeli and Palestinian national discourse. In particular, such phrases index early Zionist rhetoric, documenting the need for the foundation of a Jewish state. In particular, this song references a popular Israeli Jewish song similarly titled "Born Here," often sung by Israeli nationalists. In total, Nafar's well-crafted verse draws freely from Israeli Jewish historical texts, literature, and popular culture, reappropriating Jewish discourses of nationality and citizenship to argue for full Palestinian participation in the Israeli state.

In composing the Arabic version of "Born Here," DAM takes an entirely different approach. While the beats, soundtrack, and chorus are identical in the Arabic version, the content of the lyrics differs considerably.

For us, destroying houses is just like a whisper,
As long as we remain silent in the ears of those who encroach upon us.
But if you scream NO!, you will drown it in a sea of justice.
Listen! I can understand all the tearful eyes,
But I don't understand those who don't wipe their tears.
Lost and asking for the land, rowing through his tears.
What is happening here? Why is everyone looking at us?

Maybe because we are the ones who are opening our legs [allowing
 ourselves to be abused]?
Oh man, the last time there was a demonstration against destroying
 houses, there were 100 people, 90 of them Jews.
If today you sit and watch as they evict your neighbor,
Tomorrow they will come to your house, and your neighbor, like you,
 will sit, watching in your place.
The list is long but it has an end of falling to the power.
Power that is incapable of seeing, knowing, but scared.
If terror is living inside us, it will not live in our children.
What will we say to the weakest link in the chain? Good-bye . . .

If Nafar is especially critical of structures of racism and discrimination in his Hebrew lyrics, the Arabic version assaults a very different so-
ciopolitical issue internal to Palestinian society. Here, Nafar takes aim
at Palestinian apathy, weakness, and vulnerability. He calls for Palestinians to rise up "in the ears of those who encroach upon us" and demand justice. He strikes out against the Palestinian culture of martyrdom that bemoans lost land "rowing through the tears" but does little
to effect political change. "I can understand all the tearful eyes, but I
don't understand those who don't wipe their tears away." He is embar-
rassed that political demonstrations for Palestinian rights in Israel are
90 percent Jewish and that neighbors do little to help each other when
bulldozers arrive. There is also a certain vulgarity in imagery and text in
this Arabic version not seen in the above Hebrew. Speaking from within
a purely Palestinian frame, Nafar doesn't hesitate to attack nationalist
taboo. He goes so far as to intimate that the reason Palestinians have
been consistently abused is because "we are the ones who are opening up our legs." Rather than perpetuate the myth of the eternal victim, Nafar demands that Palestinians take some responsibility for their
condition and the initiative to constructively work for its amelioration.
Such statements reflect an interior voice of national shame and embar-
rassment in stark contrast to the idealist united front projected in the
Hebrew version.

However, both versions are built upon a sonic foundation of transnational hip-hop that significantly determines its reception among various target audiences. In composing this particular song in two versions
(Arabic and Hebrew), DAM significantly broadened its potential to have
a lasting impact among both Palestinian and Jewish ethnic communities. Through linguistic code switching, DAM could interact with two
very different audiences, utilizing social, political, and historical refer-

ences idiomatic to each group. In a very real sense, DAM can speak to and for each group in its own language, engaging a much larger audience for their work. However, simply switching languages is not enough. The potential for "Born Here" to significantly influence ethnic tensions among Israeli citizens lies not solely in linguistic fluidity. Rather, it is within the musical sounds themselves that much of the social and political work is done. DAM's very natural use of African American hip-hop as the foundation of this piece serves to redraw many of the lines separating Palestinian and Jewish ethnic communities. As African American popular culture in general and transnational hip-hop in particular gain popularity among Israeli Jewish and Palestinian youth, new social formations arise. Hip-hop communities around the world often develop independently of one another, but in the process each takes on a new vernacular for thinking about youth culture, ethnicity, subaltern empowerment, and social protest based on the images, messages, and ideas communicated in the music. Imaginings of African American urban struggle and ethnic discrimination become a neutral site, or discursive space, through which local issues may be interpreted. As audiences come to imagine the American urban battlefield through music, they join a much larger transnational community of hip-hop fans around the world. In fashion, music, movies, gesture, dance, and more, the borders of this community are marked, creating cultural cohorts based on new sets of aesthetic criteria. Communities of hip-hop fans congeal and interact across the world independent of the traditional limitations of the nation-state, creating a sense of social synchrony and community. Much of this intercommunication comes through new technologies and media. Online dissemination of music, videos, and information supplements media-based communities of hip-hop fans. Online social networks (Facebook, Bebo, MySpace, and others), blogs, fanzines, and discussion forums structure collaborative social environments for cohorts to communicate and interact with increasing ease. Such technology allows smaller undiscovered artists access to a global community of potential consumers and collaborators beyond traditional dynamics of production, distribution, and marketing.

For Israeli youth (Jewish and non-Jewish), "Born Here" offers a unique aesthetic space for all to come together based on a shared affiliation as hip-hop enthusiasts. This aesthetic space exists as a neutral site of cultural engagement, devoid of traditional lines of division and conflict. Hip-hop culture in general and rap music in particular cannot be claimed as part of the national canon of music and dance of either Jewish or Palestinian communities. It exists outside traditional discourses of the nation-state. As such, it can be interpreted without the traditional baggage of the "dual society model" that positions Jews and Palestinians as mutually exclusive national communities.[21] Rather, in hip-hop Jewish and Palestinian youth may come together and explore shared aesthetics, affiliations, and mutual experiences in ways unavailable in virtually any other social context. In performance, DAM facilitates a collaborative social environment drawn along new lines of affiliation where Palestinian-Jewish interaction may be imagined through American popular culture.

Moreover, in using rap as the primary sign vehicle for this song, DAM very clearly encourages a cultural association between African American and Palestinian communities, each suffering from rampant drugs, crime, and urban neglect. To an Israeli Jewish audience, such an association is a powerful tool for changing the way Palestinians are conceptualized in the mainstream Israeli media. Articulated in rhymes and beats and buttressed by a transnational discourse of African American civil rights, Palestinians are presented not as an external national threat, but rather as a minority community within the Israeli state seeking equal opportunity as Israeli citizens. In its various musical attributes (rhymes, beats, gestures, language, and so on), hip-hop enables a specific cultural association to take place, imagining Palestinian enfranchisement within the frame of the African American civil rights movement. Such an imagining allows for new ways of seeing the struggle to emerge beyond the boundaries of the "dual society model."

Imagining America in Palestinian Hip-Hop

As a final example of DAM's artistic work for social and political change, I offer the widely successful "Mâlî Hurîa" (I don't have freedom). Released in 2006 on their internationally distributed studio album *Îhdâ* (Dedication), this song offers important insight into how these artists have attempted to reconcile pervasive feelings of dispossession through transnational popular culture. In particular, "I Don't Have Freedom" offers a unique reconciliation of indigenous Palestinian music and transnational cosmopolitan values and aesthetics. In sonic form, this song attempts to bridge the margins between the indigenous and cosmopolitan, allowing for a more nuanced understanding of Palestinian hybridity and interaction to emerge.

The song opens with a small musical ensemble introducing a well-known Palestinian folk tune on the Arab classical instruments the *qa-*

nûn and the *'ûd*. A male chorus then performs the song to the accompaniment of the Arab goblet drum, the *dharbûkka*, in the traditional rhythmic mode *wahda*. Although the melody and rhythm remain intact, the original lyrics have been altered to reflect the current political context:

> Wherever I go I see borders imprisoning humanity.
> Why is it that all of the children of the world are free,
> But I don't have freedom?

Upon completing the first stanza, the song immediately shifts to a hip-hop beat track and bass line. The original melody line is then taken over by a synthesized *'ûd*, syncopating the original melody to align with the new hip-hop beat pattern. Although the original Palestinian folk tune is significantly altered, it remains the melodic foundation of the piece and serves as its recurring chorus. The first verse opens with Tamer Nafar singing:

> We have been like this for more than 50 years . . .

> We haven't seen any light
> And if we peek between the bars
> We see a blue sky and white clouds
> In the center a star reminds you that you are restrained
> But no, I'm steadfast, staying optimistic
> You won't limit hope with a wall of separation . . .

> I will remain connected to Palestine
> Like an embryo to the umbilical cord
> My feet are the roots of the olive tree
> Keep prospering, fathering new branches
> Every branch grown for peace
> Every branch under the pressure of occupation
> Refusing to give up

> So why don't I have freedom?
> Because I refuse to live in slavery.

In this first verse Nafar very clearly references Palestinian Israeli feelings of imprisonment living in a predominantly Jewish state. The "blue sky and white clouds" seen between the bars of the prison index Israeli hegemony via the Israeli flag: "in the center a star [the Jewish star of David]." In the next lines Nafar makes a concerted effort to proclaim (and reclaim) his Palestinian identity. Stating that he is "steadfast" (*sâmid*) and optimistic (*'aîsh matafânal*) and confronted with a "wall of separation" is an extremely common trope in Palestinian nationalist poetry and music. He further references the great tradition of Palestinian resistance music and poetry through a recurring metaphor of the olive tree. His "feet are the roots of the olive tree," "fathering new branches" in peace, under the pressures of the occupation. The olive tree is the preeminent signifier for the Palestinian nation and its asserted primordial ties to the land. In associating his body with the roots and branches of the olive tree, Nafar promotes an image of himself, and by extension the community of Palestinian Israelis, as a vital part of the Palestinian nation living under Israeli control. The final two lines reveal the underlying theme of the entire song, questioning why it is that in today's global context of progressive democracy and liberalism, Palestinians do not have freedom. His answer to the question, "because I refuse to live in slavery," frames much of the political discourse of the piece as a whole and further reveals a transnational vocabulary for thinking about the Palestinian-Israeli conflict.

Throughout "I Don't Have Freedom" recurring themes of "freedom," "slavery," and "children" reflect a unique fluency in common tropes of social protest, youth culture, and minority empowerment found in African American hip-hop. Couched within a standard hip-hop beat pattern, verbal articulation, and bass line, this song very easily fits within the canon of American urban protest song. Asking the initial question—"Why is it that all the children of the world are free, but I don't have freedom?"—itself references a transnational imagining of America through discourses of human rights, freedom, and democracy. For DAM to even ask this question presumes an intimate awareness of and affiliation with American ideals of human and civil rights, racial equality, and democratic enfranchisement.

The relational use of American history, culture, and politics in "I Don't Have Freedom" continues throughout each of the three main verses. While it is apparent that DAM fluidly shifts between Israeli Jewish and Palestinian cultural frames, the underlying musical and textual foundation of this piece relies predominantly upon a transnational knowledge of American history, society, and politics. In particular, Suheil Nafar makes a clear comparison between America's history of ethnic cleansing and its Israeli counterparts:

Here's another massacre
And a wall that is separating me, myself, and I
The US has made Israel its 51st state
Cleaning the Middle East of its Indians
Hitting us, then blaming us
But all the armies of the world
Are weak against the hope of children

In this verse Suheil Nafar lashes out against an America in collusion with Israel to prevent Palestinian self-determination. In making Israel the fifty-first state, the United States has abandoned a position of impartiality in brokering an end to the conflict. Rather, Nafar positions Israel similarly to America in its period of colonial expansion. As the United States was forced to make hard decisions regarding the presence of millions of Native Americans, so too has Israel been forced to clean "the Middle East of its Indians" in the project of colonial expansion. The use of the word "massacre" (*majzarah*) in the first line is especially important in carrying forth this imagery of shared ethnic cleansing, as it is the word most typically used to describe both the historical treatment of Native Americans as well as the tragic events of 1948. In previous lyrics and interviews DAM has been careful to point out the similarities between Palestinians and African Americans, each suffering from ethnic discrimination. Here in this lyric is a powerful reference to America's historical treatment of its indigenous populations interpreted within the frame of Palestinian history. In composing this lyric Suheil Nafar seeks to draw upon common interpretations of American colonial expansion so as to reposition common interpretations of Israeli colonial expansion. In each case America provides the fulcrum through which interpretive shifts of meaning are imagined and articulated.

Conclusion

In seeking to explore the "relational" histories and identities of Palestinian Israelis, a critical understanding of the processes of popular culture can be especially important. Through DAM's work we see that popular media structure social spaces where the social and political effects of the occupation are not only expressed but also confronted and debated. These "texts" of popular culture (songs, poems, paintings, dances, videos) demarcate the boundaries of a discursive field where ideas of self and the world may be further engaged, refashioned, and naturalized within or against the dominant order. DAM's potential for meaningful social impact depends largely on its ability to express its messages in Arabic, Hebrew, and English, drawing upon common vernacular phrases, slang, obscenities, and references indigenous to each cultural group. In each instance, a carefully orchestrated usage of American history, politics, and values frames the intended meanings of the music.

Through performance DAM has attempted to align itself within the nationalist trajectories of its target audience. Yet at the same time, in refashioning popular conceptions of Palestinian suffering and seeking dialogue with the Israeli mainstream, DAM confounds nationalist dogma. In its usage of highly stylized Hebrew slang, DAM makes a play for the incorporation of Palestinians into the Israeli state imaginary. The music reveals to Israeli Jews how their native language can be appropriated and refashioned into an ideological weapon against Jewish hegemony. In the face of Palestinian nationalists, DAM speaks out against the prevailing discourse of the "righteous victim" and allows for new forms of music and media to be included in the Palestinian resistance movement. But perhaps most important, DAM reveals the relational histories of interaction and influence between Palestinians and Jews. Growing up in Israeli schools speaking Hebrew and living within an ethnically Jewish state, these young rappers identify themselves as Israeli citizens. In style, dress, politics, and cultural practice, they feel more similar to Israeli Jews than to Palestinians in the West Bank. As DAM's visibility in the mainstream Israeli music scene increases, and as more and more Jewish and Palestinian rap fans flock to their performances, these young rappers bring to the fore the historical, social, and cultural interconnections between Palestinians and Jews in Israel and further contradict the mythologized nationalist histories of Jewish and Arab autonomy in the region.

But the means through which these young artists are able to so freely navigate between national narratives is due primarily to their usage of American popular music and media. Hip-hop, circulated globally through transnational circuits of flow and exchange, constitutes an essential discursive space for these dialogues to take place. In a fascinating twist, transnational imaginings of a uniquely American popular culture now enable a relational dialogue to emerge between Israeli Jews and Palestinians through music, dance, and other performative media. American popular culture and media serve to broker a unique conversation beyond the borders of the nation-state, bringing together hip-hop fans traditionally separated by nationalist politics and an entrenched "dual society model."

Captured in the tragic events of "Black October," DAM experienced a profound crisis of identity. The dominant "dual society model," revived in the early stages of the al-Aqsa Intifada, could not account for the cultural hybridity experienced by a young population of Palestinian Israelis struggling to understand the violence of October 2000. For these young artists, hip-hop became a powerfully appropriate means of communicating intense feelings of dispossession and dislocation. Imaginings of American history, society, and politics in hip-hop allowed for these performers to frame their argument within a common transnational vernacular of racial equality, ethnic violence, and minority empowerment to an audience of Israeli youth (Jewish and non-Jewish). In this sense, America served as a neutral site for interpreting the ongoing violence of the occupation. In music hip-hop captured the attention of Israeli youth outside the prevailing dogma of the nation-state, allowing for a unique cultural conversation of hybridity and interaction to emerge.

Understanding the unique ways in which America is articulated and imagined in popular culture offers a new direction in American studies. Such a move repositions our focal awareness away from the self-reflexive pursuit of American power and instead strives to better understand the nuanced ways America is interpreted around the world. As has been detailed in this chapter, popular culture offers a new terrain for studying America as a negotiated concept among those most affected by its far-reaching influence. In the ongoing struggle of power, politics, and identity, popular culture is an important tool for understanding what "America" means to communities around the world.

Notes

Portions of this manuscript were presented at the fiftieth annual meeting of the Society for Ethnomusicology in Atlanta and appear in David McDonald, "My Voice Is My Weapon: Music Nationalism and the Poetics of Palestinian Resistance" (PhD diss., University of Illinois, 2006). In researching this project, financial support was generously provided by the Fulbright-Hays Commission, the University of Illinois, and the American Center for Oriental Research.

1. Official crime statistics from Lyd are difficult to obtain, but several articles in Israeli newspapers have documented the problems of drug addiction

and drug-related crime in Lyd. For this, see Ori Nir and Lily Galili, "The Jews Can Leave but the Arabs Have Nowhere to Go," *Ha'aretz* (Jerusalem), December 3, 2000.

2. DAM was named with a sense of hybridity in mind. First, DAM is derived from the Arabic root word *dûm*, meaning "everlasting" or "eternal." In Hebrew, as well as in Arabic, *dâm* means "blood." In English DAM is an acronym for Da Arabic MC. As described to me by Suheil Nafar, when juxtaposed together DAM has the total meaning, "Even if you come at us with blood Da Arab Microphone is eternal" (personal communication, 2005).

3. The concept of the "dual society model" is introduced in Zachary Lockman, *Comrades and Enemies: Arab and Jewish Workers in Palestine, 1906–1948* (Berkeley: University of California Press, 1996). In addition, several other fine researchers have expanded and developed the concept such as Joel Benin, *The Dispersion of Egyptian Jewry: Culture, Politics, and the Formation of a Modern Diaspora* (Berkeley: University of California Press, 1998); and Rebecca Stein and Ted Swedenburg, "Popular Culture, Relational History, and the Question of Power in Palestine and Israel," *Journal of Palestine Studies* 33, no. 4 (2004): 5–20. For a more recent ethnographic study of Jewish Palestinian relations in Israel, see Jonathan Cook, *Blood and Religion: Unmasking the Jewish and Democratic State* (Ann Arbor, MI: Pluto Press, 2006).

4. For a very thorough study of this phenomenon, see Nadim Rouhana, "Accentuated Identities in Protracted Conflicts: The Collective Identity of the Palestinian Citizens of Israel," *Asian and African Studies* 27, no. 1 (1993): 149–170; Nadim Rouhana, *Palestinian Citizens in an Ethnic Jewish State: Identities in Conflict* (New Haven, CT: Yale University Press, 1997); and Rhoda A. Kanaaneh, *Birthing the Nation: Strategies of Palestinian Women in Israel* (Berkeley: University of California Press, 2002).

5. For a history of Palestinian nationalist and resistance music, see McDonald, "My Voice Is My Weapon," 42–161.

6. Tamer Nafar, interview by the author, July 9, 2005, Lyd, Israel (emphasis added).

7. Bruce Knauft, *Genealogies for the Present in Cultural Anthropology* (New York: Routledge Press, 1996), 141–176; Alan Barnard, *History and Theory in Anthropology* (Cambridge: Cambridge University Press, 2000), 139–157.

8. Knauft, *Genealogies for the Present*, 177–218.

9. Stuart Hall, "Gramsci's Relevance for the Study of Race and Ethnicity," *Journal of Communication Inquiry* 10, no. 2 (1986): 5–27.

10. Ted Swedenburg, *Memories of Revolt: The 1936–39 Rebellion and the Palestinian National Past* (Minneapolis: University of Minnesota Press, 1995), 5–15; Stein and Swedenburg, "Popular Culture," 6–10.

11. Thomas Turino, *Nationalists, Cosmopolitans and Popular Music in Zimbabwe* (Chicago: University of Chicago Press, 2000); Harris M. Berger, *Metal Rock and Jazz: Perception and the Phenomenology of Musical Experience* (Hanover, NH: University Press of New England); Harris M. Berger and Michael Thomas Carroll, eds., *Global Pop Local Language* (Jackson: University Press of Mississippi, 2003).

12. Walter Armburst, *Mass Culture and Modernism in Egypt* (Cambridge: Cambridge University Press, 1996); Walter Armburst, ed., *Mass Mediations: New Approaches to Popular Culture in the Middle East and Beyond* (Berkeley: University of California Press, 2000); Rebecca Stein and Ted Swedenburg, eds., *Palestine, Israel, and the Politics of Popular Culture* (Durham, NC: Duke University Press, 2005).

13. "Creative Environments" (joint interview between Dave Watts and Tamer Nafar), *Blag* (2004). This quotation was originally written by Tamer Nafar in a thick urban dialect. For ease of reading, I have changed many of his spellings. The original text is as follows:

> and till da age of 17 i was writin' all kinda luv songs till i met Pac's music, so i created a bubble called "hey, im da nigro of da middle east" when pac say "how many brothers fell victems 2 da streets" i was answerin' him wit' names of my late friends dat keeps dyin' here from drive by's as a result of a ongoing war of "which arabic will control da drug market," so i published my 1st lp "stop sellin' drugz" den i studied crime knowledge and noticed dat der's a reasons of crime, like poverty, un imployment, hunger 2 knowledge, basicly political reasons, but still i chose 2 ignore poletic cuz i wanted 2 "succeed," ya, i was kinda of an cowered, till da Sunday—11/9/2000, when 1 of my closest friends died from a drive by so i said "fuck it, even if im not touchin' it its touchin' me" and began my lyrical war, began 2 be real, but i was missin' knowledge and till dat day (4 years after) im only eatin' books, history and street wisdom, and what throw more gas 2 my fire was dat same mounth, when da second Intifada began (black october), dat got me gettin' back 2 my Palestinien roots, and i noticed dat all my life (tv, books, skool, envierment) was created by Israel only 2 make me a un-connected 2 my roots, so i started writin' songs 4 da young arabs here 2 shorten der prossess and gett'em 2 der roots in a ways dat i didn't had.

14. Tamer Nafar, interview by the author, June 8, 2005, Lyd, Israel.

15. Marius Schattner, "Violence with Israel Further Isolates Arab Minority," *Agence France Presse* (Paris), October 2, 2000.

16. Ibid.

17. *Ha'aretz* (Jerusalem), November 12, 2000; *BBC* (London), October 11, 2000; *Guardian* (London), October 6, 2000.

18. On September 15, 2005, the Police Investigations Department concluded its inquiry into the deaths of the twelve Israeli and one Palestinian victim of "Black October." Their conclusion was that the killings were not a crime and that no charges would be brought against police responsible for the deaths. Throughout the investigation the Or Commission was highly criticized for its handling of the situation. Israeli newspaper *Ha'aretz* reported that in the month following the incidents, the Police Investigations Department conducted only two interviews with police officers involved in the shootings, did not attempt to gather any evidence from the scenes of the riots, and did not conduct any autopsies on the victims. All of these decisions severely limited the amount of evidence available to the Or Commission in making its ruling. See,

for example, Yoav Stern, "Arab Victim Families: Review of Oct. Probe 'Stinking Maneuver,'" *Ha'aretz* (Jerusalem), September 29, 2005. For an in-depth analysis of the events of "Black October," see Cook, *Blood and Religion*.

19. This translation was the result of collaboration between the author and DAM. I have made every effort to provide a clear translation that maintains and preserves the artists' preferences for certain words and phrases. In this example I would not have translated *khayân* as "renegade." I felt that their intent was more "traitor." However, DAM was clear in their wish that this word be translated as "renegade." They felt that "renegade" had more of an urban hip-hop connotation and better matched their original inspiration.

20. In Tupac Shakur's famous song "Everything They Owe," he makes a very similar point. By striking out at the structure of ideology and power, which defines African Americans as "drug dealers and empty souls," Tupac was the inspiration for Nafar's belief that "he didn't break the law, the law broke him." Tupac's original rhymes state,

> Supreme ideology, you claim to hold
> Claiming that we are all drug dealers with empty souls
> That used to tempt me to roll, commit violence
> In the midst of an act of war, witnesses left silent.

21. Lockman, *Comrades and Enemies*, 3–15.

PART IV

CLASSROOM ENCOUNTERS

CHAPTER 8

American Studies in the Arabian Gulf: Teaching American Politics in Bahrain

COLIN CAVELL

From the perspective of having taught political science and related courses for eight years in the American Studies Center (ASC) at the University of Bahrain in the Kingdom of Bahrain, I offer the following observations on teaching American politics to students there. Related courses I taught during my tenure there included US history, political economy, law, minority cultures, and geography.[1]

The Kingdom of Bahrain: The Country and Its Peoples

The nation of Bahrain is a thirty-three-island archipelago situated in the Arabian Gulf,[2] approximately halfway between the Strait of Hormuz near Oman to the south and the mouth of the Tigris and Euphrates Rivers in Iraq to the north, and is buttressed between the much larger nations of Saudi Arabia to the west and Iran across the Gulf to the east. It hosts the US Navy's Fifth Fleet, which sustains the kingdom's monarchy while acting as a forward deployed base—or, in Pentagon parlance, a "forward operating location"—for the United States.

Bahrain has just over 580,000 citizens (of both Arab and Iranian descent) and more than 220,000 expatriate workers (mostly Indians from the southern Indian state of Kerala, Filipinos, and Bengalis but also a smaller mix of Lebanese, Yemenis, Pakistanis, Tunisians, Algerians, Moroccans, Egyptians, Palestinians, Jordanians, Iraqis, Syrians, and others), the latter holding more than 63 percent of all jobs there. The feeling on the part of the United States that it needed to legitimize the al-Khalifa family and its rule—by whose authority the Americans park their ships in Bahrain—was satisfied in 2002, when the kingdom held its first parliamentary elections in twenty-seven years.[3] However, the election was marred by the boycott of many of the Shiite Muslim parties who are outspoken against the forty-seat Shura (or consultative) Council (the upper chamber), whose members are appointed by the king. The Shiites wanted all members of the newly established bicameral legislature to be elected by the citizenry rather than solely by the forty-member lower house, called the Chamber of Deputies, and saw little need for the presumed advantages said to result from "experienced and professional members to give advice" in the appointed upper chamber. In effect, the construction of Bahraini democracy takes a page from the US model, in that the members of the US Senate were also appointed, albeit by state legislatures, for more than 125 years, until the adoption of the Seventeenth Amendment of 1913, which instituted the direct election of the US upper house. In the November 2006 Bahraini parliamentary elections, Islamic political societies, which had boycotted the 2002 elections, participated and garnered nearly half of the total elected representatives. The outcome of the November 2010 parliamentary elections replicated the 2006 results, with the Shiite majority again supporting the campaigns of Islamist candidates running against Sunni supporters of the monarchy. The political establishment quietly stokes the Shiite-Sunni tension, as it effectively obfuscates the basic contradiction between rich and poor in Bahrain. The two labor or Marxist-oriented secular parties that do address the growing material inequities in Bahraini society—the National Democratic Action Society, successor to the Popular Front, and the al-Menbar Progressive Democratic Tribune, successor to the National Liberation Front—are marginalized by the existing political establishment, even though these two political societies feature perhaps the most rational and enlightened minds in Bahrain.

The al-Khalifa family—which has ruled in Bahrain for more than two hundred years, even when Bahrain was a formal British protectorate from 1916 to 1971—are Sunni Muslims. Sunnis constitute only about 30 percent of the citizenry of Bahrain; 70 percent, or a majority, are Shiites.[4] Despite the fact that the Shiites want both houses of the parliament to be elected directly by the people, it is in fact *they* who are labeled "antidemocratic" by the local media because of their boycott of the 2002 Bahraini elections, carried out in a show of protest.

As in the political realm, so too in the academic realm is there an underlying tension along the Sunni-Shiite religious divide; however, there is unity among the native Bahraini population in its pronounced opposition to the current US occupation of Iraq as well as to the United States' continued support for Israel. This anti-Americanism at times flares up at marches and rallies, usually directed at the US Embassy in Manama, though at times at the university as well. Historical admiration for the United States—including its technological and scientific prowess, military capability and hegemony, and presumed democratic institutions—still holds sway among a number of Bahrainis, enough to support the establishment of the American Studies Center at the University of Bahrain and annually supply a constant, albeit small, cadre of students since the program's inception in 1998.

The University of Bahrain

The University of Bahrain currently has approximately twenty thousand students at two campuses,[5] with its main campus in Sakhir sporting a modern architectural style and stocked with modern teaching facilities, computers, high-speed Internet, library, and the like. As at most universities, there are plenty of eager students willing to learn and improve themselves, with most looking down the road for well-paying jobs. Many of the structures of the university appear similar to their US counterparts, with a division into colleges, departments, administrative sections, and so on. Expatriate faculty, however, are hired on a two-year contract basis with renewal contingent upon mutual agreement, while native Bahraini faculty have sinecures until they retire. This dual employment scheme for faculty has its logical consequences in the form of unequal salaries, unequal possibilities for promotion, unequal workloads, and so on. Concomitantly, though Bahraini faculty members are favored over expatriates in the above-mentioned ways, their elevation has led to a general feeling among expatriates that many Bahraini faculty are simply dead weight and nonproductive.[6] In contrast to their US counterparts, there is virtually no faculty participation in the governance of the university as a whole, though there is a semblance of faculty participation in the governance of the departments. There are no faculty or staff unions. In fact, there are generally only a few unions in Bahrain, mostly in the few dominant industries—oil and aluminum, for example—and they are closely tied to the management of those industries.

Though the university's student population is predominantly Bahraini (more than 99 percent), the workforce of the country, as indicated above, is quite diverse. The University of Bahrain, however, restricts its student population primarily to Bahrainis, some Arab nationals from Gulf Cooperation Council[7] states, and a select few from other Arab states. In the 2001–2006 period, a number of private universities were allowed to establish themselves in Bahrain—with curricula primarily oriented toward business, information technology, banking, and finance. Unlike the UOB, however, these private institutions will accept almost anyone who has the financial means to pay. And because they are graduating a number of former UOB students who left the university due to poor grades, the rigor of their academic programs has recently been called into question. In 2008 the king issued Royal Decree No. 32, creating the Quality Assurance Authority for Education and Training (QAAET)[8] to ensure that quality standards prevail at each university. As of this writing, at least ten private universities have been warned to rectify their standards or be shut down.

The Teaching Environment

What is it like teaching at the predominantly Arab-populated University of Bahrain? Aside from the language difficulties one who is not fully conversant in Arabic might encounter, there are also cultural differences that may be unusual for some Americans, Europeans, and Asians and Africans who are not part of the Muslim world. For example, imagine entering a classroom where all of the female students are dressed in black *abbayas* (dresses designed to hide the female form) and *hijabs* or *sheilas* (head-covering scarves), some with their entire faces covered by a *niqab*, leaving only the students' eyes visible. As for the males, imagine many of them dressed in blazing white *thobes* (similar to a cassock worn by a Catholic priest) with a headdress called a *guttrah*, which is fastened to the head by a black ropelike hoop called an *agal*. Such a sight might be unusual at first—unless, as in my case, you grew up in a heavily Catholic region of the United States (southern Louisiana, that is) and went to Catholic schools, were taught by nuns, preached to by priests, and served many a mass as an altar boy, and thus are used to similar fashions. Displaying one's religiosity and an appearance of virtue are very important to Bahrainis, especially those who wish to "succeed." Indeed, a Western visitor's vision of modernity will be immediately confronted with this apparent premodern reality (see Cavell 2006a).

Regarding academics in particular, note that the University of Bahrain has neither a political science program nor a philosophy program, as university officials have stated that these topics are already covered by the Department of Arabic and Islamic Studies. Students tell me that only in American studies courses are they allowed to debate and voice their own opinions. Individual expression of opinion, students say, is forbidden, shunned, or simply not encouraged in all other areas of the university. In fact, it is because of the American Studies Center's openness to diverse views—which is perhaps no greater than that of most US colleges and universities—that our program is thriving, despite the level of anti-Americanism arising out of current US actions in the Middle East. Indeed, the American Studies Center attracts some of the brightest and most capable students at the university. We invite many speakers, sponsor special field trips, host events and sometimes parties for our students, and, through the US State Department, provide scholarships for students to study and teach in the United States—activities and programs that are not available elsewhere in the university. Of even more importance, much of the center's success can be attributed to the fact that the ASC is the one place on campus where students feel they can speak their minds without fear of reprisal.

While governmental reprisals against its opponents—real or imagined—frequently do occur in Bahrain, one American studies professor's successful defense against one attack has given ASC students some pride of association, as well as providing the ASC with a degree of freedom found in few other settings in the kingdom.

Teaching as an American in the Middle East thus has been a new experience, both exciting and educational. Also, having some distance from one's native country allows one to be simultaneously more critical of one's government—especially one like that of the United States, which is involved all over the world—and more appreciative of some of the rights we often take for granted, such as those embodied in the First Amendment to the US Constitution, in addition to the due process rights provided by the Fifth and Fourteenth Amendments. Moreover, I have gained new insight into and appreciation of Bahrainis in particular and Arab peoples in general: their world, their struggles, and their worldviews. And Bahrain—also known as the ancient land of Dilmun, to which King Gilgamesh traveled seeking immortality, as told in *The Epic of Gilgamesh* (the oldest extant work in literature)—while not paradise, is definitely full of life. Indeed, where else do nearly 365 days of blue skies and sunshine describe the climate, with no tsunamis, hurricanes, tornadoes, or earthquakes, located only three degrees north of the Tropic of Cancer?[9]

Language: English Is a Core Component

In this age of information and intellectual property, packaging, distribution, and marketing of ideas is more key than their development. Language is the vehicle through which this packaging and distribution is accomplished. Hegemony of language is therefore comparable to control of ideas by controlling their distribution. Since language is ultimately a "game" of contexts and meanings, whoever defines the language of discourse controls the rules of the game. (Malhotra 2001)

At the present time English, to a much greater extent than any other language, is the language in which the fate of most of the world's millions is decided. English has, in the twentieth century, become the international language par excellence. (Phillipson [1992] 2003, 5–6)

Bahrain's citizenry comprises both Arab and Iranian descendants. While the minority Sunni Arabs dominate the politics of the country, it is tempting, though incorrect, to classify all Bahrainis as Arab; many of them hail from Persian ancestry. While Arabic is the official language of Bahrain, many of its Shiites still speak Farsi as a second language. The national curriculum now requires English be taught as a second language in all public schools; nevertheless, most entering college freshmen possess only a beginner's level of mastery, though graduates of the kingdom's several private high schools usually come to university with advanced English proficiency. And while the level of English proficiency is slowly improving—aided by the establishment of at least three English daily newspapers, a similar number of English magazines, and at least two local radio stations broadcasting in English, in addition to a saturation of English-language television and radio satellite providers—Arabic remains the most widely spoken language in Bahrain.

For those wishing to reach most of the population, magazines and telephone answering systems usually begin with an Arabic message followed by the same message in English. This dual-language messaging is also employed in many advertisements, especially billboards, which depict the message in Arabic on the right side (as Arabic is read from right to left) and the English message on the left. Similarly, in certain magazines and textual publications of the educational and commercial sectors, both English and Arabic versions are provided, with the English version being read from left to right to the midpoint of the publication and an Arabic version that can be read from right to left until one reaches the last English text page.

At the University of Bahrain, English is the language of instruction in the Colleges of Business, Engineering, Education, Computer Science and Information Technology, Science, and, increasingly, Law. In the College of Arts, passing basic English courses is required of all graduates, though Arabic remains the language of instruction in the Departments of Arabic and Islamic Studies, Social Sciences, and Mass Communications. The American Studies Center is part of the Department of English Language and Literature; consequently, students minoring in American studies are usually proficient in both Arabic and English. The existence of a body of English-speaking students makes possible the American Studies Center and its curriculum, as most texts used in American studies are from US publishers and are printed in English, although the US State Department from time to time does publish certain texts on American government, history, economics, geography, and literature in Arabic, which are sometimes helpful.

While those students proficient in both English and Arabic enjoy their bilingual capabilities, resentment is widespread among other, solely Arabic-speaking, students who are required to pass basic English courses in order to graduate from the College of Arts. Failure rates in introductory English courses among these students surpass 50 percent every semester. One major reason for the high failure rate is the practice of passing most students in their English courses from grade school through high school, a practice encouraged by the Ministry of Education. However, once students are at the university, faculty members are encouraged to fail any student who cannot master basic English. Politically, this unwritten policy allows the government to appear magnanimous in granting the sons and daughters of the kingdom's citizenry widespread admission to the UOB while knowing that the job market will not be saturated with university graduates, as many fail to pass the basic English requirements and end up dropping out of the university. Rather than hold the government responsible for this situation, some students instead blame the faculty of the English Language Department for the high failure rates. The consequences have led to student protests, letter-writing campaigns to local newspapers, and the expected bureaucratic directives to placate student unrest by requiring the chair of the English Department, as well as English-language faculty, to repeatedly address student concerns.

Why Teach American Politics to MENA Students?

For decades, students of the Middle East have had to contend with the United States as a superpower that operates in and about their home-lands. During the Cold War, the Soviet Union shared this role with the United States, as each country was caught up in the game of choos-ing which superpower to ally with while being treated as a pawn in the deadly game for world power.

With the demise of the Soviet Union at the end of 1991, the United States moved rapidly into the Middle East and North Africa region, seeking to implement procapitalist liberal regimes favorable to the United States, in order to ensure continued American access to the re-gion's oil reserves on favorable terms. At the same time, this strategy al-lows the United States to support its long-term ally Israel and declare an indefinite global war on terrorism—specifically against what has been dubbed "Islamo-fascism," "Islamic radicalism," or "militant Jihadism" (see Bush 2005)—and simultaneously proclaim that it is promoting freedom and democracy (see Cavell 2002).

Building on its entrance into the region in the early part of the twen-tieth century,[10] the United States sought to consolidate its hold on the Middle East and its resources, particularly as the world enters the pre-dicted period of "peak oil,"[11] with the price of one hundred dollars per barrel of oil becoming the norm in 2008 before declining to around seventy-five dollars per barrel by 2010, as many newly industrializing nations joust with established industrial nations for what remains of earth's hydrocarbon reserves. Bolstered by a neoliberal agenda that had advocated US intervention in the region in the late 1990s,[12] the admin-istration of George W. Bush used the September 11, 2001, attacks on the US mainland as provocation enough to launch a war in Afghanistan to oust the Taliban regime, which had provided safe haven for Osama bin Laden and his al-Qaeda religious jihadists, and replace it with the pro-US regime of Hamid Karzai by 2002. Then, in March 2003, Bush launched a second war against Iraq, claiming the regime of Saddam Hussein possessed weapons of mass destruction, was pursuing a nuclear weapons program, and had assisted al-Qaeda operatives in the 9/11 attacks against the United States. In its eighth year of occupation of Iraq, the United States had between 50,000 and 92,000 troops in the country, down from a peak of 170,000 in 2007, as President Obama pledged to stick to a timeline for military withdrawal by the end of 2011 (Wilson 2010). Troop withdrawal was completed in December of that year. In Afghanistan, however, US troop levels rose from 26,000 in 2007 to 68,000 by November 2009 and upward to 94,000 by May 2010, as the Taliban continued to press an insurgency in its quest to return to power ("Pentagon to Extend" 2007; Pugliese 2010).

Faced with the omnipresence of American power in the region and the concomitant commodity- and consumer-oriented culture imposed there, it is nearly impossible for Bahrain to ignore the United States. Thus, it is not surprising to find students eager to learn about the US government and American politics. While some are perhaps motivated by the adage of Sun Tzu Wu to "know thy enemy," others are genuinely interested in learning about democracy, how the US government works, and why it became so powerful.

Their country having declared its independence from Britain in 1971, Bahraini students can somewhat identify with the United States in its war of independence (1775–1783), although Bahrain's nominal independence was more about shifting international patronage from Britain to the United States. But aside from this point of quasi-related identificafion, almost everything else about US politics is relatively new to them, although there is a shared understanding of why the United States initially opted for a confederacy after living under the tyrannical and arbitrary rule of the unitary government of King George III of Britain; the vagaries and annoyances of monarchical rule are quite the norm for Bahrainis. The United States' eventual move to a federation under the 1787 Constitution has its adherents among students—though with limited applicability to the small island nation of Bahrain—as does the constitutional separation of powers among the executive, legislative, and judiciary branches, each with coequal powers and checks and balances. Periodic fixed-date elections for governmental representatives, who derive their authority from the consent of the governed, many students find intriguing, though most are as yet unconvinced of the virtues of liberal democracy, preferring instead to defer to their imams, or religious leaders, while a few still opt for monarchy.

The one feature of American democracy that most Bahraini students can support with enthusiasm is the principle of constitutional supremacy and its related consequence that no one is above the law. Why

Americans read, study, and often memorize their constitution appears initially strange to many of them, even though Bahrain itself has a fairly modern written constitution as well. The apparent reason for this reaction among Bahraini students, as is often lamented in classes, is that their constitution is rarely followed, for it is not the supreme law of the land. Indeed, the mind-set of the average Bahraini is that if you want to get anything done in Bahrain, you need *wasta*, or connections to powerful people, who are either part of or connected with the monarchy. Thus, not only are the structures of a republican form of government and its theoretical bases important subjects for Bahraini students to ponder, but the associative checks and balances, along with the doctrine of constitutional supremacy and the rule of law, provide them with ample food for thought as well.

Further Considerations on Teaching American Politics to MENA Students

Ensuring access to the Arabian Gulf region's oil reserves on favorable terms appears to be a key component of current American strategy there (see Cavell 2007). However, in order to do so, and because this entails a long-term process, the United States must likewise transform the region—technologically, economically, and ideologically—so that it, its allied governments, and multinational corporations can operate in the region on an ongoing stable basis. The quid pro quo in this relationship is thus one of offering the tools of modernization in exchange for the region's hydrocarbon resources while securing and guaranteeing the stability of cooperative Arabian Gulf regimes. This relationship with the Gulf countries remains vital for continued US hegemonic aspirations and indeed for the consumption-based, growth-oriented, capitalistic society of the United States.

While some characterize the threat of "peak oil" as a sort of commodity fetishism (see Caffentzis 2008) or downplay the immediacy of the potential shortfall, as some oil industry apologists do,[13] others, including many scientists, take the threat of a finite reserve of oil seriously, as reflected in policies undertaken by current American political leaders. New megabarrel-producing oil fields are rarely found; meanwhile, older fields are maturing or drying up, failing to yield enough oil to satisfy increasing worldwide demand (see Whipple 2007). The industrializing powers of China, India, and others, not content to forgo the advantages of an oil-based economy, thus compete with postindustrial Western societies for the earth's remaining hydrocarbon resources. The control and management of these remaining energy resources are currently being keenly fought over. Middle Eastern oil reserves thus appear essential to US security, and strategists are acting accordingly.

Not long after the British pulled out of the Middle East in the early 1970s and the Iranians forcibly removed the shah of Iran in the revolution of 1979, US president Jimmy Carter proclaimed the doctrine that would bear his name, stating, "An attempt by any outside force to gain control of the Persian Gulf region will be regarded as an assault on the vital interests of the United States of America, and such an assault will be repelled by any means necessary, including military force" (1980). To back up the Carter Doctrine, a rapid deployment force, operating out of MacDill Air Force Base in Tampa, Florida, had been set up four months prior. Then, in January 1983, President Ronald Reagan "converted the Rapid Deployment Force (still based in Florida) into the US Central Command (CENTCOM), the first regional command created in thirty-five years" (Johnson 2004, 223). Between the end of the Iraq War of 1991 and the beginning of the Iraq War of 2003, the United States extended its presence in the Persian Gulf region tremendously. While CENTCOM remains based in Florida, a forward headquarters was established at Camp as-Sayliyah in Qatar in 2000, on the outskirts of the capital city, Doha. Camp as-Sayliyah now constitutes the largest prepositioning base outside the US mainland and allows for the rapid movement of personnel, equipment, and supplies by land, sea, or air to other countries in the region. In 1995 Juffair Naval Support Activity in Manama, Bahrain, became home to US Naval Forces Central Command[14] and the United States Fifth Fleet. Acting as both a prepositioning site for US troops and matériel, the Fifth Fleet has particular responsibility for securing US hegemony in both the Indian Ocean and the Arabian Gulf.[15] As Chalmers Johnson notes in *The Sorrows of Empire*, the United States currently has or operates out of at least twenty-eight permanent military bases in the Middle East (Johnson 2004, 216–253).[16]

Given the strategic location of their island nation, Bahraini students both understand and lament US support for their country's monarchy. While many Sunni students see such support as necessary, most Shiites, of course, see it as an impediment to majority—that is, Shiite—rule, and hence a drag on the country's political development. Bahraini students understand the importance of Middle Eastern oil resources to current international relations. They also understand how this predicament presents the region and their country with both positive and neg-ative prospects. While Bahrain was the first country on the Arabian side of the Arabian or Persian Gulf to strike oil in 1931, it will also likely be the first Arab country to run out of oil, in approximately ten to fifteen years.[17]

Diversification is therefore a pressing issue for the country's eco-nomic leaders. So far, investment has gone into constructing and oper-ating the largest aluminum smelter outside of eastern Europe, operating a gas liquefaction plant and, most especially, making Bahrain a regional financial hub; it hosts more than 370 offshore banking units, 65 Amer-ican firms, and 32 Islamic commercial, investment, and leasing banks, as well as Islamic insurance companies. Bahrain is now said to host "the largest concentration of Islamic financial institutions in the Mid-dle East" (Bureau of Near Eastern Affairs 2007). Still, the yearning for citizen input into determining the country's future is quite high, espe-cially as it experiences rising incomes, fosters a more mobile and asser-tive middle class, and becomes technically savvy, culturally aware, and conversant in both Arabic and English. Stifling such aspirations will not only be disconcerting to the Bahraini population but present problems of stability for the continuation of the monarchy as well.

Thus, Bahrain is rich with political problems and opportunities lo-cally, nationally, and internationally, and many of its students are seek-ing answers to such political questions. Without an established program of political science or a program in philosophy at the University of Bah-rain, it is logical for some of the most politically aware and articulate students to gravitate to the American Studies Center—the only place on campus to learn about and freely discuss politics and diverse ideas—to pursue their courses.

What Should Be the Posture of American Studies Programs in the Arab World?

Given this understanding of Bahrain's position in current world affairs, the role it plays, and how this influences its citizens and their college-age students, what should an American studies program in the Arab world focus on in its curriculum as well as in its methodological ap-proach and disposition?

To be certain, the American Studies Center at the University of Bah-rain is a program supported by the state of Bahrain. The ASC does receive substantial funding from the US taxpayer through the US State Department in the form of scholarships, speakers, travel opportunities for students, computers, books, and other instructional materials; however, the two professors primarily associated with the daily operations of the center and the teaching of most of its courses are, in fact, faculty members of the UOB and hence have an economic interest in being loyal to the Kingdom of Bahrain, its citizens, and the country's development. Moreover, as academics, we should take a critical view toward whatever material is being studied in conjunction with the courses presented. A critical approach thus entails examining, as thoroughly as possible, every aspect of American society: its political institutions—including its laws, policies, and governmental structures; its historical development and major conflicts and whether and how they were resolved; its literary and cultural productions and their effects; the components of its population and the various cultures represented and whether and how they are assimilated; its economy and stratification; its religious diversity and various ideological orientations; its foreign policies and international relations; and so on. The orientation we have taken at the UOB ASC involves presenting students with a broad, multidimensional perspective on American society in a comparative, transnational way, with views of both adherents and detractors included, and allowing students to judge critically what aspects of the American experience they deem useful and what can be dispensed with.

Still, to chart one's role correctly, one must envision or imagine one's demise. In this respect, the UOB American Studies Center will have fulfilled its mission when the university incorporates a critical approach to both teaching and learning in all of its curricula, when freedom of speech and expression are not only allowed but encouraged at the university and in society at large, and when a Department of Political Science and a Department of Philosophy are gladly welcomed into the curriculum of the UOB and not seen as a threat to either the government or Bahraini society.

In a March 2003 article for the Egyptian weekly *al-Ahram*, Professor Edward Said related the story of Saudi prince Ibn Al-Walid donating ten million dollars to the American University in Cairo that same year in order to establish an American Studies Center, commenting that "apart from a few courses and seminars on American literature and politics scattered throughout the universities of the Arab world, there has never been anything like an academic centre for the systematic and scientific analysis of America, its people, society, and history, at all. Not even in American institutions like the American Universities of Cairo and Beirut." It is understandable that Said, as most everyone else at the time, was unaware of the American Studies Center at the University of Bahrain, established in 1998; Bahrainis, especially political leaders, were unsure of just exactly how such a program would be welcomed given the strain of anti-Americanism that has pervaded the region for decades and was greatly exacerbated during the eight years of the Bush administration. Yet the UOB ASC has grown steadily; current enrollment is approximately sixty student minors. In addition, the center has expanded its course offerings (approximately five every semester), established a speaker series, opened a theater that regularly shows popular American films, established a website (http://userspages.uob.edu.bh /asc/), built and maintained an email distribution Listserv,[18] started a biannual news magazine, graduated at least seventy students who minored in the program, and established an alumni association. It is thus a consequence of hard work and some luck that the ASC celebrated its tenth anniversary at the UOB in October 2008, making it the oldest American studies program in the entire Middle East.

Thus, while admittedly the program as outlined above is relatively new to the region, it is incumbent on such programs to seek to foster a critical approach to learning at all levels of the university and society in general, meanwhile envisioning the eventual completion of their mission. It should go without saying that American studies programs that attempt to act as cheerleaders, apologists, or propaganda arms for America and its policies, without approaching the subject scientifically and objectively, will be ignored by MENA students and societies at best and attacked vociferously at worst.

What Tools Are Available to Teach US Politics in the MENA?

Ordering books from the United States can at times prove difficult. Efforts to order course textbooks through the UOB bookstore did not succeed. Eventually, some professors opted to order the books themselves and sell them directly to the students. In fact, for at least three years, almost no faculty members in the Department of English Language and Literature ordered their textbooks through the university bookstore; in 2009 the university mandated that faculty order class texts only through the UOB bookstore. The UOB bookstore waits until the first day of classes to place the order for course books—which means that often the books come in a month after the semester has started—and systematically orders only half of the number of books that faculty members request. Its perennial complaint and justification are that "books don't get sold" and that they have "no way to return unsold books to the publishers." Apparently, this complaint is true not only for books ordered from the United States but also for books ordered from other countries. After many memos and meetings, it is still unclear whether this is due to general incompetence or if there are postal barriers and the like slowing down the process. Nonetheless, we have had little problem in ordering textbooks from the United States directly and getting them shipped in a timely manner to Bahrain, although we have also encountered publishers who say that they cannot ship textbooks to this part of the world. However, there are other alternative publishers and booksellers who are willing to ship books to Bahrain.

As mentioned above, most of the textbooks used in the American studies program at the UOB are ordered from US publishers. Also, the US State Department periodically supplies a limited number of books on American government, history, literature, geography, economics, and so on. While these texts can sometimes be used as supplementary class materials, the one very useful item periodically supplied by the State Department was a CD-ROM entitled *InfoUSA*. In the Introduction to American Studies courses, we regularly used many of the readings from the CD-ROM's "Basic Readings in U.S. Democracy,"[19] which incorporates founding documents, court cases, famous speeches, policy determinations, and the like.

In addition to these textual materials, satellite television continuously broadcasts American news and cultural programs into the region. Since November 15, 2006, the Arab-owned and Qatar-based al-Jazeera Television has also been broadcasting around the clock in English, presenting a much-welcomed balance to the slew of distorted and biased news emanating from US-based broadcasters. Similarly, more than a half year later, Tehran-based Press TV began broadcasting around the clock in English as well. Though the launch of the Iranian government–funded Press TV was not as well advertised or as widely reported on as the al-Jazeera English launch, its programming has begun to catch on among many viewers in the region, though the channel itself is not officially accessible within Iran due to the Islamic Republic's ban on the use of satellite dishes since 1995. Nevertheless, Press TV generally broadcasts more critical coverage of Western government policies and thus acts as a check to al-Jazeera's more favorable coverage of the West. Both of these English-language television broadcasters are not only bringing regional concerns to the attention of Western audiences but relaying Western ideas and history back to local populations as well. Together, they form invaluable tools in the instruction of regional peoples about American politics in the English language.

What Problems Occur in Teaching Politics in the MENA?

Despite having the assets of being Muslim (marrying my Moroccan wife required my conversion) and of being able to operate in Arabic, one of the main problems I shared with others teaching American politics in the Arab world is that both the person and the program he or she is associated with—namely, an American studies program—are seen initially as suspect and perhaps as part of a secret, seditious plot to undermine Arab interests and to promote American imperialism. It is not that the idea of establishing an area studies program at an Arab university so as to obtain a better, fuller understanding of the particular area under consideration is a new, and hence potentially dangerous, undertaking. There are at the UOB, in addition to the American Studies Center, a German Studies Center, a French Studies Center, and a Japanese Studies Center as well, though these other centers are predominantly language oriented. Rarely does one hear negative student comments suspicious of the intent of these other cultural centers or of the faculty associated with them. Rather, it is that the Arab peoples are quite aware of which country has been and is currently dominating them and perpetuating the status quo political arrangements under which they are forced to live. It is America that is currently fighting a war in Afghanistan, which is strongly influencing the governments of Pakistan, Lebanon, Jordan, Saudi Arabia, the Gulf kingdoms, and others; that is occupying Iraq while attempting to police its civil war; that unquestioningly continues to support Israeli aggression against Palestine and its peoples; that is heightening its rhetoric, imposing sanctions, and rattling its saber toward Iraq; that keeps the region's monarchs and autocratic leaders in power, seemingly forever; and that strolls and polices its waterways as if they were American ponds. This history of US intervention in the region is growing longer and more pronounced every year; hence, it is only natural for folks to become defensive, wary, and cautious about things American. Such is the environment one can expect in establishing an American studies program in the Arab world. Presenting the positive aspects of the American experience is thus often complicated by present US government policies and actions.

What Is to Be Taught, Politically?

Each semester I usually[19] teach three of the following twelve courses focusing on political science, history, political economy, law, culture, or geography:

1) AMST 201: US History I: From the Colonial Period to 1877
2) AMST 202: US History II: From 1877 to the Present
3) AMST 205: American Government I: National and Local
4) AMST 206: American Government II: National and Local
5) AMST 211: Introduction to American Studies I: Aspects of American Culture
6) AMST 212: Introduction to American Studies II: Aspects of American History and Government
7) AMST 224: History of US–Middle East Relations
8) AMST 250: American Law and Institutions
9) AMST 411: Minority American Cultures
10) AMST 413: American Political Economy
11) AMST 420: America's Role in International Affairs
12) AMST 225: US Geography

AMST 211 and AMST 212 are both required courses for the American studies minor at the UOB; as such, I usually teach the American culture introduction in the fall semester and the American history and government introduction in the spring semester, supplementing each course with two additional courses drawn from the list above every semester. As these courses are American studies students' first introduction to US politics—and, indeed, to any course on politics from a scientific perspective ever—the remainder of this chapter will focus on the pedagogical approach taken in these two introductory courses, so as to provide a basic template for understanding, comparison, and critique.

Because the political, economic, and historical aspects of US development are intrinsically linked and mutually supportive, in telling America's story in these two introductory courses, an instructor must touch on the following facts of American development:

1) the European conquest of the New World, the resulting contest for empire in the Western Hemisphere, and the establishment of a colonial-settler apartheid regime
2) the war for independence from Britain and monarchy and the establishment of a constitutional republic with checks and balances, a Bill of Rights, and especially the First Amendment rights of freedom of speech, press, belief, peaceable assembly, right to petition the government for a redress of grievances, and the establishment and free exercise clauses that separate church and state while forbidding the state from impeding the free exercise of religion
3) industrialization, inventions, the push-pull factors of immigration and urbanization, and the rise of an organized labor movement
4) expansion of the country from the Atlantic to the Pacific under the doctrine of "Manifest Destiny" and the resulting genocide against Native inhabitants
5) the free flow of immigrants, the importation of indentured servants, and the forced kidnapping and enslavement of Africans and resulting class stratification of the US political economy
6) the contradiction between an acclaimed free society and the enslavement of blacks and the attempt to resolve this breach with the 1861–1865 Civil War
7) the use of war to expand the nation: the Mexican-American War, the Spanish-American War, World Wars I and II, and so on
8) the cultural mythology of individualism, the self-made man, pulling one's self up by one's own bootstraps, from rags to riches, and the eventual transformation of a community-oriented social ethic to self-centered egotism
9) the enfranchisement of blacks, women, Native Americans, and eighteen-year-olds
10) minority rights movements

Racism and genocide, the capitalist exploitation of labor, white Anglo-male supremacy, and American imperialism run deeply throughout the development of the United States. Utilizing a historical-materialist approach, I attempt in these two introductory courses to depict examples of the struggles and controversies surrounding each of these historical moments through the perspectives of both the victors and the vanquished, while emphasizing the developing class struggles underlying each of these contests for power, economic dominance, and supremacy. While portraying America's story, I attempt to relate the American historical experience to either past Arabic history or ongoing struggles in the region.

Many of the ongoing struggles in the MENA region have antecedents in US history, thus providing a treasure trove of strategies, tactics, philosophical arguments, and the like available for appropriation by students of the region who wish to advance their societies. In class presentations in these two introductory courses, three of the topics most often spoken on are the historical plight of the Native Americans, the African American struggle against slavery and subsequent civil rights movement, and, most especially, the women's rights movement. Specific readings that touch on these three topics and are utilized in these two introductory courses include the following:

Readings: Thomas Jefferson, "'Laws': The Administration of Justice and Description of the Laws," in *Notes on the State of Virginia* (1781)

Readings: "Black Hawk Surrender Speech" (1832) (*InfoUSA* n.d.)

Readings: "Declaration of Sentiments" (1833) (*InfoUSA* n.d.)

Readings: The American Anti-Slavery Society, "The *Amistad* Revolt: A Historical Legacy of Sierra Leone and the United States" (1839) (*InfoUSA* n.d.)

Readings: Alexis de Tocqueville, "How the Americans Understand the Equality of the Sexes," *Democracy in America* (1840)

Reading supplement: "Argument of John Quincy Adams before the Supreme Court of the United States in the Case of the *United States, Appellant, vs. Cinque, and Others, Africans, Captured in the Schooner Amistad, by Lieut. Gedney*" (1841)

Readings: Henry David Thoreau, "Civil Disobedience" (1846) (*InfoUSA* n.d.)

Readings: Seneca Falls Declaration (1848) (*InfoUSA* n.d.)

Readings: Frederick Douglass, "What to the Slave Is the Fourth of July?" (1852)

Readings: *Dred Scott v. Sandford* (1857) (*InfoUSA* n.d.)

Readings: Abraham Lincoln, "A House Divided" (1858) (*InfoUSA* n.d.)

Readings: Abraham Lincoln, "Emancipation Proclamation" (1863) (*InfoUSA* n.d.)

Readings: Abraham Lincoln, "Gettysburg Address" (1863) (*InfoUSA* n.d.)

Readings: *Bradwell v. Illinois* (1873) (*InfoUSA* n.d.)

Readings: *Plessy v. Ferguson* (1896) (*InfoUSA* n.d.)

Readings: Harry S. Truman, Executive Order 9981 (1948) (*InfoUSA* n.d.)

Readings: *Brown v. Board of Education* (1954) (*InfoUSA* n.d.)

Readings: Martin Luther King Jr., "I Have a Dream" (1963) (*InfoUSA* n.d.)

Readings: Civil Rights Act (1964) (*InfoUSA* n.d.)

Readings: NOW Statement of Purpose (1966) (*InfoUSA* n.d.)

Readings: George M. Fredrickson, "Models of American Ethnic Relations: A Historical Perspective" (Colombo, Cullen, and Lisle 2001)

Readings: "True Women and Real Men: Myths of Gender" (Colombo, Cullen, and Lisle 2001)

Readings: Ronald Takaki, "Race at the End of History" (Colombo, Cullen, and Lisle 2001)

Note that at least fifteen of the above readings are—from the previously mentioned *InfoUSA* CD-ROM—at one time supplied by the US State Department. True, the CD-ROM includes neither Thomas Jefferson's *Notes on the State of Virginia* nor Frederick Douglass's "What to the Slave Is the Fourth of July?"—arguably two important critical readings affecting US development, and, for this reason, can be said to be deficient in its rendering of significant US political texts. But what one cannot find on the CD is usually available elsewhere, and I have attempted to compensate for some of the CD-ROM's failings in the list above as well as on the course syllabi.

Given the capitalist orientation of the Arabian Gulf states and the current weak status of the region's labor movement, it is understandable that labor rights fail to generate as much enthusiasm as do the above topics at the university level. As for specific selections, the most often chosen reading presented in class is Martin Luther King Jr.'s 1963 "I Have a Dream" speech. This is usually followed by Henry David Thoreau's "Civil Disobedience" essay and the Seneca Falls Declaration of 1848. Another popular reading available on the *InfoUSA* CD, though not mentioned above, is Ralph Waldo Emerson's 1841 essay "Self-Reliance."

By studying the original complete essays or excerpts from significant books, speeches, or court cases that play a determining role in the American experience, students are able to quickly read, analyze, and identify with the particular issues under discussion. Emphasizing that rights are won through effort and struggle, and not given, orients students to the necessity of struggle to freedom by clearly setting one's goals, assessing one's opposition, and defining one's tactics in accordance with one's strategy. Presenting numerous examples of various people overcoming difficult odds to advance freedom in some form acts as a reinforcement of the chosen material and stimulates students to reflect on the possibilities for their own struggles.

In addition, while it is not often chosen for in-class presentations, it must be mentioned that Benjamin Franklin's maxims from his *Poor Richard's Almanack* make an indelible impression upon most of the American studies students, as they often repeat the aphorisms in class, papers, or everyday conversation. Franklin's values of frugality, thrift, hard work, discipline, practicality, shrewdness, efficiency, selfless service, integrity, and the like appeal to many students as appropriate to their personal integrity and security in their rapidly changing and highly commercial world. Furthermore, when the students are tested on these adages, they generally are able to complete the following matching exercise correctly (taken from the AMST 211 midterm exam):

51. A good Lawyer _____
52. He that can compose himself, _____
53. If you'd have a Servant that you like, _____
54. Men meet, _____
55. Tis better leave for an enemy at one's death, _____
56. He that speaks ill of the Mare, _____
57. To whom thy secret thou dost tell, _____
58. When Knaves fall out, honest Men get their goods: _____
59. The Creditors are a superstitious sect, _____
60. Have you somewhat to do to-morrow; _____
61. Well done _____
62. After crosses and losses _____
63. There are no ugly Loves, _____
64. At the working man's house _____

65. The greatest monarch on the proudest throne, _____
66. The Use of Money _____
67. What maintains one Vice, _____
68. The nearest way to come at glory, _____
69. A countryman between 2 Lawyers, _____
70. Early to Bed, and early to rise _____
71. Don't misinform _____
72. Three good meals a day _____
73. Tell a miser he's rich, and a woman she's old, _____
74. The noblest question in the world is _____
75. There are no Gains, _____

a. is bad living.
b. makes a Man healthy, wealthy and wise.
c. What Good may I do in it?
d. great observers of set days and times.
e. To him thy freedom thou dost sell.
f. your Doctor nor your Lawyer.
g. a bad Neighbour.
h. you'll get no money of one, nor kindness of t'other.
i. without Pains
j. When Priests dispute, we come at the Truth.
k. is to do that for conscience which we do for glory.
l. is like a fish between two cats
m. than beg of a friend in one's life.
n. do it to-day.
o. mountains never.
p. men grow humbler & wiser.
q. is wiser than he that composes books.
r. hunger looks in but dares not enter.
s. is oblig'd to sit upon his own arse.
t. is all the Advantage there is in having Money.
u. will buy her.
v. nor handsome Prisons.
w. serve your self.
x. is better than well said.
y. would bring up two Children

Answers: 51=g, 52=q, 53=w, 54=o, 55=m, 56=u, 57=e, 58=j, 59=d, 60=n, 61=x, 62=p, 63=v, 64=r, 65=s, 66=t, 67=y, 68=k, 69=l, 70=b, 71=f, 72=a, 73=h, 74=c, 75=i

Again, these proverbial bits of wisdom from *Poor Richard's Almanack* are included in the following *InfoUSA* CD-ROM readings:

Readings: Benjamin Franklin, "Hints for Those That Would Be Rich," in *Poor Richard's Almanack* (1737) (*InfoUSA* n.d.)

Readings: Benjamin Franklin, "Rules of Health and Long Life and to Preserve from Malignant Fevers, and Sickness in General" and "Rules to Find Out a Fit Measure of Meat and Drink," in *Poor Richard's Almanack* (1742) (*InfoUSA* n.d.)

Readings: Benjamin Franklin, "The Way to Wealth," in *Poor Richard's Almanack* (1758) (*InfoUSA* n.d.)

The African American struggle for equality and the women's rights movement touch a nerve here in the Arabian Gulf countries, as many of the UOB's middle-class families employ expatriate, usually female, domestic servants—Indians, Bangladeshis, Pakistanis, Filipinos, Indonesians, Ethiopians, and so on—paying them a pittance of a monthly salary though demanding their labor power twenty-four hours a day, seven days a week. Indeed, the process of securing domestic servant labor in the Arab Gulf countries often acts as a cover for much of the region's human trafficking as well as a large percentage of its sexual abuse and even murder cases. The typical wage for a domestic servant in Bahrain is between BD40 and BD60 (about US$106 to US$159) per month. The servant is generally provided with a small room, or a shared room with other servants, in the employer's house, usually on the lowest floor and specifically built for and referred to as "the servants' quarters." The servant or servants are expected to be on call seven days per week, twenty-four hours per day, with no official free time for themselves. Servants' passports are usually confiscated by the employer upon entry into the Gulf countries and returned only if the servant travels with the employer's permission outside of the country—generally when dismissed or, rarely, for a vacation after several years of employment. Rifling through the servant's belongings is a frequent practice by employers who build up and harbor a distrust of their domestic servants, particularly after the harsh treatment the employers mete out upon them. Consequently, domestic servants have little privacy, little free time, and little hope. Many regret their decision to come to the Gulf and spend their nights crying in isolation, which often leads to suicide. Like the expatriate workers imported for construction jobs, most domestic servants are lured to the Arabian Gulf countries by unscrupulous labor companies who promise riches for only a few years' worth of labor. Most of these blue-collar laborers become indebted before they even depart their country of origin, agreeing to exorbitant fees for the chance to work in the "exotic Gulf." As the Arab Gulf countries are generally rentier states,[20] much of the domestic population refuses to hire itself out for manual labor—hence the constant need for imported migrant labor. The above-described abuse of immigrant blue-collar workers and domestic servant labor is widespread and rampant, yet appears to be unquestionably accepted by most Gulf nationals. In fact, observing how the local Gulf culture protects this institution, one can begin to understand how the nineteenth-century American South protected slavery while likewise proclaiming its virtuous character, humane civilization, and religious piety. Nonetheless, the existence of a separate caste of mostly dark-skinned (darker than most Arabs) menial workers building the countries of the Gulf region and performing every imaginable manual labor job and service, including acting as domestic servants in the home, is an undeniable reality to Gulf-country residents. Asserting the humanity of these expatriate blue-collar workers, and hence a normative standard of fair treatment, is a new phenomenon, though many UOB students are cognizant that an attack on this institution hits close to home. That this practice is highly exploitative, however, cannot be denied, even by the locals.

Likewise, women of the Gulf countries are well aware of their second-class status in the Arab world. Though justified by many as part of the edicts of the Holy Koran, and hence the commands of Allah, most of the oppression of women in this part of the world lies in the people's tribal history, the harsh conditions of the desert, and the long practice of male supremacy among Arabs. The Koranic allowance of up to four wives for each male has its historical etiology in the number of females made widows in the early days of Islamic expansionist wars. Forced covering of the female form with the black *abbaya*, with every female required to wear a *hijab* or *sheila* over her head, likewise owes its origin to the hot desert environment. Modern plumbing, electricity, communication, transportation, and the expansion of educational opportunities are calling many of these practices into question, with many females adopting downright defiant attitudes toward what may accurately be described as simply medieval mores, customs, and attitudes about the role of women. As the UOB is populated predominantly by females (at least 80 percent)—males in these rentier states do not see as much value in higher education as females do—a future of retaliatory measures against such chauvinistic practices can be assuredly predicted.

A religious worldview is dominant in the Arab Gulf countries. With most of the male citizens mimicking the Prophet Muhammad by wearing white *thobes* to cover their bodies, their heads wrapped in *guttrahs* and sandals on their feet, while females are draped in black *abbayas* and *hijabs*, the average Arab citizen of the Gulf countries consciously strives to be seen as pious. Many still harbor a religious frame of mind and interpret developments or world events as the will of Allah. For example, a widely shared view in the Middle East at present is that the April 20, 2010, explosion on a British Petroleum oil rig in the Gulf of Mexico—which killed eleven workers and injured seventeen others in addition to causing the leakage of thousands of barrels of oil into the gulf, thus destroying fisheries and endangering other wildlife, fauna, and vegetation while damaging much of the local tourist, restaurant, and subsidiary industries—was Allah's punishment of the United States for its continuously aggressive policies in Iraq and Afghanistan. Challenging this religious worldview or simply prodding students to question cause-and-effect relationships in the world is an uphill battle, as the scientific method is largely foreign to the academic culture of the Arabian Gulf region, even among many university professors.[21] An attempt by me to provoke student thought on the subject can be seen in the following research paper question, one of several that students in AMST 211 can choose to write on:

> Benjamin Franklin was born in 1706 in Boston, Massachusetts, in the Puritanical religious culture of early America, where superstition reigned and Calvinist theology had a strong influence. Mankind was believed to be governed by fate, with some predestined for heaven and others for hell from the moment they were born. Just fourteen years before his birth, nineteen people had been hanged in nearby Salem, Massachusetts, during the Salem witch trials. One of the prevailing cultural beliefs of his time was that a person was born into a particular class and could not escape one's situation; if you were born into a poor laboring family, you could not rise above your station in life, just as you were predestined for either heaven or hell. Though he was trained early in his life for the religious ministry, Franklin was yanked out of school at age ten to work for his father's candle and soap shop, work that Franklin did not enjoy. When the boy was twelve, his father indentured him to work in the printing shop of his half-brother James, and there Franklin encountered and read many of the new novels of the time, such as *Robinson Crusoe* and *Treasure Island*, which were becoming popular. Growing up in what historians call "the Age of the Enlightenment" or

"the Age of Reason," Franklin jettisoned many of his early religious beliefs and focused instead on improving human life in this world. His secular orientation was considered sinful by many religious ministers of the time. Yet, utilizing his rational faculties and following the scientific method, not only was Franklin able to explain the principles of electricity, which subsequently transformed the world, but in addition he fostered many new inventions and was a key player in establishing the modern American democratic republic, believing that self-rule of the people was preferable to the autocratic rule of a monarch. Today, religious beliefs still dominate certain parts of the world, where people believe that our fates are decided by a deity and that we have very little to absolutely no role in determining how our lives will be lived. Using Franklin's life and subsequent American culture as a guide, contrast the positive and negative aspects of following a secular way of life based upon reason versus a religious way of life based upon faith. Are these two ways of life diametrically opposed? If so, how? Or can a synthesis of these two ways of life be realized? And, if so, how? Explain which way of life you think should be taught to students today.

While few students ever choose the above question as the topic for their term papers,[22] it nonetheless provokes thought among them, as they often bring up local controversies of secular challenges to religious ideas and customs in class discussions.

Intrigued by struggles for personal and group rights, students are often eager to learn how the United States has been able to protect and extend its political gains. Here the focus on US governmental structures becomes salient. While aware that the structure doesn't offer heaven on earth, many of the students do become convinced, or at least intrigued by the proposition, that the limitation of political power by separating it into three different branches, executive, legislative, and judicial; instituting a federal government and thus dividing power into one national and fifty local state bodies; adding checks and balances, fixed terms, and set election dates; and having a written constitution applicable to all may arguably be the closest that humanity can get to political perfection here on earth. It is admitted by most that it is at least preferable to the political arrangements they currently live under. Whether politics and political theory as practiced by Americans can convince Arabian Gulf students is secondary to the goal of provoking them to, at a minimum, begin pondering their own political structures and their relationship to them.

Notes

1. Part of this paper draws from a previous article titled "Teaching in the Kingdom of Bahrain," *MCCC Newsletter* 6, no. 11 (2005). The University of Bahrain is the only coeducational public university in the Kingdom of Bahrain.

2. Most Arabs refer to the body of water between Saudi Arabia and Iran as the Arabian Gulf, while most Iranians refer to it as the Persian Gulf. This term has been one of contention for some time between the Arabs on the peninsula and the Persian people of Iran.

3. Bahrain's first parliament, elected in 1973, two years after independence was declared in 1971, was disbanded by the emir in August 1975 when it attempted to legislate an end to the al-Khalifa monarchy and expel the US Navy from Bahrain.

4. Shiites constitute the second-largest denomination of Islam. Their dominant counterparts, the Sunni, believe that the heirs of the first four caliphs (from the Arabic word *khalifa*, meaning "successor" or "representative"), or heads of the Islamic nation, as well as their successors, were rightly chosen leaders of the faithful until the new Turkish Republic under the leadership of Mustafa Kemal Atatürk abolished the Ottoman caliphate in 1924. The Shiites instead believe that Muhammad's (570–632 CE) true successors are only those of his bloodline (one should note that while most Shiites are against the hereditary monarch of Bahrain, they apparently see no contradiction in supporting the hereditary succession of their religious guides), which included his daughter Fatima Zahra and a cousin, Ali, as well as his grandsons. In 680 CE, Ali's son Hussein and seventy-two others were killed in an uprising against the existing caliph, who was deemed "illegitimate." The divide between Sunnis and Shiites has continued ever since.

5. The UOB's smaller Isa Town campus is currently being phased out and converted into a separate polytechnic college, as most UOB departments have already relocated to the Sakhir campus.

6. The same attitude prevails in regard to the hiring practices of local industry, where the government has instituted a scheme of "Bahrainisation," through which private industry is continuously exhorted to employ more citizens. As one local writer put it: "Not unlike the majority of business people in Bahrain, we have been suffering from the Bahrainisation policy adopted and enforced by the government, which regulates the labor market and shoves unqualified, unwanted, unproductive and completely useless Bahraini job seekers down our throats and penalises us if we dare fire them, thus disregarding the basic premise of business which is to make a profit and sustain the economy. The private sector has been used for decades as the scape-goat and the virtual geriatric unit in forcing us to absorb the unqualified labour force" ("The Failure of the Bahrainisation Policy" 2004).

7. The Gulf Cooperation Council was created in 1981 and includes Saudi Arabia, the United Arab Emirates, Kuwait, Qatar, Bahrain, and Oman. In 2003 the GCC established a customs union, which was followed by a plan for the establishment of a monetary union and a single currency by 2010; however, relatively uneven trade and lack of economic integration among member states

and soaring inflation make it questionable whether these predominantly hydrocarbon-based economies, which boast some of the highest gross domestic products in the world, can achieve this goal. In fact, in February 2008, Oman withdrew from the planned monetary union, though this may be a temporary measure. In addition, political union will likely take much longer, as the competing monarchs of the member states are each vying for dominance.

8. The official website of the QAAET is http://en.qaa.edu.bh/.

9. Bahrain's geographical location is N 26°00′, E 50°33′.

10. Though Gulf Oil was the first American company to gain an oil concession in the Middle East, that concession lapsed in 1928 before the company could act on it. Their concession was taken over by the Standard Oil Company of California in 1931, and, fortuitously, its subsidiary the Bahrain Oil Company successfully struck oil in Bahrain on May 31, 1932. Bahrain thus became the first Arab Gulf country to strike oil. British oil firms Burmah Oil and Anglo-Persian Oil were the first oil companies in the Middle East, following the discovery of oil in western Persia—that is, on the Iranian side of the Gulf—in 1908.

11. Geologist Marion King Hubbert was the first to publicize the idea of "peak oil" when in 1956 he accurately predicted that US oil production would peak between 1965 and 1970. The Hubbert peak theory is the basic model upon which current assessments of oil supply worldwide are now formulated. As geologist and first president of the Association for the Study of Peak Oil & Gas Colin J. Campbell states, "The term *Peak Oil* refers [to] the maximum rate of the production of oil in any area under consideration, recognising that it is a finite natural resource, subject to depletion" (2006). Campbell predicted that world oil production would peak in 2007. Given that demand would then outpace production, not only will the depletion of world oil reserves drive prices upward, but the foreseeable end of the oil age is likely to have grave consequences for humanity as well. See Campbell 1988.

12. These analyses include Brzezinski 1997; Project for the New American Century 2000; and Institute for Advanced Strategic and Political Studies 1996.

13. See Harte 2010. See also "Producers Move" 2006; and Bahree and Ball 2006.

14. US Naval Forces Central Command is responsible for securing US hegemony in the Red Sea, the Gulf of Oman, the Persian Gulf, and the Arabian Sea.

15. Note that the US Pentagon uses the term "Arabian" Gulf rather than "Persian" Gulf.

16. These US bases in the Middle Eastern region include Camp Doha, Camp Arifjan, Ahmed al-Jaber Air Base, and Ali al-Salem Air Base in Kuwait; Juffair Naval Support Activity and Shaikh Isa Air Base near Manama, Bahrain; Prince Sultan Air Base, King Abdul Aziz Air Base, and Riyadh Air Force Base in Saudi Arabia; al-Udeid Air Base, Camp as-Sayliyah, and Camp Snoopy near Doha, Qatar; al-Dhafra Air Base, Jabel Ali Seaport, and Fujairah International Airport in the United Arab Emirates; Masirah Air Base, al-Musnana Air Base, Seeb International Airport, and Thumrait Air Base in Oman; Camp Le Memonier in Djibouti; unspecified "secret" bases in Jordan; well over one hun-

dred camps, air bases, and forward operating bases, albeit many perhaps temporary, in Iraq (see Pike n.d.); and Incirlik Air Base in Turkey. Other regional bases from which the United States operates include ones in Egypt, Afghanistan, Pakistan, Kyrgyzstan, Uzbekistan (the Uzbek base was formally shut down in November 2005), and the island Diego Garcia.

17. See Bureau of Near Eastern Affairs 2007. *New York Times* foreign affairs columnist Thomas Friedman asserts that the expectation that Bahrain will be the first Arab Gulf state to run out of oil is the reason it became the first state in the Gulf region to sign a free trade agreement with the United States in September 2004 (Friedman 2006).

18. The ASC e-mail Listserv currently has more than 325 subscribers, including students, alumni, faculty, and staff, as well as interested observers from five continents.

19. Per UOB rules, if a course fails to have a minimum of ten students sign up, the class will be canceled unless there is a graduating student in the class.

20. "A *rentier state* is a term in political science and international relations theory used to classify those states which derive all or a substantial portion of their national revenues from the rent of indigenous resources to external clients. The term is most frequently applied to states rich in highly valued natural resources such as petroleum; however it could also be applied to those nations which trade on their strategic resources (such as permitting the development of an important military base in their territory)" ("Rentier State").

21. It is interesting to note that Palestinian Authority president Mahmoud Abbas and Prime Minister Salam Fayyad, in their recent calls for reform in the educational sector, repeatedly stressed the need to promote critical thinking while criticizing trends within educational establishments toward rigid social practices, "particularly in relation to interactions between male and female students." As Ziad J. Asali, president of the American Task Force on Palestine, stated, "From a reform point of view, this effort will be a microcosm of what to expect if (and hopefully when) other Arab governments decide to initiate their own sorely needed educational reform processes. From a political point of view, education is one of the major areas where fundamentalist Islamist ideology and humanistic secular ideology vie for ownership and definition of the public discourse—and ultimately political power—in the Arab world" (Asali 2010).

22. It should also be noted that this author has been told repeatedly by students and professors alike that he is the only professor at the UOB who requires students to write and submit a research term paper.

References

Asali, Ziad J. 2010. "Fighting for a Culture of Enlightenment in Palestine and Beyond." *Huffington Post*, August 13. http://www.huffingtonpost.com/ziad-j-asali-md/fighting-for-a-culture-of_b_681665.html.

Bahree, Bhushan, and Jeffrey Ball. 2006. "Producers Move to Debunk Gloomy 'Peak Oil' Forecasts: Saudis, Exxon Say Supplies Are Ample as Policy Makers Begin to Weigh Substitutes." *Wall Street Journal Online*, September 14.

Brzezinski, Zbigniew. 1997. *The Grand Chessboard: American Primacy and Its Geostrategic Imperatives.* New York: Basic Books.

Bureau of Near Eastern Affairs. 2007. "Background Note: Bahrain." US State Department, October. http://www.state.gov/r/pa/ei/bgn/26414.htm.

Bush, George W. 2005. "President Discusses War on Terror at National Endowment for Democracy." October 6. http://www.whitehouse.gov/news/releases/2005/10/20051006–3.html.

Caffentzis, George. 2008. "Remarx: Peak Oil Complex, Commodity Fetishism and Class Struggle." *Rethinking Marxism* 20, no. 2. http://www.informaworld.com/smpp/title~content=t713395221~db=all~tab=issueslist~branches=20-v20.

Campbell, Colin J. 2006. Association for the Study of Peak Oil & Gas. http://www.peakoil.net/.

———. 1988. *The Coming Oil Crisis.* Essex: Multi-science.

Cavell, Colin S. 2002. *Exporting "Made-in-America" Democracy: The National Endowment for Democracy & US Foreign Policy.* Lanham, MD: University Press of America.

———. 2005. "Teaching in the Kingdom of Bahrain." *MCCC Newsletter* 6, no. 11.

———. 2006a. "Clarification Regarding the Letter from English 112 Students." Memo, November 2.

———. 2006b. "Liberalism and Its Implications for the Middle East and North Africa." *Journal of Strategic Studies* 2, no. 5: 59–80.

———. 2007. "American Strategy in the Gulf." *Journal of Strategic Studies* 3, no. 6.

Colombo, Gary, Robert Cullen, and Bonnie Lisle. 2001. *Rereading America: Cultural Contexts for Critical Thinking and Writing.* 5th ed. Boston: Bedford/St. Martin's.

"The Failure of the Bahrainisation Policy." 2004. *Mahmood's Den*, September 23. http://mahmood.tv/2004/09/23/The-failure-of-the-Bahrainisation-policy/.

Friedman, Thomas L. 2006. "The First Law of Petropolitics." *Foreign Policy* (May–June). http://www.foreignpolicy.com/story/cms.php?story_id=3426.

Harte, Julia. 2010. "DOE Still Disavows Peak Oil Forecast, Despite New Studies." *Solve Climate, Daily Climate News and Analysis*, May 10. http://solveclimate.com/blog/20100510/doe-still-disavows-peak-oil-forecast-despite-new-studies.

InfoUSA: Information USA [CD-ROM]. n.d. Washington, DC: US Department of State, Bureau of International Information Programs.

Institute for Advanced Strategic and Political Studies. 1996. "A Clean Break: A New Strategy for Securing the Realm." Last modified June. http://www.iasps.org/strat1.htm.

Johnson, Chalmers. 2004. *The Sorrows of Empire: Militarism, Secrecy, and the End of the Republic.* New York: Metropolitan Books, Henry Hold.

Malhotra, Rajiv. 2001. *Language Hegemony and the Construction of Identity.* Princeton, NJ: Infinity Foundation.

"Pentagon to Extend Troops in Afghanistan." 2007. *CBS News*, February 9.

http://www.cbsnews.com/stories/2007/02/09/terror/main2457144 .shtml.

Phillipson, Robert. [1992] 2003. *Linguistic Imperialism*. Oxford: Oxford University Press.

Pike, John. n.d. "Iraq Facilities." GlobalSecurity.org. http://www.global security.org/military/facility/iraq.htm.

"Producers Move to Debunk 'Peak Oil' Forecasts: Report." 2006. *People's Daily Online*, September 15.

Project for the New American Century. 2000. "Rebuilding America's Defenses: Strategies, Forces, and Resources for a New Century." http://newamerican century.org/RebuildingAmericasDefenses.pdf.

Pugliese, Dave. 2010. "US Troop Levels in Afghanistan Reach 94,000: More than in Iraq." *Ottawa Citizen*, May 25. http://communities.canada.com /ottawacitizen/blogs/defencewatch/archive/2010/05/25/u-s-troop-levels -in-afghanistan-reach-94–000-more-than-in-iraq.aspx.

"Rentier State." n.d. *Wikipedia*. http://en.wikipedia.org/wiki/Rentier_state.

Said, Edward W. 2003. "The Other America." *Al-Ahram Weekly*, March 20– 26. http://weekly.ahram.org.eg/2003/630/focus.htm.

Whipple, Tom. 2007. "The Peak Oil Crisis: Connecting the Dots." *Falls Church (VA) News-Press*, February 8.

Wilson, Scott. 2010. "Biden: US Troops Will Leave Iraq on Deadline." *Washington Post.com*, May 27. http://www.cbsnews.com/stories/2010/05/27 /politics/washingtonpost/main6523510.shtm.

CHAPTER 9

Waiting for Hasan: Lewis Hine, Service Learning, and the Practical Pedagogy of American Studies

KATE SAMPSELL-WILLMANN

So, I have it on good authority that this is how it happens. A Qatari guy, let's call him Hasan, goes to Pakistan, Sri Lanka, Nepal, India, maybe even Bangladesh. He is a labor recruiter who is scouting for some folks willing to work for a sheikh, driving, gardening, something like that. He'll pay three hundred dollars per week, including a place to live. That's a lot of money in Sri Lanka. Hasan gives a willing recruit a plane ticket and an entrance visa to Qatar and says he'll meet him at the airport. Every night, men pour in to Doha from the subcontinent carrying everything they own in bundles and emerge from the airport into the sultry Doha dark looking for their ride, for the man who recruited them. He's never there. They don't have a return ticket, and since their visas were sponsored, they need permission to leave the country from their sponsor, who is nowhere to be found. The airport staff is rude (because they've heard it all before) and eventually has security show the men out. Scene fades to black as bewildered, frightened men squat against the wall of the Doha airport, waiting for something to happen. Not quite *Waiting for Godot*, but . . .

This is not to be a criticism solely of Qatar. This kind of labor "recruitment" happens all over the Gulf. The failure is twofold: political and social. The political will to protect guest workers is weak because citizens are socially accustomed to unrestricted power over the lives of the powerless, which has led to abuse. The solution? Take a page from a hundred years ago, from immigrant-overloaded New York. Teach your students about social documentary photography (SDP), especially about Lewis Hine.

Act I, Scene 2: Two Days Later, Doha Airport, 13:00, 43°C

Five of the men who have been waiting for someone to meet them, who have spent the pocket money the man gave them back in Nepal on water and some food, have formed a small collective. They have shared their experiences and have realized how each was promised a similar job. The reality of the situation has begun to sink in. Fear has turned to resignation, anticipating what is next. Some students from the university came by, gave them some food and water, and explained the situation. The men have the number of their embassy, but there is little anyone can do.

Soon after, a big white Land Cruiser pulls up. A man in a *thobe* steps out—let's call him Said—and through his friend who speaks Nepalese asks if he can help. He listens to the story about Hasan and sympathizes. He tells the waiting men that he can transfer their visa to his company and give them a job and a place to stay, but he can't pay three hundred dollars per week, and they won't be working for the sheikh. They'll do construction work or something like it. He'll pay them one hundred dollars per month (or some such paltry amount), but they will have to pay to transfer the visa and pay for the housing. It will take some time before he will be able to get them an exit visa, and then they will be responsible for their own ticket home. All this will be docked from their pay. Looking at the sidewalk where they have been living, the men agree and go. What they never find out is that Hasan and Said work for the same construction company, paid to get workers to build Doha. And they will live in super-substandard conditions, will be overworked in conditions of virtual slavery, and will be unable to save money, quit, or go home. Some will die because of unsafe working conditions and the casual violence of unchecked power.

Service Learning

At one of the American universities that have established campuses in Doha, the Office of Student Activities put together a service learning organization.[1] The home institution is big on service to the wider community, and when its liberal group arrived in Doha, they were appalled by the labor conditions they witnessed. What they did not immediately see eventually shocked them even more. Overfamiliarity had caused willful blindness among local students and staff. Bad things happened to guest workers, but bad things *always* happen to guest workers. Abuse had become normalized during the rapid change from an ethnically homogeneous cottage-industry economy to ethnically stratified, post-industrial world megapower. Qatar, and all the fossil fuel–rich countries in the Gulf, skipped a period of industrialization. Suddenly, Qatar had all of the elements of a postindustrial economy without having learned the lessons so painfully taught by industrialization. And this is where American studies is relevant to teaching in the Middle East.

Qatar and the United States actually have an enormous amount in common: they are both postindustrial economic superpowers, great numbers of their workforces consist of immigrant labor, their economies depend greatly on fossil fuels, and the richest 2 percent own 90 percent of the wealth (actually, Qatar distributes more to a higher percentage, but these beneficiaries are all Qatari, which is the same everywhere in the Gulf; spoils are distributed according to ethnic, national, and tribal background). American studies can help teaching in the Gulf by drawing attention to these parallels and teaching how the United States coped with similar problems in its industrial period. Teaching of this content as securely contextualized within American history also helps avoid the pitfalls of encouraging service-related learning: offense to one's host country. At the end of the day, we're teaching American studies, not issue-specific activism.

The service learning staff asked me if I would be willing to give a lecture and volunteer to work with the service learning program. I was a naïf regarding the labor recruitment scheme described above, but I had witnessed (everyone can) the conditions in which people labor. Perhaps a blue-collar union background made me pay more attention from inside my air-conditioned sport-utility vehicle truckosaurus. Safety measures were nonexistent; every day the newspaper published reports of "blood money" being paid to the families of dead workers (who finally found repatriation), people suffering in the desert heat, and the virtual absence of women in some ethnic communities. I was instantly reminded of many labor practices in the early twentieth century: US Chinese men were recruited for coolie labor, but Chinese women were excluded. Immigrant workers were ensnared in company towns and debt servitude. Children worked in all industries at the earliest ages, robbed of childhood and education. Immigrant labor was terribly exploited by low wages, substandard housing, child labor, domestic labor assault, and so forth. I found it easy to develop a topic and content and to lead these eager young people. I am a photographer and a photographic historian, so Lewis Hine and the social documentary photographers who followed him jumped to mind.

Lewis Wickes Hine (1874–1940), the father of social documentary photography, was an intellectual activist for social justice. As a public intellectual, he can be understood as a product of his thinking environment. The battles he picked were some of the core causes of the Progressive movement: expanding education, combating nativism, treating urban poverty, creating decent working conditions, abolishing child labor, encouraging equality in work, finding the moral equivalent of war, and, fundamental to all, celebrating the dignity of work itself. Although Hine did participate integrally in many of the social movements of his time, the circumstances unique to his life shaped his place in them. Hine emerged from study with John Dewey at the University of Chicago prepared to enter the teaching profession. Frank Manny convinced Hine to take a position in 1901 at the experimental Ethical Culture School. He taught at ECS until 1908 when he began photographing full-time for the Progressive weekly *Charities and Commons*. Soon thereafter, Hine became a photographer for the National Child Labor Committee, which was under the direction of Owen Lovejoy. The period of Hine's greatest notoriety, impact, and professional success came when he became the director of photography for the NCLC.[2]

Hine is most well known for his portraits of children laboring in the places of adults and for his pictures of the builders of the Empire State Building. Hine moved from "social" to "interpretive" photography (his terms) when the collapse of Progressivism in the 1920s forced him to restyle his political agitation to fit the ruling ideas about labor. Although his photographic style noticeably changed after he returned from photographing World War I refugees for the Red Cross in Europe, his fundamental subject never really did. Before 1920 Hine photographed mostly children and other victims of industrial excess, even going so far as to call the product of such exploitative systems "human junk," but after 1920 Hine shifted to making "work portraits" of adults. Still his fundamental subject remained essentially the same. Hine defended the dignity of work, first by criticizing those who would debase it and then by celebrating those who performed it.

Lewis Hine dedicated his working life to imaging work and those who did it. In his work portraits, Hine raised the skilled craftsman to the zenith of modern civilization and introduced his patrons to a new heroic ideal. The most sublime output of that intention was the collection of photographs he made documenting the building of the Empire State Building and those who built it. In his estimation, the workers who built modern cities manifested the spirit of Hine's own credo, found in the "Moral Equivalent of War" and other writings by William James. And although Hine's Empire State Building photographs brought him renown in his time—being the subject of his only published book, *Men at Work*—they certainly were not the sum total of Hine's work portraits. He had been working for the decade of the 1920s on his project of elevating the men and women who made industrial society run to a central place in the pantheon of modernity. He also photographed workers on railroads in the central Atlantic corridor, especially the Pennsylvania Railroad, for whom he photographed his stunning *Power House Mechanic* (fig. 9.1).

Hine is especially relevant to the conditions that guest workers in the Gulf are subject to because he photographed at Ellis Island, the gateway for millions of immigrants to America, where he portrayed new immigrants not as Lady Liberty's "huddled masses" and "wretched refuse" swept through "the golden door," but as confident, competent travelers seeking a new life in a foreign land, no matter how exploited they were by their own countrymen and native-born boosters once they arrived. However, Hine photographed Ellis Island to capture a moment of history and to defeat anti-immigrant sentiment. His pictures are uplifting. Students who would affect conditions in Doha would need to learn how to look at scenes to which they had been normalized and find a way to use images to argue for social change. For this reason, I start teaching with the most easily defended argument, that children should go to school rather than work in adult conditions.

Preparation: Content

My plan was to teach the students to use social documentary photography to discover conditions and form conclusions and then to use their photographs to agitate or educate, whatever was needed to accomplish the goals they had decided to pursue in helping the people they photographed. I chose Lewis Hine as an example because he cared for his subjects as more than aesthetic objects, and he identified himself as more than a muckraker or journalist; he was an investigator of and commentator on sociological conditions. The social documentary photography that he practiced was an involved action that emphasized learning

Figure 9.1. Lewis Hine, "Power House Mechanic Working on a Steam Pump" (1920). From the National Archives and Records Administration, Records of the Work Projects Administration, 69-RH-4L-2.

as much as advocacy. The first step was to teach what went into making a social documentary photograph.

Social documentary photography is not journalism. Whether journalism actually achieves objectivity or not, certainly journalists, especially photojournalists, would argue that objectivity is their goal. Not so for social documentarians. Social documentary photographers are guided by sociological principles of research, but the reasons for pursuing that research are not objective. Speaking directly to Hine's work, and not sociologically generated work of the present, Hine was a nascent sociologist who focused on child labor and industrial situations, including home tenement work. Hine championed the sanctity of labor and (to a lesser extent) the importance of a safe home as refuge.

What makes Lewis Hine (and not Jacob Riis) the first social documentary photographer is his innovative, compassionate perspective. Although the Progressive Era ruling idea, even among reformers like Jane Addams, was based in the dubious tenets of social Darwinism, Hine did not adhere to the "survival of the fittest." Reforms from Hull House to Carnegie libraries were fueled by a desire to help people in their death struggle for limited resources. Like the minority voice (and sociology pioneer) Lester Frank Ward, Hine did not blame people for their poverty. His photography and writing express the view that technology removes societies from the biological struggle for society, and economies are built to serve those societies and their members, not the other way around.[3] Rather than operating within the rubric of social Darwinism, as Riis did, Hine rejected the scientistic for the pragmatic.[4] His honest concern for the people he photographed is what distinguishes Hine from those who came before, no matter their good intentions.

Social documentary photography was conceived in the crucible of industrialization and immigration in the first decade of the twentieth century. Lewis Hine, at the urging of his mentor at New York's Ethical Culture School, Frank Manny, voyaged to Ellis Island to have a look around. According to Hine, "Manny conceived [the] idea of visualizing school activities in a camera."[5] As an intelligent person with a natural gift for observation, living in New York, and working at a predominantly Jewish school, Hine did not fail to notice the enormous social changes wrought by Ellis Island immigration. He headed to the immigration hub with his camera and Frank Manny as an assistant and recorded what he witnessed on one of the greatest migrations in human history.[6]

When Hine left the ECS shortly after his stunning Ellis Island series, it was not "to give up teaching" but "to engage in a new kind of teaching, *visual teaching*."[7] Hine became interested in social welfare because of his trips to Ellis Island.[8] Felix Adler suggests that Hine "set up as a sociological photographer," and "this meant child labor work."[9] The National Child Labor Committee was just starting up in 1904, the year Hine made the shift to sociological photography (his terms), and became interested in Hine for the organization. At the same time, Hine met Paul and Arthur Kellogg, publishers of what would become *Survey Graphic*, around the same time. Paul Kellogg had just secured funding for his Pittsburgh Survey project, arguably the first social science investigation of living conditions in a large industrial center, from the newly formed Russell Sage Foundation.[10] So we look to Hine's Ellis Island portraits and photographs for the National Child Committee and Pittsburgh Survey to see how American reformers went about using visual education as both a tool of social science data collection and political agitation to help improve the status of recent immigrants and unregulated working conditions. The social documentary photograph was born in the work of Lewis Hine.

Naturally, Hine knew that he could not capture all of industrial experience through even a set of pictures, so he set about recording what was in front of him with a thesis in mind, to represent accurately what he saw (meaning using "straight," unmanipulated photographs) that would be "fireproof." If the photographs reproduced Hine's perceived experience, then they would do the most good politically. He disdained the dominant photographic aesthetic, the expressly nonutilitarian, metaphoric style of the Photo Secession as led by Alfred Stieglitz. Nonetheless, Hine took Paul Strand, his student at ECS, to Stieglitz's gallery, 291, as part of an ECS excursion. Strand quickly became a disciple of Stieglitz's, but he forged ahead with a straight, unmanipulated visual aesthetic, mirroring his photography teacher's style.

Separating Hine from the Photo Secession (and Jacob Riis) was Hine's use of captions, especially as he grew as a photographer with the NCLC. The image was proof, evidence that the witness was present to make the notes and to defeat arguments that such conditions as depicted did not exist or were not the norm. The context, what existed outside the picture, was nearly as important as the visual text. Although the two could be disconnected and used separately (as picture and text have been—too many historians rely on the written evidence and do not address the image as narrative generating but only as illustrative), to-gether they made a much stronger explanatory argument that was also open to less interpretation.

Another element of SDP was the overt rejection of the social Darwin-ist paradigm.[11] Hine never blamed the poor for their poverty; rather, he recorded first-person conversations with willing subjects. Using a finely tuned sense of incongruity, Hine captured a sense of grace in a sea of tragedy. With very few exceptions, Hine represented individuals as still capable of redemption. From image to image, Hine's little workers flash innocent or playful smiles; the young boys, sometimes mouthing a sto-gie, show a stoic bravado; young women peek demurely out from their piecework.[12] Unlike those before him (and many after), Hine showed the best in the human condition, no matter how degraded the envi-ronment. That incongruity, the outrageously flirting berry picker in a stained dress and bare feet (despite the thorns of her crop) or the very urge to play in a moment stolen from work, indicates to the viewer that Hine had not abandoned the children.[13] His pathos is real.

And finally, although Hine used his cameras to collect data, many of his individual images, in fact most of them, can be read as iconic representations of the whole through the experience of the individual. Again, the subjects of SDP are just that, subjects in their own drama. Fueling and fueled by an "everyman" ethic, a democratic culture, these individuals (especially in Hine's later postwar "work portraits" and in Dorothea Lange's images for the New Deal [the Resettlement Admin-istration, Farm Security Administration, and Office of War Informa-tion]) came to be identified as archetypes of working-class legitimacy, possessing the quintessence of American determination. Although this represented a maturing of SDP, the sacred nature of work can be found in the earliest Hine image celebrating a new immigrant as an element of invigoration or harshly criticizing the corruption of any work ethic that occurs when a child works in place of an adult.

Both Lange and Hine saw their photographs spur action, and both suffered deep disappointment at the limits of what they achieved. None-theless, viewed from a historical perspective, both are credited with ini-tiating a paradigm shift in documenting not only the poor but how so-ciety thinks about working people and people out of work. Especially in Hine's case, lasting reform came in the United States—the types of la-bor and working conditions he opposed have, to a large extent, been regulated out of existence—but that reform is still sorely needed in in-dustrializing and postindustrial economies.

Figure 9.2. Lewis Hine, "Laura Petty, a 6 year old berry picker on Jenkins Farm. 'I'm just beginnin'. Picked two boxes yesterday.' Gets 2 [cents] a box. Rock Creek, Md." Date: 06/07/1909." Library of Congress, Prints and Photographs Division, National Child Labor Committee Collection, LC-DIG-nclc-0003.

Reading Photographs: Child Labor

Once the students learned the background of how so many guest workers had been brought to Qatar and had seen presentations of the conditions in which they lived and worked, I wanted to empower them to investigate within that framework and make their own presentations with the images they captured. We spent some time examining the work of our two paragons and determining what made their photographs such powerful political weapons, in addition to being great works of art.[14]

Starting with Lewis Hine and his ability to evoke an emotion through a still photograph, I showed them his masterpiece 1909 image of a little girl who could still be captured by childlike curiosity and wonder, despite her troubling surroundings (fig. 9.2).

Without context, this image would mean very little to students unfamiliar with American history, climate, and botany. The first thing I register is Laura's smile and body language. Vicki Goldberg wrote in the introduction to her *Lewis Hine: Children at Work* (1999) of her smile and stance, "A six-year-old berry picker flirts outrageously with the man who will immortalize her." When contrasted with this natural childlike pose, the stained dress and bare feet create a sense of dislocation, made even more uncomfortable by the carefully tied but wilted bow. This is a happy picture transformed through context into an indictment. How does one make sense of such a complex photograph?

Ask the analytical questions of the image. Where is the photographer standing? Well, he wasn't standing. Hine (then in his thirties) knelt on the ground with his cumbersome camera to photograph this diminutive berry picker. Hine's career-long stylistic and intellectual choice to engage those he photographed, both physically and culturally and on their own level, is evident. Quite literally, Hine did not look down at people, especially children. His philosophical perspective led to a visual choice: he was on his knees and eye to eye, even with the littlest.

Hine needed time to arrange himself on the ground to make the image. Knowing that the NCLC photographer was not usually welcomed by many who employed children, one can infer that this particular employer had no qualms about Hine making pictures, believed a piece of subterfuge that Hine had offered to gain access, or was simply absent. Hine did not have to gain entry to a factory under the gaze of a foreman to make a picture of berry pickers. The process of employing migrants from East Coast US cities (Baltimore in Laura's case) to pick at harvest time was pretty well ingrained in the collective mind of a then still agricultural nation; many saw nothing wrong with seasonal farmwork. The on-again, off-again nature of agricultural work combined with the still living myth of the beneficence of farmwork for children rendered Hine's agricultural labor pictures less effective politically than those he made of children in mines and factories. With this picture and others like it, Hine was undertaking a Sisyphean task. Nonetheless, this has become an iconic child labor image. When we accept it as that, we also accept Hine's argument for the necessity for national regulation of hours and universal education for all children, be they farm- or industrial or mine workers. The conditions Hine documented of tiny miners and spinners had greater impact on the Progressive mind, but the same arguments against child labor can be read into Laura Petty's situation. So the next question is to ask what exactly is in the image, and what is not?

Hine made this image in the very strong natural light of the Maryland late summer to early fall and thus would have had enough light to shoot the image with both a stop-action shutter speed and a narrow aperture to capture as much depth of field as possible. Hine, an excellent technician, would have accomplished this by using a longish shutter speed (but not more than 1/60 of a second—otherwise Laura would not have appeared with stopped action; children move around). Using his knowledge of his craft, however, Hine isolated Laura and the bushes around her as the dominant elements of the image using a narrow plane of focus and thereby draws the eye of the viewer to the child and her immediate surroundings. The background recedes immediately and indistinguishably into blurred focus. Neither Laura's parents nor her coworkers are in the image, giving a more intimate feel to the interaction with the photographer. Yet there is a small, uncomfortable sense of abandonment. Laura is alone in the berry fields; the ghosts of other pickers are barely visible on the horizon.

Turn to the incongruities in the image. Laura's overall bearing stands in stark contrast to the conditions in which we find her. The magical innocence of childhood has not been extinguished. To Hine's audience, Laura would still appear to have the opportunity to have a healthy childhood and productive adulthood, if only those with power to do so acted to end her exploitation. She is outrageous as only those untainted by the crushing realities of poverty can be. Laura, however, is very visibly stained—tainted—by her life as an underpaid, overworked laborer. She remains emotionally unscarred in this image, but Hine offers very tangible evidence of how her optimism conflicts with her circumstances, and he relied on viewers to see what he wanted them to. Laura's carefully tied ribbon and combed hair wilt in the heat of exertion. We surmise that she works in her pretty dress because it is likely the only item of clothing she owns, despite the fact that when her mother dressed her, she would have known the condition it would be in after days of picking raspberries.

Perhaps the most shocking mismatch between child and her working conditions is one that Hine did not overtly emphasize (as he sometimes did in other child labor images). Laura stands barefoot among the bushes. Hine probably assumed that his audience would have been well aware of the barbs and thorns that make raspberry picking so treacherous (those teaching in desert climates cannot make the same assumption). Yet little Laura does it in bare legs and feet.

In the caption, Hine reinforced for the viewer the substance of the ideas communicated in the image. He drew no conclusion, but rather simply stated facts he had gathered (which is so much different from how editors treated his images). He relied on the visual evidence, carefully composed and presented, to communicate what was to him the obvious evil of child labor. As the first social documentarian—he called his style "social photography" and later the "human document"—Hine recorded what he saw and simultaneously testified to its veracity. His captions are largely a presentation of facts gathered near the time when he made the image.

Hine added yet more poignancy to the composition, and reinforced her subjectivity, by quoting the little girl in the caption (rather than making an editorial comment). Laura enthusiastically reports her productivity. Like many children, her aspiration is to be grown-up, if only so she can work harder and contribute more to her family's income, a sweet sentiment that evokes pathos. By allowing the child to speak, Hine crafted an argument that emphasized this selfless innocence. In the face of social Darwinist apathy (or enmity), Hine sought to entice viewers into a feeling of parental protection.

Again, he faced a tough crowd; the wealthy industrialist, so fond of apocryphal rags-to-riches stories, would probably have patted Laura on the head, praised her industry, and sent her back into the fields to keep trying. Hine succeeded in changing minds with his photographs of children in new industrial situations (like the textile mills) and in presentations of visual evidence of the damage inflicted on America's youth by mining, the energy source of the Second Industrial Revolution. As noted above, he enjoyed far less success in persuading his contemporaries of the exploitation of children in traditional farm labor. Most still saw farmwork as healthy and beneficial for children.

Students today would probably agree that nonindustrial family farm labor (no matter how strenuous) is not a social evil. Having indicated how to read a photograph and to determine what is social documentary, the students then consider images that have more relevance for the specific social situation they wish to investigate. Industrial conditions in the early-twentieth-century United States are startlingly familiar. That Hine's photographs of the street trades, tenement homework, mills, and mines are easily compared with current conditions is a sober reminder of the gulf between Europe-America and the developing world.

Textile mills sprouted from the Industrial Revolution. In fact, the demographic that staffed the southern textile mills consisted in overwhelming numbers of poor whites drawn from Piedmont farms, where impoverished conditions tended to expose the truth behind the myth of self-sufficiency farming, that it was more productive of debt servitude than republican virtue. White sharecroppers and their families left the fields in droves to labor in the new southern textile industry. And, as before, everyone in the family worked.

Notwithstanding developments prior to the Civil War (and indeed the central place of cotton in that conflict), textile millwork took on the same character as other industrial labor in the postbellum era. Rather than resembling guild-dominated craft work, textile mills involved both large-scale manufacture (in New England and then in the South) and take-home piecework (in New York City); as a cog, the textile worker's life became one of unskilled or semiskilled drudgery. The work was repetitive, often speeded up, always poorly paid. Working conditions, while less obviously dangerous than in the mines, posed their own hazards. One unseen danger came from the minute fibers the workers inhaled. Like coal dust, they did not break down. Instead, they too coated the lungs, leading to "white lung" disease. And most often, women and children bore the brunt of these poor conditions and low wages. Once the day of the Lowell Mill Girl passed, that is, once New England textile mill owners turned to Irish, French Canadian, and other immigrant sources of labor in the decades before the Civil War, women and children made up the bulk of the labor force in the industry.

Quite different from his pictures of young miners and street-trades children, Hine did not have to worry about normalizing conditions in the eyes of his viewers. Instead, he went to the mills to gather evidence that children were working—sometimes in contravention of state laws—and to gather evidence of their widely varying working conditions in support of the NCLC's campaign for a national child labor law. This led to the Keating-Owen Child Labor Act, passed by Congress in 1916 (and found to be unconstitutional by the Supreme Court in *Hammer v. Dagenhart* [1918]).[15] Even though southerner Alexander McElway directed the NCLC's cotton mill campaign, his fellow white southerners grew sensitive to the very public criticism of what the NCLC often presented as a "southern" problem. Responding in a way similar to how their grandfathers had answered the abolitionists' condemnations of slavery, southern governors, legislators, and mayors alternated between excusing child labor as a family decision and defending it as a positive good that would instill a sense of industry into poor white children. I am not aware of any single Hine photograph of an African American mill child, which reflects in large part the rampant segregationism characteristic of these nonunionized shops as implemented by bosses and legislators alike.

Georgia's one African American legislator said in 1906, "Our children are not employed in the cotton factories. . . . I for one am in favor of doing something for the protection of the little white children of Georgia."[16] Reinforcing the racial homogeneity of the labor force of the mills was the reluctance of Samuel Gompers's American Federation of Labor and other labor unions to alienate southern lawmakers with demands they would never even consider. The unions realized that campaigns to eliminate segregation in the workplace would go nowhere. Union calls for child labor reform in the mills applied only to white children, which made it less threatening.[17] But the entrenched poverty in the postbellum South, combined with the disdain for "white trash" by gentlemen legislators—child labor proved an effective way to control their social inferiors—slowed even the modest reforms introduced by labor.

In comparison, the NCLC campaign was fairly radical. As noted earlier, Hine's true ire rarely showed in public, but by just training his camera in his conversational, nonsentimental, and noncondescending way, he overcame the hesitancy of organized labor and the class bias of southern legislators and transformed "white trash" children into fully human subjects. Although Hine also visited New England mills, the vast majority of his mill photographs are from Georgia and the Carolinas.

Textile mills' apparent lack of danger and exploitation was a challenge. Hine would not be able to rely on faces obscured with soot to get his message across. And since the mills were not unionized, either there was no limit on the hours and ages of the workers or such regulations were simply ignored by the mill boss. No union meant no agitation, no vigilance. Families needed to send their children to work because of the low wages the father and older siblings could earn, and the younger children sacrificed their childhoods by working twelve-hour days. As Dave McCarn sang in 1926:

> No use to colic, everyday at noon,
> The kids get to crying in a different tune.
> I'm a-gonna starve, and everybody will,
> 'Cause you can't make a living at a cotton mill.[18]

Because of publicity the NCLC campaign generated, Hine had difficulty getting into the mills. So he had to resort to subterfuge and invent devices to help him gather data to accompany his pictures. It is not usually good practice to start one's picture analysis with the caption, but Hine's caption of the girl in figure 9.3 stands out as a bit strange. Why did Hine start with the fact that she was "51 inches high"? Such little details can yield interesting history and in this case tell us something

Figure 9.3. "One of the spinners in Whitnel Cotton Mill. She was 51 inches high. Has been in the mill one year. Sometimes works at night. Runs 4 sides—48 [cents] a day. When asked how old she was, she hesitated, then said, 'I don't remember,' then confidentially, 'I'm not old enough to work, but do just the same.' Out of 50 employees, ten children about her size. Whitnel, N.C., 12/22/1908." Library of Congress, Prints and Photographs Division, National Child Labor Committee Collection, LC-DIG-nclc-01555.

about how Hine operated. We do not know how he gained entrance to this particular mill while carrying a very large camera. We can be confident that he did not identify himself as a representative of the NCLC. We do know how he measured the girl's height. He kept a piece of paper in his pocket on which to make notes and which he used to measure the distance from the floor to each of the buttons on his jacket. As he stood next to a child, he counted premeasured buttons; thus, he could calculate the child's height.

Both boys and girls worked in the mills. Boys, generally, had jobs that required a lot of energy for short periods. Between doing their jobs, like sweeping the floor, changing spools (doffing), and cleaning clogged machines, they rested and waited to be called for work. However, the girls and women toiled at lighter industry, mostly spinning raw cotton into thread and loading it on spools, but their tasks were con-

Figure 9.4. Lewis Hine, "Rhodes Mfg. Co. Spinner. A moment's glimpse of the outer world. Said she was 11 years old. Been working over a year. Lincolnton, N.C., 11/11/1908." Library of Congress, Prints and Photographs Division, National Child Labor Committee Collection, LC-DIG-nclc-01345.

tinuous and gave no intermediate respite from the work. They stood all day long, breathing white fibers that filled the air, performing the same monotonous work, day in and day out. Hine often found adolescents whom he occasionally called "human junk" after having their child-hoods stolen by the mills. And he was more attentive (and therefore sympathetic) to the girls, women, and small boys.

One must look at the date and location of each of the photographs in figures 9.3 and 9.4 to be sure they are not pictures of the same child. In addition to monotony in the days of child workers, Hine's photographs of mill children in the new South are often framed in a similar way, with a small child in front of a machine that, in effect, looms over the diminutive subject of the photograph. Stretching through planes of focus, the loom itself is the instrument of torture, and Hine placed it in the picture not only to gauge the height of the child he photographed but also to represent her in the context of her imprisonment. Yet the machines are not the subjects; they are the context, the important background (both literally and figuratively) that the viewer needs to understand the message Hine sends.

Hine's message is more blunt in other mill child photographs, and because of his consistency we can read these images keeping his overall mission in mind. Neither child in figures 9.3 and 9.4 is at imminent risk or far down the slope to turning into so much "human junk." Hine made both of them in natural light coming from behind where each girl stood.

Turning to figure 9.3, while the pretty clothes seem very much out of place in a spinning mill, the child was a worker. Hine did not have to depict her actually at work on the spinning machine to invite the viewer to see something amiss here. Although Hine's captions reveal that many children prevaricated when asked about their ages or work status—"She's just bringing my dinner," said one mother disingenuously—this little girl is a textile worker. Even though her frilly dress was most definitely a work hazard—clothes and body parts quite often got caught in the workings of a machine and injured the child—she and most girl workers in Hine's child labor images wore to work their Victorian-era best. Mill families did not bend to the practicality of trousers and simple shirts for women until the Depression and World War II. Hair pulled away from the face was no doubt safer for the children, but there seems to have been an effort to secure the braid over her left shoulder. Given the thick coating of cotton lint on her right hand, perhaps spinners had to lean in toward the machine with their dominant hand. Nonetheless, her hair has begun to fall out. She had probably been working since before dawn (as Hine made the photograph in December with the sun fairly high in the sky—around the lunch hour?—so as to cast shadows at a slightly downward angle, left to right across his subject). If the dress had been pressed before she began work, hours of toil in a humid factory had taken its creases out.

The child's bearing is a bit disconcerting. Like almost all of Hine's portraits, she faces him directly—engaged with the photographer. He had to have been kneeling or crouching to do so. There is no classic nineteenth-century pose or occupational portrait here (or anywhere) in Hine's images. Although Hine photographed adult workers later, his treatment of toilers in his later "work portraits" has a disturbing precursor in this portrait of the little spinner. The child, this wee girl, who, by her own admission, was not old enough to work, *had been* working long enough to acquire the bearing of an experienced spinner. Her sleeves pushed up, resting her hands in equipoise (so not leaning or otherwise seeking support), she could be a heroine of Hine's interwar years when he often photographed women at work in textile factories, but as a matter of celebration, not protest. To see a small child with such stolid stature is in and of itself a criticism.

Her face is set in the mask of the determined, momentarily asked to move away from her work. She still has bright, playful—and indeed intelligent—eyes, but her lips are pursed and shoulders set in a way that can be easily read as a presentation of competence, not suffering. Different from the shy glances and childlike flirts that Hine often evoked, she evinces instead the work ethic that fueled the South's Progressive Era industrialism. She seems pretty far from the "white trash" accusations of the moneymen who would treat her and her family as disposable people, fit only to have their labor extricated for the least possible sum and then their futures discarded as so much industrial waste. The shame here, and Hine recorded it, lies in the fact that she would not reach *actual* working age with the same level of skill, confidence, and conspiratorial trust indicated by her premature working-class deportment. Such maturity and pride in one so young—she was four foot three—is more than evidence of regulatory need; it is a wholesale criticism of the philosophies of a civilization that would allow it.

Although in a nearly similar setting, Lincolnton, North Carolina, is larger than Whitnel and lies one county away. The girl in figure 9.4, however similar in appearance to the child in figure 9.3, is in a completely different world. Whitnel's caption carries the information needed for the NCLC to compile statistics and to expose the mill owners for intentionally employing children too young to work under state regulations. Juxtaposed with Whitnel's, Lincolnton's daughter stands as an exception in Hine's repertoire. She does not face the camera; there is no one near her to indicate that she had been recently working with others on the line; except for the soiled rag in her tiny hands and her proximity to the loom, she cannot be objectively observed to have been working. Hine tells us in his caption that she had been, and for far too long—at age eleven working for "over a year." Perhaps these atypicalities are the reason that this tiny spinner has not become one of the mass-produced Hine iconographs. Perhaps the depth of field is too shallow or the glass-plate negative too broken. So far as technique is concerned, the image is not a great one. It seems likely, however, that Hine had wanted to make a stop-action picture; he had to use a fast shutter speed and a wide aperture—thus the shallow depth of field.

What is so remarkable about this image is what it reveals about the photographer as well as the subject. The child in figure 9.4 is neither a political tool nor an idealized image of childhood. She is fragile, and the political needs of the day demanded that Hine photograph children who were still capable of rescue. To have used her as a political tool seems wrong. Although it appears that this child is still very much a little girl and not a tiny grown-up worker, the picture would have been bathetic in anyone else's hands, emotionally manipulative, and easily dismissed as oversentimental. But Hine did not photograph her that way. His technique was atypically bad, which indicates that the image is more candid than posed. He did not have in his tool kit fast film and a super-high shutter speed (my digital Nikon records in 1/2,000 of a second). She caught a glimpse of something, and Hine photographed her displaying an unguarded, purely childlike expression of wonder. In a sense, Hine caught a glimpse of the child within. She saw the outer world; Hine saw the inner. It's a magnificent moment, comparable to the best of later geniuses such as Henri Cartier-Bresson and Alfred Eisenstadt, who roamed pre– and post–World War II Europe with their 35mm Leicas and abundant Kodak film speed. Hine accomplished this on a glass plate, on a winter's afternoon, inside a dreary cotton mill, seventeen years before Oscar Barnack at Leica invented the 35mm camera. Extraordinary.

When I show this image to students, invariably they try to construct a narrative of what is happening outside the window, to fill in the gaping visual blank. They also want to read an emotion on her face, one that reflects what they feel when they look at the picture. Neither is objectively defined nor confidently assumed. She sought a subject all her own. We are concerned with Hine's: childhood threatened. The delicate, shy curiosity so familiar to middle-class parents was being wasted in favor of a few more dollars in the pocket. Hine must have seen the potential power of this image, but it remains a rather obscure example of his work. Perhaps there was too much intimacy; this little girl trusted the older man who watched her to the extent that she could turn away and be honestly kid-like for a moment. Sometimes we see such vulnerability in Hine's pictures of the very littlest ones selling papers, but by introducing such heart-wrenching pathos he could have opened himself to a charge of bathos. There is a sweetness, an innocence—bottom lip tucked under, posture straight but head tilted slightly forward, totally engaged in the spectacle that caught her eye—that would have been threatened by literally making her a poster child for child labor reform. Here, childhood was still triumphant as a human universal. It becomes a photograph not of a child working but rather of a moment in the natural course of life that eventually extinguishes pure awe in favor of the wonderless sophistication of reason. That she could still manifest this complete absorption born of curiosity is unbelievably touching. That Hine caught it is a testament to his skill and sensitivity as a photographer, and it shows us how truly carefully he composed his other images. Hine wanted the viewer to see exactly what he put in the frame. We can rely on that when we analyze his images.[19]

Photography Excursion 1: Central Bus Station

Before taking the students into the heart of the immigrant worker community of Doha, Industrial City, a bleak and foreign place to the mostly wealthy students, we planned a trip to the one other place in Doha that guest workers were able to congregate without interference by the internal security forces, the Doha main bus terminal. Guest workers from the subcontinent were banned from visiting shopping malls through limiting mall visits to whole families or only women, thus excluding the overwhelmingly male population. The weekend in Doha is Friday and Saturday, because Friday is the Islamic holy day. Most of the population the project sought to investigate had only Fridays or half of Saturdays (or both) off and spent much of the day socializing or traveling to other work centers.

Members of the student activities staff had made well-received overtures to the embassies that represented the target nationalities.[20] Officials from Pakistan, India, Bangladesh, Nepal, and Sri Lanka were eager to receive help and have the plight of their nationals recognized and publicized. Some of the goals of the program were to raise funds for legal fees and to lobby the government to grant exit visas for workers caught in limbo (having been dismissed from a job without first obtaining an exit visa) and to enforce existing labor laws. So, to some extent, the path was cleared for our investigations.

The need for good photography became clear when a group of stranded Indian workers was asked to come and talk to the faculty involved in the service learning activity. The men told a terrible story of despair and horrid living conditions. They were still working but had not been paid for six months. Their living conditions were fetid and unsanitary. Some lived in shipping containers or semitrailers, with no running water or sanitary facilities. Often, workers lived on construction sites in shacks built out of discarded lumber. These men were gracious, welcoming, and intensely proud. One of the student activities assistants (an ethnic Indian) had accompanied the men to their "compound" and made a video of some of the conditions. The video was inadequate to give a sufficient emotional impact, although it was explicit and immensely saddening. What was missing was the kind of sympathetic pathos evoked by SDP in the hands of Lewis Hine and others. As Hine said around 1906, "There is a crying need for photographers with even a slight degree of appreciation & sympathy."[21] We had the sympathy; what we needed were the photographers.

As the photography leader, I had to balance the safety of the students, educational benefit, subject matter, available light, and ethics. Most of our student volunteers were women, all of them fearless. Although being dressed in *abayas* and *hijabs* guaranteed that the women would be safe in our excursions, several of the students did not wear traditional Islamic dress, and others were not Muslim. This left us a narrow spectrum of subject events and a very short window of opportunity to shoot, from late fall to early spring, three to five o'clock, in a public place. We could not take the women into the housing compounds of the male workers (although they were willing to go) because our goal was to help the unempowered, not embarrass them. As a married Western expat teacher (teachers are highly valued in all of these cultures), I could have traveled to the camps with or without a male escort, but it would have been enormously insensitive to take students into the camps. Work sites were unsafe, as the huge death and injury toll testified, and were off-limits to photographers anyway, so we had to choose an unregulated space where we could meet and photograph those who built Qatar's wealth.[22] To limit the contact to a controlled area, we chose the bus station. Students and workers interacted in a positive manner. The students collected both images and explanatory captions that illuminated the guest-worker experience and framed for them the kinds of photographs and interactions they thought would be the most helpful to achieving goals as discussed in class.

At the Bus Station

The following weekend, the group met to show and discuss the pictures made at the bus station. Conversation about the trip on campus attracted several more students to the next trip. In evaluation we discussed how the workers received the students, if they accomplished what they had set out to, how they would approach the exercise if repeated, and how would they change the parameters of the exercise. Unanimously, the students found it to have been a positive experience. Many bemoaned the fact that they had not taken a "serious" camera with them; a few had disregarded advice (as students are wont to do) and brought mobile phones as cameras. They agreed that after a short while, the workers warmed to their presence. Through interpreters, youthful idealism, and exuberance, many had conversations. Also unanimously, the students wanted more time to make the images and to encounter a larger group of workers. They were happy with their photographs, but did not see the immediate application of the images to the task at hand, urging reform and enforcement of current labor laws. We planned a larger outing for the following weekend, an hour earlier in the day (to extend the light), and to the crowded ghetto known as Industrial City.

That left three questions to discuss: the emotional difficulty of making photographic portraits (it is hard to stick a camera in someone's face without depersonalizing him, at least momentarily and at the crucial moment, when the photographer makes the image), the ethics of exploiting the less fortunate for photographic excellence, and how to turn pictures of smiling, nice people into an indictment of the labor situation in Doha. Hine's example thankfully provided the answers.

All of Hine's portraits were "staged," meaning that they were not and were never meant to be candid. Technological limitations alone are not the explanation for the face-to-face contact and the seeming ease of those who people Hine's portraits. Hine's bulky equipment took some time to set up, yes, but even when he moved from glass plates to film and shot outdoors to avoid the necessity for magnesium flash powder, his subjects were comfortable with being photographed. Almost all smile or display pride, bravado, or innocent curiosity. As with our students' pictures, Hine's images were conversations. Hine managed to make searing visual condemnation while portraying the individual strength of each conversant.[23]

This fact helped the students to understand the questions they asked: one overcomes the discomfort of sticking a camera in a human being's face when that person's humanity is being preserved, not appropriated, exploited, abstracted, or denied by the action. And once a photograph becomes a conversation between equals, no matter how culturally unfamiliar, people smiling despite objectively difficult (to put it in its most mild incarnation) circumstances becomes its own indictment of the ones who put them there or maintained the unacceptable conditions.

The smiles remind the viewer that the human spirit is not dead and efforts at reform will not be too late. Also, trust on the part of the photographed (including a desire to help in the cause but not to be identified; we promised to obscure individual identities) helped us make images, again following the example of Lewis Hine, into political montages.

As we discovered, however, the difficulty truly came when the smiles faded. There was more than location difference between the bus station and Industrial City; there was a disconnection between the numbers and receptivity of skilled workers and the unskilled mass. Those at the bus station, of course in retrospect, had the money and freedom not only to travel outside Doha but also to travel *around* Doha. This is something the leaders (myself included) of the project should have taken into consideration. Mass transit and sidewalks (and reasonable temperatures) in early-twentieth-century New York still provided an opportunity, limited as it was, to move about the city. The vast underclass of guest workers in Doha did not even have the luxury of sidewalks.

Photography Excursion 2: Industrial City

The following weekend, and with a few more chaperones, the group went to Industrial City for a two-hour shooting session. We were overwhelmed by the vast difference in the group of workers we encountered. The true nature of the skilled-versus-unskilled divide in labor systems was brought immediately into focus. The sheer numbers of people milling about in the waning sunshine of a hot November afternoon shocked us, as did the relative aggression of that group. Where we had encountered maybe one hundred people at the bus station, there were at least (an unexaggerated) ten thousand men shuffling idly about, playing games, window-shopping, talking—celebrating the time off from onerous labor—and gathered in ethnically determined groups, not all friendly with others. Animosity among disparate nationalities unfortunately persisted despite sharing a common plight. And the project participants suddenly became the major distraction for a large group of bored, overworked, and increasingly angry people.

Initially, our group was met with curiosity. Luckily, the character of the students involved kept the situation from devolving. They showed no condescension, only concern. Their experiences from the bus station and postmortem (and possibly their sense of privilege—nothing bad could have happened, mostly because of the serious toll the reprisal would have taken on the population we were trying to help—just one of the many ethical questions raised by the exercise) allowed them to see the men who encircled the group as individual human beings seeking distraction and attention rather than as a dangerous mob. That the young people stayed calm and friendly, much as Hine had in his forays into Five Points and some of the more notoriously "dangerous" (to the middle class) sections of New York, created an environment where the people we were there to photograph became participants rather than objects. Through interpreters, we explained why we were there, and many quickly volunteered to be photographed (and spread the word of our intent) to help the intruders tell the story of how the Middle East is built.

We broke up in groups with one chaperone for each group. I kept watch on five women and one man. Interestingly, I was one of the tallest people there (five foot ten), so I had a vantage that many of the students did not (see figure 9.6, in the following section). My group had no interpreter, so we needed to communicate in other ways (as did Hine with his largely immigrant subjects). Digital technology helped enormously. We were able to show our photographs immediately to our subjects to demonstrate how we were making their pictures. Also, I had loaded an image I made after the trip to the bus station onto my memory card and was able to explain through a few people who spoke English what we were trying to do. Like a stone cast into water, one could actually watch as the information was relayed outward in a concentric wave. That we, the children of Muslim privilege and products of the unattainable West (all the chaperones were American), were there to make art intended to help *their* cause transformed the event; to the workers, we no longer represented only a diversion from an otherwise Sisyphean existence. Inadvertently, our presence had caused a moment of agitprop theater, in which we were the audience to be educated.

As the feeling changed from a subaltern group bemused by supposed slummers to a group that sensed an opportunity to seek empowerment, *their* cameras came out, to both challenge our visual appropriation and to record the moment as an event. This also served to remind the student photographers that pointing a camera can be a hostile act; suddenly, the men felt we were not a threat to them and they could express themselves in what the top caste would no doubt have seen as uppity aggression. Afterward, the students remarked that they felt a tidal wave of frustrated emotion release and specifically *not* gratitude (after all, ethnically we represented the sources of both their oppression [Gulf Arabs] and the thing they coveted most [Western affluence]).

Despite a mishmash of subcontinental ethnicities and religions, one student identified the emotional shift as a sudden expression of consciousness, of *class* consciousness. Most assented to that analysis. All agreed that the conditions we witnessed, even though they were light-years from the worst, not only represented injustice but also contained the seed of a dangerous idea, even if expressed peacefully. We thought our experiment might actually work if it could help create a unified voice from the heavily stratified and controlled society of Gulf guest workers. The students, many of whom were freshmen, were committed for the long haul.

Making Political Art Montage

Again, I planned a session for debriefing, a student photo show, an evaluation, and a photomontage workshop for the following weekend. To plan the event, I met with two especially active student helpers, one an accomplished photographer, the other a moving force in the service learning project. My lesson plan for the following Saturday included a workshop to apply the discussion we had had two weeks earlier on Lewis Hine's photomontage as political education and agitation. We had examined exhibition panels Hine made for the NCLC exhibit at the 1915 Pan-American Exposition in San Francisco, advocating the national child labor law (see figure 9.5). Following the workshop, the students were to have taken their own photographs and used them to make posters advocating the kinds of change they perceived as necessary and expressing their own political and artistic vision. I planned for the next session to be a discussion of media, communication, advocacy, and political science in order to give students guidance on how, if they wished, to use their creations to attempt political change. As a template, I created two more posters, using my own images with input from my student helpers.

From the beginning of the project, I had emphasized that this was an educational exercise guided by community service ideology but that it would rest on the ethics of intellectual property: each person's work was his or her own. Thus, in addition to Hine's examples, I used my own ideas as an example of how one *might* marry pictures, color, and

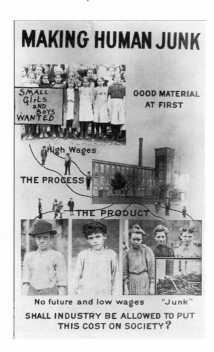

Figure 9.5. Lewis Hine, exhibit panel: "Making Human Junk," ca. 1914.

text to create an artistic document with a guided conclusion. I emphasized the differing elements in the images, using photographs of the students themselves, to create a visual expression of my intent to teach, how the use of art can free not only the subjects but the photographers as well (figure 9.6). I also used an image from the moment just after I detected the shift in our subjects' understanding of the project to grab their own cameras and record us as a moment of cultural empowerment (figure 9.7). With color and text, I sought to draw these conclusions for the viewers.

Doing so, I narrowed the scope of my expression to demonstrate what I had personally sought to accomplish with the exercise. In addition to working toward social justice for our target community, my primary goal (and responsibility) was to educate *my students* as to how art had been used in American history, and therefore how it could be used again, as a powerful tool of personal expression. Ultimately, I sought to empower the students to express themselves visually and to teach them the enormous power of art. My opinions on the politics of Qatar were irrelevant; my job was to teach the students to think critically and ex-

Figure 9.6. Kate Sampsell-Willmann, "Art Is a Weapon of Freedom" (Industrial City, Doha, 2008).

Figure 9.7. Kate Sampsell-Willmann, "Art Is Power" (Industrial City, Doha, 2008).

press themselves articulately in a tried-and-true medium that was new to them.

Results

Lewis Hine's campaign against child labor collapsed with Progressivism. Although the Progressive Era was a time of enormous success in the attempt to reform society (although not all reforms were, upon reflection, wise, Prohibition being exhibit number one), reform movements lost steam after 1918. As noted earlier, the Keating-Owen Child Labor Act of 1916 was ruled unconstitutional in *Hammer v. Dagenhart*, and although agitation continued for a child labor amendment to the Constitution, public support (and funding) evaporated after 1920. Hine shifted his focus on work as a "human value" from agitation against abuse to promotion of "the man behind the machine." What Hine and the NCLC lacked was a greater political will to interfere with state regulation of labor, perhaps especially in the wake of the Russian Revolution. In essence, the same lack of political will (on a micro scale) derailed the photography project.

The governments of the nationalities represented in the study were very supportive of the investigation, and the Qatari government (a reform- and arts-supporting government) was very interested in seeing the results of the excursions, especially since members of the royal family were among the participants. Nonetheless, the project was canceled by the university administration; the posters were literally ripped from the walls and torn up in front of my student helpers in a stunning rebuke to academic freedom. The students were in the process of hanging the posters to advertise the upcoming discussion when they were torn up and thrown away. No satisfactory explanation was given for the action except an arbitrary one from a dean and assistant dean (both Americans from the main campus) who simply did not "approve" of the artwork. The project ended abruptly there, much to the students' dismay. It and this discussion therefore remain uncompleted and therefore unsatisfactory. Rather than agitprop, the exercise indeed became theater of the absurd and emphasized the limits of liberalism, even a liberal arts education.

Notes

1. For reasons that will become clear, the institution will remain unnamed.
2. For basic biographical background, see Daile Kaplan, introduction to

Photo Story: Selected Letters and Photographs of Lewis W. Hine (Washington, DC: Smithsonian Institution Press, 1992), xvii–xxxvi; and Alan Trachtenberg, "Ever—the Human Document," in *America and Lewis Hine* (New York: Aperture, 1977).

3. Lester Frank Ward, "Mind as a Social Factor," *Mind* 9, no. 36 (1884).

4. For a brief discussion of Jacob Riis and social Darwinism, see Kate Sampsell-Willmann, "Lewis Hine, Ellis Island, and Pragmatism: Photographs as Lived Experience," *Journal of the Gilded Age and Progressive Era* 7 (April 2008), http://www.historycooperative.org/journals/jga/7.2/willmann.html; and Jacob Riis, *The Battle with the Slum* (1914; reprint, New York: Dover, 1998) and *How the Other Half Lives* (1890; reprint, New York: Dover, 2004). For Riis generally, see Peter Bacon Hales, *Silver Cities: Photographing American Urbanization, 1839–1939* (1984; reprint, Albuquerque: University of New Mexico Press, 2006); and Bonnie Yochelson and Dan Czitrom, *Rediscovering Jacob Riis: The Reformer, His Journalism, and His Photographs* (New York: New Press, 2008).

5. Elizabeth McCausland Papers, Archives of American Art, November 19, 2010, http://www.aaa.si.edu/collectionsonline/mccaeliz/overview.htm, AAA _mccaeliz_746786; Lewis Hine, "Biographical Notes," reprinted in Kaplan, *Photo Story*, 177–180.

6. See handwritten notes, AAA_mccaeliz_746807.

7. Ibid. (emphasis in original).

8. Ibid.

9. Ibid. Although Hine wrote in 1906 that Adler was not sanguine about Hine's chances at first. See Lewis Hine to Frank Manny [1906], reprinted in Kaplan, *Photo Story*, 2.

10. AAA_mccaeliz_746789. The Russell Sage Foundation has a substantial bibliography of publications and has engendered much criticism since its founding in 1907. For the Pittsburgh Survey, see Maurine W. Greenwald and Margo Anderson, eds., *Pittsburgh Surveyed: Social Science and Social Reform in the Early Twentieth Century* (Pittsburgh: University of Pittsburgh Press, 1996); Elizabeth Beardsley Butler, *Women and the Trades* (1909; reprint, Pittsburgh: University of Pittsburgh Press, 1984); Crystal Eastman, *Work-Accidents and the Law* (New York: Russell Sage Foundation, 1910); John A. Fitch, *The Steel Workers* (1910; reprint, Pittsburgh: University of Pittsburgh Press, 1989); Margaret Byington, *Homestead: The Households of a Mill Town* (1911; reprint, Pittsburgh: University of Pittsburgh Press, 1969); and Paul U. Kellogg, *The Pittsburgh District: Civic Frontage* (New York: Russell Sage Foundation, 1914) and *Wage-Earning Pittsburgh* (New York: Russell Sage Foundation, 1914).

11. For an allegation that the NCLC did embrace elements of social Darwinism, see Alan Derickson, "Making Human Junk: Child Labor as a Health Issue in the Progressive Era," *American Journal of Public Health* 89 (September 1992): 1280–1290.

12. I thank John McClymer for "stoic bravado."

13. For "flirting outrageously," I thank Vicki Goldberg.

14. For the sake of length, only Lewis Hine will be addressed herein.

15. Both the finding of the Court's majority and the dissent make for in-

teresting reading in light of continuing battles over states' rights. You may find the Court's opinion here: http://supreme.justia.com/us/247/251/case.html.

16. Quoted in Walter I. Trattner's classic *Crusade for the Children: A History of the National Child Labor Committee and Child Labor Reform in America* (New York: Quadrangle Books, 1970), 86–87. See also Hugh Hindman, *Child Labor: An American History* (New York: Sharpe, 2002); Juliet Mofford, *Child Labor in America* (New York: History Compass, 1970); and Russell Freedman, ed., *Kids at Work: Lewis Hine and the Crusade Against Child Labor* (New York: Sandpiper, 1998). There is a dearth of analysis on Hine's contribution to child labor reform.

17. See Shelley Sallee, *The Whiteness of Child Labor Reform in the New South* (Athens: University of Georgia Press, 2004), 50–57.

18. For Dan McCarn, see Patrick Huber, *Linthead Stomp: The Creation of Country Music in the Piedmont South* (Chapel Hill: University of North Carolina Press, 2008); and William F. Danaher and Vincent J. Roscigno, "Cultural Production, Media, and Meaning: Hillbilly Music and the Southern Textile Mills," *Poetics* 32 (February 2004).

19. Although I showed the students many other examples of social documentary photography over a period of two weekends, especially Dorothea Lange and others in the New Deal, I hope that the reader will get the idea of how I teach SDP to prepare students for shooting excursions. For the sociological partnership between Lange and Paul Schuster Taylor, see Linda Gordon, *A Life beyond Limits* (New York: W. W. Norton, 2010). Although I disagree with Jan Goggans's characterization of Paul Taylor as the origin of social documentary ideas, see her *California on the Breadlines: Dorothea Lange, Paul Taylor, and the Making of a New Deal Narrative* (Berkeley: University of California Press, 2010); and my review in *Journal of Agricultural History* (2011). For using Lange's pictures in the classroom, see Linda Gordon, "Dorothea Lange: The Photographer as Agricultural Sociologist," *Journal of American History* (December 2006), http://www.historycooperative.org/cgi-bin/justtop .cgi?act=justtop&url=http://www.historycooperative.org/journals/jah/93.3 /gordon.html; and the "Teaching the *JAH*" Web project at http://www .indiana.edu/~jah/teaching/.

20. Doha guest workers are caught in a relatively strict hierarchy based on nationality. One cannot become a nationalized Qatari citizen, so no matter how many generations of families live in Qatar, their ethnicity determines their nationality. The hierarchy is (roughly) from bottom to top: Bangladeshis and Pakistanis at the bottom; Sri Lankans, unskilled Indians, and Nepalese; Indonesians; Filipinos; educated Indians; Islamic Africans; Levant Muslims (educated Palestinians and Lebanese) and Turks; expats (English-speaking Westerners and highly educated Asians and Africans—mostly oil, higher-education, or technical sectors, living in secure compounds); non-Gulf Arabs (Yemenis mostly); Gulfies (Arabs from other Gulf states) and Qataris; and members of the royal family at the top.

21. Hine to Manny [1906], reprinted in Kaplan, *Photo Story*, 2.

22. For photographs and statistics on Nepali workers in Qatar, see http:// www.mikeldunham.blogs.com/mikeldunham/2010/01/death-rate-for

-nepali-workers-reaches-record-high-in-qatar.html: "According to a new report released by MigrantRights.org, Qatar, the rapidly developing Gulf state, is becoming a death chamber for Nepali workers, with the number of Nepalis dying in Qatar increasing in the last three years."

23. For individual identity in Hine's Ellis Island portraits and why maintaining it was politically important, see Sampsell-Willmann, "Lewis Hine, Ellis Island, and Pragmatism."

CHAPTER 10

Teaching in the Middle East:
Partial Cosmopolitanism

EDWARD J. LUNDY

The Princeton University professor of philosophy Kwame Anthony Appiah, in his 2006 book, *Cosmopolitanism: Ethics in a World of Strangers*, examines the contrast between strict cosmopolitans who see themselves primarily as members of the cosmos, as a kind of global, universal people, and those who center their identity with their city, their language, their food, their nation, their exceptionalism. The strict cosmopolitan or globalist decries provincialism in favor of a world without borders, where we live in the cosmos rather than be restricted by the local community. The counterparts root themselves in their nation, their traditions.[1]

In Appiah's thinking the strict cosmopolitan, in a positive sense, accepts the unity of humans in the spirit of Saint Paul, whom he quotes: "There is neither Jew nor Greek, there is neither bond nor free, there is neither male nor female: for ye are all one in Christ Jesus."[2] He faults the cosmopolitan's emphasis on the global, which is "to abjure all local allegiances and partialities in the vast abstraction, humanity."[3] Although he agrees that we ought to maintain traditions and honor our national culture, he argues that those who value only locality and regionalism can slide toward a totalitarian view in which the nation or the people are paramount or exceptional. Appiah points to Hitler and Stalin as examples of exaggerated provincialism or tribalism.[4]

Professor Appiah opts for a position he calls "partial cosmopolitanism," a vision that honors the local, the tribal, the national, and at the same time values the ideas, cultures, and traditions of others who inhabit our cosmos. This "partial cosmopolitan" position is neither unprincipled nor uncritically accepting but in a comparative, transnational approach requires scrutiny, openness, an ability to appreciate common values yet retaining one's respect for locality, for the national, for one's own heritage. As a personal example, Appiah points to his Ghanaian father, a professor at the Duke University School of Medicine who refrains from wild meat, meat killed in the forest, holding to one of many ties to his Asante tribe.[5] At the same time that Appiah smiles at his father's honoring this ancient tradition or taboo, he points to him as an example of "partial cosmopolitanism." His father is open to the world while respecting his tribal traditions, even traditions that are strange to many of us.[6]

Appiah's "partial cosmopolitanism" seems to me to be a required vision or direction for all teachers of American studies but especially for faculty residing outside the United States. As transnational, this approach lifts us from our own world to examine other regions and nations, their politics, foreign affairs, economies, family structures, women's roles, patriotism, music, entertainment, and all the segments that are included in American studies. Following this comparative approach, students and faculty place the host nation's structures and traditions side by side with US structures and traditions. In this study, we follow the accepted focus of American studies to include the other countries of North and South America.[7] However, in a significant change we expand the focus of American studies to include the nations and cultures of the Middle East, Turkey, and the Gulf.

The process of honest comparison explores differences and similarities as a method of understanding and appreciating both worlds. This approach encourages questions, dialogue, and disagreements and can form the basis of a valid, serious encounter through "American" studies. Neither solely cosmopolitan (embracing only the global community) nor solely exceptional (valuing only one's own nation, people, and culture), American studies, in the framework of Professor Appiah, will be "partially cosmopolitan."

This chapter is based on my experiences in American studies classrooms at the University of Jordan in Amman, at Bilkent University in Turkey, and in classes that I visited at other universities in the Middle East and the Gulf. In these classrooms I heard many students seriously engaging the United States, particularly its foreign policy, its secular culture, and its political, cultural, and military power in the Middle East, questions and insights that both criticized and praised what they were studying. I saw how successful faculty presented a broad vision to their students by comparing their local culture and policies to US culture and policies, faculty who aimed to strengthen the students' critical thinking and exploratory writing skills by being "partial cosmopolitan." It became clear that successful faculty avoided what had sometimes been charged, that they sought to propose the United States as exceptional. Partial cosmopolitan faculty (comparative and transnational) also learned from their classroom investigations. For example, in Jordan I appreciated how closely personal family and extended family relationships lay at the center of student lives, how strong was their sense of Arab pride, why many identified themselves as Muslim or Palestinian rather than Jordanian, how imaginatively they, like many students, could abide by rules while bending them to their own needs. I also learned how often they were offended by our acceptance of gay and lesbian marriage, with our continued struggles with racism, with our gun culture that seemed to them an inordinate emphasis on individual liberty and a lack of respect for the community.

I will begin with a University of Jordan poetry class. Then I will move to an American literature class, a Dialogue and Persuasion class, and two graduate American studies classes—American Culture and American Politics—before concluding with insights gained from classrooms in other Middle Eastern and Gulf countries. My thesis is that a partial cosmopolitan approach, transnational and comparative, can create a classroom that is interactive, open to other viewpoints, and far more interesting than a one-sided approach that either overly praises or overly faults the United States or diminishes in any way the host country.

The faces in a photo of a University of Jordan poetry class smile back at me today as I sit at my writing desk. Most of the students' names have slipped my memory, but many of the faces help me recall personal conversations and classroom incidents that form a composite of my two and a half years in Amman, as a Fulbright scholar, then employed for an additional year by the university, and finally through an ACOR grant that allowed my wife, Dr. Eileen T. Lundy, and me to visit the American studies programs in the Middle East and the Gulf.[8]

I pay special attention to this one, of about sixty-five, mostly positive, faces. Maybe the smiles reflect the Jordanian students' cheerful acceptance of the eccentricities of an American professor who suggests, "Let's go outside for a class picture." They laugh loudly, "If he wants our picture, strange, but why not?" Certainly, these students had a sense of humor, and, besides, our Jordanian students saw American professors as different. "What will they think of next?" The photo reflects the general custom among women in Jordan, where the majority, but not all, wear the *hijab* and a few the *nikab*. Like any mosaic, our classes show diversity. Most are smiling. Most, if not all, are open to our examination of American poetry, especially its themes. They are also prepared to disagree.

Back to our photo: a senior information technology (IT) engineering student hangs his arm over my shoulder. He used one of his few electives to take our poetry class because he wanted to expand his thinking and writing capabilities. Many, but not all, literature classes emphasize the single meaning of a poem or the single correct lesson of a story. I recall this IT student laughing when I asked a puzzled classmate, on the first class day, what she heard when the speaker of the poem spoke the last lines. He always sat close to the first row and, like most Jordanian students, did not hide his reactions. He chuckled when he talked to me after the first few weeks of the semester: "How different from science where there is one answer. And you asked for many answers, different answers, and you called it 'ambiguity.'" And he added, "I still laugh how my classmates murmured on that first day. But we got used to this and now realize that there might be more than one answer to many questions, like love, or loyalty, or many other intangibles." These might not be his exact words, but he understood that the voice of the speaker is an important clue, leading us to more insights. After a few classes the students found that ambiguity could be fascinating although daunting. We needed to hear the speaker and grasp the setting, both questions asked in reader-response criticism.

I think that this question of ambiguity was the first of my transnational contributions to the intellectual growth of my classes. I asked, "Who's right? Zeinab or you? Maybe, both of you are right. Read it aloud, all of you. Yes, ALOUD." And the class breaks into groups of students reading the poem, aloud. Then a knock on the door tells us that our loud reading is interrupting other classes. There are a lot of laughs about how the American professor has finally gotten himself into trouble. Times like this remind me of the charming ability of most Jordanian students to adapt, to try something new, to show youthful excitement, to begin to trust their own insights. And then I am brought back to our comparative earth: "Professor, you ask us to hear the voice of the speaker, but we hear her differently from you. In our next class, tell us what you hear." We compare our different experiences. We realize that there are many "voices" in this one classroom, even though we listened to one speaker. We compared how voices carry over distant and disparate borders.

I am often surprised by my students. For example, I remember the tall woman dressed totally in black, from head to foot, including gloves. When she came to me at the end of a class, her stiffened body and her formal Islamic dress warned me of a serious complaint. I suspected she did not approve of that day's poem.

In Mary Oliver's poem "Five A.M. in the Pine Woods," a woman sees deer tracks in a local woods.[9] She decides to arise early the next morning, to be in the woods before the deer stir, to await them. And the two deer do come. One draws near. But at the urging of the other, they both move away, wary of her as a nondeer. The speaker sits quietly, for how long she does not know. Maybe she dozed, but she calls the experience when the female deer almost touched her as a kind of prayer. "I was thinking: so this is how you swim inward; so this is how you flow outward; so this is how you pray."[10] She had experienced a religious moment, a contemplative sensibility, what the romantics understood as a spiritual intuition grounded in nature. Because the university rules did not permit classroom discussions of politics or religion, I figured the covered student would complain that we had introduced religion, prayer, contemplation, and religious intuition into the classroom. However, to my relief, she vehemently stressed a much different complaint. This intense, intelligent veiled woman told me that she understood how a sacred time and place can be created by the encounter with the deer, that the divine can be present in nature as well as in traditional sites. Her anger? Not with me, thankfully, but with traditions that prevented her, a mature mother of three children, from enjoying this kind of spiritual knowing, alone in the forest at five in the morning. She was thanking me for introducing our class to an example of poetry that honored a kind of Sufi spirituality. That some Western poetry spoke to the sacred surprised most of the class, especially when I explained that Rumi, the Sufi poet, was well known in the United States—another transnational connection. At the end of the semester I gave her my volume of Mary Oliver's poetry. She trumped me with her English translation of Rumi's poems.

The picture of the American woman sitting alone in the forest at five in the morning opened a discussion of cultural differences our class tactfully explored. We had touched on the traditional, sometimes limiting, roles of Jordanian females without suggesting any opposition to their culture. At the same time, the class questioned what they saw as the comparative freedom of Western women. "Was she safe, alone?" One young woman laughed, "Maybe the deer ran because the woman was dressed immodestly," another reminder of the importance of Arab modesty since the poet never described the woman's clothes, or lack thereof. But clothing was clearly on the minds of the students, especially, as I thought, because they instinctively judged that I, a Western male, would not understand many of their traditions. I decided to try another poem, in a similar vein but about horses, an animal much revered in the fine art and poster art of Arab countries. The noble, electric Arab stallion is known to all. But I inserted a cowboy theme in place of the fine Arab stallion.

"The Blessing," by James Wright, tells a simple narrative of two young men returning to their ranch after a day's work, probably in a local small town.[11] As they walk up the path to their house, one pauses by the pasture to greet two female ponies. One pony shows a marked affection for the man. This pony moves forward and nuzzles its head into the open arms of the man. He touches her ear and thinks that the ear has the softness, the tenderness, of a girl's wrist. "And the light breeze moves me to caress her long ear / That is as delicate as the skin over a girl's wrist."[12] The man feels profoundly touched by this gesture, hence the title, "The Blessing."

"The softness, the tenderness of a girl's wrist." This metaphor startles the class. "Is he in love with the pony?" "Is this a social protest poem, denouncing his life away from the ranch, working in the town?" "Is he thinking of his girlfriend?" "Why a blessing?" "Does he have a wife?" "Yes," I say, "maybe you are all right. Maybe this is a social protest poem in which a cowboy resents urban living because his girlfriend married his wife, and they have drifted away to the city and his only friend is the pony." This was the closest I have come to having poetry books or shoes thrown at me. They thought that I did not feel the wonder of the "wrist" metaphor. I never said that convincing students of the worth of ambiguity was easy or quickly accepted. Touching the pony's ear, although not overtly sexual, is, in some surprising way, incredibly personal, suggesting intimacy. The students talked about this image as magical. At the end of the semester when I asked them to remember one line from everything we read, most remembered "soft and tender as a girl's wrist."

What's more, to understand that the young man identified his experience as a blessing added to the mystery of the poem. Again, we seemed to be extending the experience of religion into the world of nature, of deer and ponies, of prayer and blessing. We noted that the majestic Arabian stallion communicates its own feelings: admiration, heroism, pride.

This tiny Indian pony also communicates feelings, a transnational comparison we thought about for a minute. As class ended, I think I see most students touching their wrists, smiling, understanding the cowboy, hopefully open to the possibility of "blessings" during everyday experiences. For me, I enjoyed a moment of effective teaching and learning. We had touched Islamic spirituality, on feelings of romantic love that many students saw as central to every relationship, on experiences from another culture to which they could relate, on shockingly beautiful language, on poetic ambiguity that lay at the heart of our curriculum. I thought that they understood how touching a pony's ear could be a blessing. We had crossed borders, both geographical and spiritual. Mary Oliver's and James Wright's nature experiences echoed Islamic Sufi experiences. We saw similarities in our differences—transnational and comparative insights.

The poem that created the most negative reaction touched on the issues of personal responsibility, independence, and the possibilities of existing apart from one's family. The poem clearly set Western values against those of the students, a clear transnational conflict. In Richard Wilbur's poem "The Writer," a father watches his daughter sitting at her writing table, wrestling with her manuscript.[13] As he stands on the stairway, unseen, he remembers a bird caught in that same room, how many times the bird crashed into closed windows before he, the father, finally opened a window, allowing the bird to fly away. The father thinks reluctantly that his daughter needs to suffer pain, like the bird, before she finds, or does not find, her opening, her window, into her own creative imagination, her ability to fly. He resists his fatherly impulse to help her and continues up the stairs, deeply feeling for his daughter's pain but allowing her the freedom to find her own answers.

Students reacted negatively to the father who did not stand by his daughter. "My father—my mother—my sister—my aunt would not abandon me." "What a failure as a father!" "How could he not open her window?" They generally concluded that they preferred their Arab family's warmth and cohesiveness to what they judged as the father's coldness, which, they thought, hid a lack of love under the cloak of independence. Their strong objections to the father showed not only that they had become deeply engaged in the situation but also that they had, in the comparative mode, appreciated their own culture that treasured family life with its unquestioned support. According to our comparative model, I attempted to explain the father's opting for his daughter's freedom and self-reliance, while they dismissed him as a cold, self-absorbed, unloving father. We realized we had discovered a clear example of cultural diversity in which we could place side by side the American parent with the Jordanian and Arab parent. We worked to see how each parent followed important traditions. The students absolutely opted for their family traditions. I wondered aloud how I would have embraced my daughter or allowed her to struggle.

Next, a literature class, on the morning our class had scheduled a discussion of Henry Thoreau's "Civil Disobedience."[14] That morning, Eileen and I had sensed a clearly charged atmosphere as we passed the university gate. Students were huddled in small groups, some of them crying. A few groups comprised female and male students, quite unusual in this conservative society. Finally, a student told us that a revered Palestinian spiritual leader, the blind, paralyzed Sheikh Yassin, had been assassinated that morning in the West Bank by the Israeli Defense Force.[15] The whole campus seemed to be in mourning. The majority of students at the University of Jordan had Palestinian roots, a reality that underscored their grief. Later, when I stood in front of my literature class, I proposed that we postpone our discussion of Thoreau's "Civil Disobedience," a topic I thought touched too closely to Sheikh Yassin's death. But after a class meeting, a student countered with an offer: "We will stay in class to discuss Thoreau if YOU march with us in the campus protest." This was an ironic proposal since the march, in itself, was an act of civil disobedience. Student marches and protests violated university rules.

We worked through "Civil Disobedience" in a subdued atmosphere. The young man who proposed continuing the class had the final comment: "Thoreau spent a night in the Concord jail before having his school tax paid. Sheikh Yassin paid with his life. I guess we need to pay in our own way." After an unplanned minute of silence during which we pondered our classmate's insight, he pinned on my jacket a memorial pin with Sheikh Yassin's face. We then proceeded to the protest march. I was very conscious about illegally parading and wondered about criticism from the university administration, but the incident quietly passed. I still have the pin, which I keep as a token of the students' ability to listen to me if I listened to them. As I marched with them, I felt that Henry David Thoreau would have appreciated our decision. These students grasped the comparative-transnational lesson in our real-life experience of civil disobedience.

During my first year as a Fulbright scholar, I spent most classes with graduate students. The university did not offer an American studies undergraduate program. Consequently, we needed to introduce students to different ways of thinking, reading, and exploratory writing that would challenge their skills. Primarily, we wanted to move students beyond their traditional papers in which they diligently researched a topic and then reported the facts, very thoroughly. We wanted them to move beyond reporting to explore what they found, to move past their sources to what they thought, what they might want others to question: "What do you think now that you have investigated your subject? Help us to see something new: a new question, a new problem, an insight." We asked for exploratory writing rather than their carefully researched reports.

Our students generally showed a surprising ability to begin dealing with exploratory writing. In an Introduction to American Culture class, one student studied the American national parks system, principally the Everglades and Yellowstone Park. How she moved from one to another, I do not recall, but she thrilled our class with her PowerPoint presentation that featured not only the animals and beauties of the parks but also their expression of American values that stress the healing possible in the outdoors, our need to connect with nature, with the spiritual silence and peace of the parks. She also saw the problems of maintaining the integrity of the parks in light of increased use, the pressures of tourism, of logging and mining interests, and the problems related to sports vehicles. At the end of her presentation, which most Americans would have appreciated, she proposed introducing a similar system into Jordan but was roundly hooted down because she did not mention Petra or the Roman city of Jerash. "I embrace Petra and Jerash, but I wish we had a Yellowstone or an Everglades." After a feisty discussion, we agreed to leave Yellowstone in the United States but to recall that Petra is one of the ten wonders of the world. In this case we compared and contrasted without choosing one over the other.

This seminar influenced at least two students. One has stayed in touch, continuing to e-mail newspaper clippings that report on the tug of war between American conservationists and snowmobiles and battles with coal mining interests. Another student, an astute young woman from Kuwait, continues to send material about the politics of Louisiana, especially related to Katrina and the British Petroleum oil spill. She has published her first book about her Kuwaiti family's history, a project she had begun to think about in our history class. She has also been appointed the chief executive officer of a major family foundation to oversee Kuwaiti cultural projects, a role for which she felt capable, as she explains, because of our critical thinking sessions. She also keeps us up-to-date with the emerging role of women in Kuwaiti politics. She wonders if a successful women's movement might lead to other social successes, as happened in the United States. But then she adds, "We are so different." I wrote to remind her that our comparative class had stressed not only our differences but also our similarities. "We Americans did not do well for a long time. And we are still trying to mirror the ideals of our Constitution."

Our American Culture seminar enrolled mostly Jordanian-Palestinian students but also students from Bahrain, Saudi Arabia, and my friend from Kuwait. It was only natural that this class heavily accented the comparative nature of US studies since we easily moved from discussing not only comparisons and contrasts between US culture and Jordan's but also culture as it differed in their respective countries. The energetic Saudi Arabian student explained how she pushed against restrictive customs and rituals in Saudi Arabia. Recently, she wrote that she drove a car in a protest movement against Saudi law. She laughs at the fact that she broke the law, like Thoreau, but was not arrested. In class, we talked comparatively about music, regional foods, movies, films, the arts, dance, male-female relationships, and clothing, topics not touched by most Middle Eastern university classes.

This cultural seminar received a real-life lesson in cultural globalism when we wondered about the power and popularity of Oprah. During our discussion, our Kuwaiti student asked about John Steinbeck. Her mother faithfully followed Oprah, who, that week, urged her listeners to read a Steinbeck novel. Oprah to Kuwait to Amman to Kuwait: "Who is John Steinbeck?"—a genuine transnational moment. This "traveling question" allowed us to explore the international influence of American culture, to ask about the attractions and influences of non-Arab sources on their traditions, to search for ways for the East to touch the West in positive ways. They seemed happy when I told them that hummus and falafel were on many Austin restaurant menus. And we smiled at the ubiquity of cell phones that allowed young people worldwide to begin and maintain clandestine romances, avoiding the restrictions of families. The students smile at this transnational subterfuge.

Because we lacked materials for our American Political Systems seminar, we developed a course in which each of the twelve students chose a US state as her or his field of study. Each followed a US congressperson through the semester. Each week students contacted the congressperson's Washington office to ask a specific question about policy or upcoming legislative debates. Each student also followed the editorials of their congressperson's local newspaper in order to understand the problems, the culture, and the needs of the home state with its various districts. And each week we reported our findings, leading to a final verbal report that stressed the diversity of the regions and the states, the job markets, the local foods and music, their person's political maneuvering, and even the conflicts among the citizens of the same states. Frequently, we returned to comparison with Jordan.

One student learned that Washington, DC, and Washington State were miles apart in many ways. Many saw the struggle between national issues and local needs. This struggle connected with Jordan's tensions between native Jordanians and the majority Palestinians who have lived in Jordan since 1948. They could also see that their US congressperson might speak differently at home than when in Washington ("Just like in Jordan" was the response). We clearly saw how regions differed, how the mountain states urged for local control of mineral and forest resources, while the New England states sought to protect clean air quality. The Jordanian students compared the US tug-of-war for resources with their national situation, citing King Hussein's creation of a political map in which tribal leaders controlled a disproportionate quantity of state resources. We recognized a comparison with the United States, that many state legislatures redrew voting districts to strengthen their own party: the same strategy for the same kind of political power, Jordan and the United States. The students nodded their heads at the similarities between Jordanian and US politics.

We also saw that in Bahrain, the minority Sunnis controlled the majority Shia despite the Shias' public protests. And the Kuwaiti student explained why Kuwait forced many Palestinians to leave Kuwait after the Palestinian Liberation Organization supported Iraq's 1990 invasion of Kuwait. In other words, these graduate students understood these political strategies. I was especially impressed with the student who had adopted Iowa as his research state. He realized that his farm state with its generally conservative fiscal, social, and anticommunist values had pushed for more open-market relations with "communist" Cuba, that Iowa's need for corn and soybean markets outweighed its conservative platform that fought Cuba's communist regime. In general, the students had no problem seeing comparisons between the Middle East and US politics, although their politicians wore different clothes and spoke different languages.

The students liked this approach to "political systems." Several students were deeply surprised and delighted that someone in a legislative office in Washington, DC, would regularly respond to their questions. On occasion, a student grumbled that Jordanian officials would not ordinarily answer a student's question. I confessed that they had been fortunate to have experienced effective communications, that I had not always been as successful trying to contact my congressional representative. And when more than one congressperson personally sent an e-mail note to a student explaining what seemed to us as a weak explanation for a position taken, we smiled at the evasion but felt good that someone answered. We also realized that a lowly staff aide probably wrote the note.

Our discussions tried to untangle newspaper versions from the formal speeches, from local editorials, general assumptions from grounded facts, posturing from actual agendas. We found this general mix to be central to our respective political worlds. The majority of students in this class also began to read Jordanian newspapers, a practice not customary for university students. They also compared Jordanian newspapers to the US ones they read for our class.

We examined some positive aspects of the American political system and understood a bit more about its complications, but saw how its ideals had not always matched its practices. Far from beatifying the United States, the class seemed to feel comfortable when they spotted nondemocratic policies and actions that revealed racial prejudice, an acceptance of widespread poverty, and the unfair power of large banks and corporations to influence national politics. That ability to freely criticize American politics seemed to allow them to scrutinize their own country and even the University of Jordan, a comparative by-product of our approach. Ironically, I found myself insisting that our classroom discussions remain within our classroom, that our classroom freedom did not extend to public criticisms of our Jordanian government or our university. They nodded in agreement.

Other classes impressed me, particularly the Dialogue and Debate class of ninety-eight students from Jordan and several Gulf nations. I still treasure a heap of papers from this class. My directions accented writing to discover reasonable material for our dialogues and debate: "We will write our ideas on these sheets that I will give at the beginning of every class. We will use them to develop and scrutinize our thoughts about the subject presented. I will collect the papers. Then we will break into small groups and 'dialogue' or discuss what we have written. We think, write, dialogue, and then debate. What do you want to say to our university president? What is Arab feminism? Would you prefer an arranged marriage? Why do you vote or not vote in national elections? What are the various positions about the Jordanian-Israeli peace agreement? Why is Islam so misunderstood?" I ended by reminding them that we were in their last university class: time to ask tough questions.

The bundle of these papers reminds me that many students learned to write clearly and to the point, distinguishing their own experiences from public sources. After a little fuss, they also began to see the value of honest discussion, of constructing a short valid argument against their own position. "If there is no valid argument against, then there is no debate." And they were certainly reluctant to share strong valid arguments against their own theses because their insights might help their opponents. I explained that in our court system, the prosecution must tell the defense attorneys all the pertinent information they had gathered, even if some information might weaken the prosecution.

These questions once again touched the boundaries that separate politics and religion from university discussions. Although no official ever cautioned me about keeping these subjects out of the classroom, the students all seemed to know of such a policy, the unwritten rule. In response to the unwritten rule, we asked, "Why should students be prevented from discussing political and religious subjects in the university?" They laughed when they saw that I might have found a way around the boundaries. "Let's talk about *why* university students cannot discuss Jordanian politics in a Jordanian university." As far as I could see, they did not look toward the corridors and doorways for Jordanian authorities when they began quietly to dialogue in preparation for a debate about the government's restrictions against political freedom. Then they decided not to continue that dialogue as a bit too threatening. Clearly, they were concerned about possible Jordanian security forces on the campus.

After two meetings in which we discussed our ideas in small groups, we arranged debating teams who would choose a leader to collect the written ideas of each participant and prepare to organize their debate against the other side. And then we debated. In this large class we suggested a grading system in which each student graded every presenter, every debater, 1 to 10. To my surprise, most students chose not to participate in the grading process, although they thought the idea was original and could benefit everyone. However, they acknowledged that they did not trust students to fairly grade a student from another tribe, from another country, from another social level. I still treasure a finely tailored *galabaya* and *kaffia*, gifts from two Emirati students after class grades had been recorded, who startled me when they thanked me for grading them fairly, not negating them as non-Jordanians. Yes, I learned from my students that class and tribal and national divisions remained important barriers. And I began to talk with them about comparable divisions in my US classrooms.

When we dialogued and debated whether family or tribal connections (*wasta*) should help students to obtain jobs after graduation, the debaters firmly agreed that the practice did not justly deal with job applicants. During our final class, we agreed that family influences, or "pull," do not seem like a healthy practice, that *wasta* negates the Jordanian sense of justice, that it should be eliminated, that students should depend on honest applications, beginning next year since they would soon depend on *wasta* to find jobs. Years later, I smile back at my photo of my Dialogue and Debate students. I wonder if they have continued to dialogue before debating or wonder about the validity of the opposite opinion. I am glad I pointed to the urgent need for honest dialogue in US political, religious, and social controversies. Again, we agreed that we shared similar concerns.

We did have at least one innovative extension of the Dialogue and Debate class when two students proposed to their Jordanian professor in an Arab-American Relations class that, in place of a written paper, they would organize a public dialogue and debate, videotaped, on an important subject: how does the West visualize the East in light of Edward Said's writings on Orientalism? They surprised their professor with their proposal and further surprised all of us with a well-developed PowerPoint presentation. Yes, they used material from our Dialogue and Debate class, but they expanded the focus of their presentation, which attracted a respectable crowd of students and faculty. They had adapted the dialogue-debate format into something of their own. Success.

Another success: I remember the symposium the American studies graduate students worked with us to organize in which they invited American studies students from other universities to the "First Students' Symposium in American Studies," hosted by the University of Jordan. Only students could present papers that a student committee approved and that they used to create a one-day symposium.

The idea was not new to Eileen and me. We had attended two international graduate conferences at Bashkent University in Turkey and saw firsthand how students experienced a sense of serious scholarship and achievement when they participated in the conferences.[16] Fortunately,

Eileen and I, while on a courtesy visit to the University of Jordan's president to thank him for the university's warm reception of us as Fulbright faculty, mentioned the idea of a graduate student conference. He smiled as he agreed this was a good idea.

When we told our program director about our conference and the permission of the president, he almost exploded: "This is not how we do things here. We follow lines of authority. You should bring this to a division meeting." Well, after the division meeting and many more meetings, we finally faced the day of the conference, one year later. We understood the Jordanian protocol and respected it but were happy that we had blundered our way to the top, to the president and his permission. So even though some members of the faculty may have opposed the symposium, the powers at the top had smiled on it, so on it went.

Our students solicited papers from other Jordanian American literature and cultural studies programs and formed themselves into committees to publicize the event, to make posters, to welcome visitors, to arrange refreshments and organize a lunch, to staff seminar rooms, and, finally, to clean up. They also organized the schedule of papers and prepared their own papers.

The paper I best remember dealt with an American professional wrestler, Eddie Rodríguez, who always wore a cowboy hat. The presenter wore a cowboy hat with no *hijab*, one of the few Muslim women in the room without one. After her interesting presentation that dealt with racist overtones in the publicity leading to matches, not a moment passed before the first question: "Why are you not wearing a proper head scarf?" The student answered, "Because wearing a head scarf is not one of the pillars of my religion, and I thought it appropriate for my topic, Eddie Rodríguez!" What an answer. A rustle of papers and we moved on to discuss the real issues in the paper.

Perhaps the most interesting sidelight at the conference happened during the grand opening, attended by the university president and his guests from other universities and the ministry, plus University of Jordan faculty. After the president offered a brief welcome, a principal critic of the symposium spoke about how important such symposia are for the university and its students. He also suggested that the idea originated with him. Our graduate students joined with Eileen and me as we smiled. We had successfully worked the system. We also told our students that such grandstanding is a comparable virus infecting some US universities as well.

On another occasion our Fulbright faculty and the US Embassy learned a lesson in the complexities and pitfalls of transnational teaching of American studies. When the US cultural attaché suggested inviting novelist Diana Abu-Jaber to visit Jordanian university campuses, including our own, we thought she would be a natural fit since her father came from Amman and she had lived in Jordan for two years. Her prominent uncle and other family members continued to live in Amman.

Abu-Jaber had recently published her second novel, *Crescent*, the central topic of our meetings.[17] In the novel set in a Los Angeles university community, Sirine, a talented Arab American cook, attracts Arab students to her simple restaurant. She understands their sadness living far from home. She brings them closer to home through her cooking. Although she does not speak Arabic and is not Muslim, she treasures her Arab heritage, which is frequently communicated to her through stories and poetry by her uncle, an Iraqi university professor with whom she lives.

Ironically, in light of what happened, American reviewers praised the novel and suggested that US Americans could learn a great deal not only about Arab values rooted in home, family, food, and language but also about Middle East tensions.

In the novel Iranian and Iraqi students did not mingle in the restaurant. They maintained the strict borders of their respective homelands until a respected Iranian florist bargains with Sirine that if she can prepare *fesenjahn kouresch*, his favorite Iranian dish, he will break the boundary line. She succeeds, and, finally, most of the students reluctantly mix. Her cooking not only satisfies appetites but also heals wounds.

Sirine has a love interest, Hanif, an attractive Iraqi literature professor who, for whatever reason, cannot return home. Again, he finds her cooking connecting with his Iraqi home. In turn, she begins studying Arabic with Hanif. The novel seemed like an inviting ground for us to discuss fiction that dealt with East and West.

When my literature students hosted Abu-Jaber for our morning class, the students immediately began to challenge the author: "How could you betray our Arab culture when you had the opportunity to teach the American public about our values?" "How could you, a Jordanian, not stand up for what is most valuable to us?" "How could you allow Hanif to drink alcohol, to have a close relationship with Sirine?" Abu-Jaber explained that this work of fiction intended not to teach but to play with real-life situations. She emphasized that these were real people who found lives in her writing, that some characters were based on her relatives. She pointed to her book as a novel, not an attempt to persuade about the value of Arab cultures. She explained that Sirine was a hero, a complicated hero, a woman who helped Iraqi and Iranian students to feel at home in America. But to no avail. The students felt severely betrayed by one of their own, who, with a US audience, did not become a standard-bearer who absolutely stood up for Arabic traditions in the face of US cultural challenges. They did not want to champion an ambiguous heroine. Clearly, their perspective overcame any literary commandment that literature intends not to teach but to illuminate the human condition.

Later that evening, Abu-Jaber faced the graduate students and faculty of the English and American literature departments. Although she was prepared for tough questions, the group repeated the brittle criticisms of the earlier classroom experience. A few days later, we sat with a large audience of the humanities students and faculty at Petra University. Again, they loudly rejected her explanation that her novel did not aim to teach Arab values. She had betrayed them.

On our part we had failed to read the novel with the sensibilities of a Jordanian reader. As with Abu-Jaber, we dealt with a fiction in which some Arabs in America slipped a little but regained their balance. But our Jordanian students and faculty tolerated no slips when on a public stage. Our cultural attaché had also fumbled the ball. And although we American faculty had thought we were culturally sensitive, we learned otherwise.

After our two Fulbright years at the University of Jordan, we became senior fellows at the ACOR center in Amman, charged with visiting American studies programs at universities in Egypt, Lebanon, Sharjah, Bahrain, Qatar, Iran, Yemen, and Palestine.[18]

These American studies classrooms stressed a comparative and transnational approach: to see one's own country and its customs and politics, warts and all, while discovering illuminating comparisons with the host country. For example, in an American University at Sharjah US history class, the professor talked about the Roaring Twenties, with its vitality, excesses, and glamour. He stressed its promise of unending prosperity, of its absolute faith in the stock market, of a building boom, of new lively dances like the Charleston, new music, new literature, and new slinky feminine fashions known as the flapper outfits. He painted a clearly positive picture of the '20s before preparing them for the next class, after spring break, which would examine how the celebrative bubble of those times was about to burst. After a moment of silence, he asked the students if they saw any resemblance between the United States in the '20s and contemporary Sharjah or nearby Dubai. He did not need to explain his point, that they as potential leaders of Sharjah might question their emirate's current optimism about its wildly expanding economy, of examples of unlimited extravagant personal spending and public building. Students looked at one another, whispering their first responses. The question was theirs to answer, not their history professor's. Could there be a comparative and transnational lesson or warning from the Roaring Twenties to them, to Sharjah?

I recall sitting in the al-Quds American studies classroom whose Palestinian students experienced daily difficulties of getting to class because of checkpoints and other hazards. We listened to presentations on the US political system, its development of foreign policies, its Bill of Rights. I felt happy but shocked that we were accepted into the class as American contributors whose answers to their honest questions seemed to be accepted. These students, mostly in their thirties, full-time workers in the West Bank, showed a high level of understanding of the United States. During one class, a student, in perfect English, presented a paper in which he explained the relationship between the US Congress and the presidency. Then he compared the US system to the Palestinian Authority. We learned how a comparative and transnational classroom succeeded in difficult economic and political circumstances, especially in light of US foreign policy that did not support Palestinian causes.

If an American visitor ever expected to be heckled on a campus or in a classroom, one might think of the University of Iran in Tehran, where Eileen and I taught one seminar and participated in another seminar organized by a group of Dutch students and faculty. Tough questions both ways but no fire, no accusations; no one left the classroom. I cherish a photo of Eileen and me surrounded by smiling Iranian students as we enjoyed our picnic lunch in the garden of their European American studies building. We had just concluded our seminar that did not evade difficult questions. In the end, on many points, we agreed to disagree. After lunch two Iranian female students, one in full chador and the other wearing a silk scarf that showed her carefully coifed hairdo, interviewed Eileen for their column in a student publication. They wanted to know more about us, not the packaged Americans. We felt honored by the hospitality and respectful investigations offered to us by the European American studies department and its faculty and students. Besides, the university paid for our hotel and made a car and chauffeur available for our convenience.

Other US faculty might have encountered disagreeable situations in the Middle East, judgmental university authorities or even the shadow of the secret police. We experienced none of that. I do not want to protest too much, but I also recall that a civilian authority of the Jordan Military College invited us to speak to the officer corps about American culture and its foreign policy. Although we never worked out a date, the Military College did publish our paper in English and Arabic.

We had similar positive experiences at the American University in Cairo and at Georgetown University at Qatar, where we attended interesting classes in public relations and another in literature. We were deeply impressed at the American University in Beirut, where we found the excellent library buzzing at ten o'clock on a Saturday night. This factor impressed us because at our University of Jordan, the library ordinarily closed in the early evening to allow students to be with their families. We attended a number of classes, but one stands out. Professor Rami Khouri and *Washington Post* journalist Anthony Shadid, recently deceased in Syria, urged students to be true scholars who take seriously authors whose negative opinions about the Arab world they would otherwise have automatically dismissed. This reminded me of the Jordanian Dialogue and Debate class in which the students reluctantly reviewed and argued the views of their opponents in order to understand and truly debate, another application of the comparative and transnational approach that we have traced in the Middle East classrooms we have visited.

In 2002 John Carlos Rowe of the University of California in Irvine argued in "The New American Studies" that American studies needed to steer a more comprehensive tack that would take the discipline into new waters. He lobbied to expand "American" to extend its vision beyond the parochial America: "The nation, especially the United States, can no longer be treated as the exclusive domain of American Studies."[19] Professor Rowe wanted to study the wider Americas, including Canada, Mexico, Central America, and Latin America, while continuing to connect with European studies, a basically western American studies.[20] Further, in his comparative model, he wanted to "avoid the one-sided, often neo-imperialist cosmopolitanism of an earlier American Studies."[21]

In summary, John Carlos Rowe sought a new American studies that expanded the study of America to all the Americas and western Europe, was transnational rather than national or cosmopolitan, and was comparative by which each culture learns from the other rather than the neocolonial function of the US government's foreign policy. Although Appiah wrote about partial cosmopolitanism years after Rowe's publications, Rowe implicitly preferred Appiah's partial cosmopolitanism to either a simple cosmopolitanism or a kind of tribal exceptionalism. Rowe foresaw the need to expand beyond the "new American studies" to the vastly more important and fascinating field of the newer American studies that we have explored.

In this study, we have seen how a comparative transnationalism has worked in our Middle East and Gulf classrooms, especially those in Jordan, although we could include Turkey, where we taught for two years at Bilkent University, in Ankara.[22] We have moved beyond Rowe, whose American studies focused on the Americas and western Europe, when we included the more comprehensive frame of the Arab and Iranian classrooms. We think the addition of these Middle Eastern classrooms is indispensable for American studies programs in our globalized world in which Arab, Iranian, and Turkish politics and cultures have called for the attention they deserve both for their understanding of themselves as comparative explorations with and for the other branches of the newer American studies.

Notes

1. Kwame Appiah, *Cosmopolitanism: Ethics in a World of Strangers* (New York: W. W. Norton, 2004), iii.
2. Ibid., iv.
3. Ibid., v.
4. Ibid., viii.
5. Ibid., 4.
6. Ibid., 54.
7. John Carlos Rowe, *Post-naturalist American Studies* (Berkeley: University of California Press, 2000), 24–25.
8. Senior Fellowships, American Center for Oriental Research (AC)R0, Amman, Jordan.
9. Mary Oliver, *New and Selected Poems* (Boston: Beacon Press, 1992), 83–84.
10. Ibid., 4.
11. James Wright, *Collected Poems* (Middleton, CT: Wesleyan University Press, 1972), 135.
12. Ibid., 136.
13. Richard Wilbur, *New and Collected Poems* (San Diego: Harcourt Brace Jovanovich, 1988), 53–54.

14. Sheikh Ahmed Yassin, a spiritual and political leader in the West Bank, although blind and confined to a wheelchair, was a vocal critic of the Israeli occupation. On March 22, 2004, he was assassinated in Ramallah, the West Bank.

15. Henry David Thoreau, *Walden, and Other Writings* (New York: Barnes and Noble, 1983), 277–302.

16. From 2000 to 2002, Professors Eileen and Edward Lundy taught American studies at Bilkent University in Ankara, Turkey; traveled widely throughout Turkey; and presented papers for three Turkish American conferences and at the International American Studies Conference in Istanbul, in 2005. While at Bilkent, they actively participated in two Student American Studies Conferences at Bashkent University in Ankara.

17. Diana Abu-Jaber, *Crescent* (New York: W. W. Norton, 2004).

18. The American Center on Oriental Research is a research organization whose Boston administrative office confers grants to those who propose studies of significant value for understanding the archaeology and culture of the Middle East. Our six-month grant allowed us to visit the American studies programs in the Middle East and the Gulf. Our final report was presented to the staff and residences of the ACOR facility in Amman.

19. Rowe, *Post-nationalist American Studies*, 1.

20. Ibid., 7.

21. Ibid., 4.

22. Ibid., 59.

Contributors

Betty S. Anderson
Betty S. Anderson is an associate professor of Middle East history at Boston University and is the author of *Nationalist Voices in Jordan: The Street and the State* (University of Texas Press, 2005), *The American University of Beirut: Arab Nationalism and Liberal Education* (University of Texas Press, 2011), and the forthcoming *A History of the Modern Middle East: Rulers, Rogues and Rebels* (Stanford University Press, Spring 2016). Dr. Anderson has published articles in *Civil Wars, Comparative Studies of South Asia, Africa and the Middle East, Critique,* and *Jordanies,* as well as chapters for a number of edited volumes. She has written about the themes covered by Islamic and history textbooks in Jordan and the politicizing role of education in the twentieth-century Middle East. Her current research examines the economic, social, and educational changes that have come to Beirut, Amman, and Ramallah in the last twenty-five years.

Colin Cavell
Dr. Cavell is an associate professor of political science and past chair of the Department of Social Sciences at Bluefield State College and an adjunct professor of Political Science at Holyoke Community College; in addition, he has taught at the University of Bahrain, the Junior Statesman Foundation Summer Program at Yale University, Merrimack College, the University of Massachusetts at Amherst, and the University of New Orleans.

At Bluefield State College, Dr. Cavell teaches Introduction to Politics; American National Government; State and Local Politics; Comparative Politics; International Relations; Political Thought; American Constitutional Law; Model United Nations; Seminar in Social Sciences; and other subjects. At the University of Bahrain, Dr. Cavell taught political science, history, political economy, and other courses in the UOB American Studies Center from 2002 to 2011.

He has published articles in *Journal of Strategic Studies*, PressTV .com, and *Global Research: Centre for Research on Globalization* and a book, *Exporting "Made In America" Democracy: The National Endowment for Democracy & U.S. Foreign Policy* (Lanham, MD: University Press of America, 2002).

Hani Ismail Elayyan

Dr. Hani Elayyan is an assistant professor of English at the American University of the Middle East in Kuwait. He holds a PhD in English from Southern Illinois University. His research interests include Arabic literature and Arab American studies. He has written articles and book chapters on Arab and Arab American literature that have appeared in collections such as *Arabs in the Americas* (2006), edited by Darcy Zabel, Peter Lang Publishing, and *People from the Desert* (2012), edited by Nader al-Jallad and published by Reichert Verlag. Currently he is working on an article on the literary representations of the experience of expatriation in the Arabian Gulf region.

Scott Lucas

Scott Lucas is a professor of international politics at the University of Birmingham in Britain. He has published a dozen books and more than fifty articles as an academic journalist.

Initially, he specialized in US and British foreign policy, but his research interests now also cover current international affairs—especially in North Africa, the Middle East, and Iran—new media, and intelligence services.

A professional journalist since 1979, Professor Lucas is the founder and editor of EA WorldView, a leading website in daily news and analysis of Iran, Turkey, Syria, and the wider Middle East, as well as US foreign policy.

Edward J. Lundy

In 1990 and 1991, during a sabbatical year at la Universidad Católica in Quito, Ecuador, Edward J. Lundy helped develop and then team-teach a bilingual graduate course titled Understanding the Two Americas. In 2004, as a Senior Fulbright Scholar, he helped establish the graduate program in American Studies at the University of Jordan in Amman, continuing for another year, at the request of the university administration, with a university appointment. For six months in 2007, he and Eileen T. Lundy resided at the American Center of Oriental Research in Amman, Jordan, as senior fellows. From there they traveled to the newly founded American studies programs in the Middle East to understand their origins and development. This book evolved from their research at ACOR. His other publications include *Islamic Movements as Seen from the West*; *Liberty and Justice: The Pilgrims and Hector Crevecoeur, A Commentary*; and an article, *Jordanians Study America*.

Eileen T. Lundy
From 2000 to 2002, Eileen T. Lundy taught in the American Language and Literature program and undergraduate American Studies program at Bilkent University in Ankara, Turkey. In 2003, she and her husband, Edward J. Lundy, received Fulbright Senior Scholar awards to teach in the newly established graduate American Studies program at the University of Jordan in Amman, the first program of its kind at an Arab university in the Middle East. The university then hired them for another year to continue to assist in the development of the American Studies program. In 2007, she and her husband resided as Senior Fellows at the American Center of Oriental Research in Amman, Jordan, positions that enabled them to travel to observe the newly developing American studies programs in several countries in the Middle East. Their research took them to nine programs that arose between 1998 and 2007. This book grew out of that research. Other publications include papers such as "Jordanians Study America"; "American Studies in the Middle East, a Growing Phenomenon"; "American Studies in the Middle East, a Call for Comparative Studies"; "The Power of the People, By the People, and For the People: Transnational Grassroots Movements for Justice"; and "Cacophony, Harmony, Unity: Voices of Women in the Middle East."

David A. McDonald
David A. McDonald is associate professor and director of the Ethnomusicology Institute at Indiana University. Since 2002 he has worked closely with Palestinian refugee communities in Israel, Jordan, the West Bank, and North America. He is the author of *My Voice Is My Weapon: Music, Nationalism, and the Poetics of Palestinian Resis-*

tance (Duke University Press, 2013), winner of the Chicago Folklore Prize recognizing the most significant work of scholarship in Folklore Studies.

Patrick McGreevy
Patrick McGreevy is Dean of Arts and Sciences at American University of Beirut. From 2004 to 2009, he was director of the Center for American Studies and Research (CASAR) at AUB. His research and writing focus on university studies, American higher education in the Arab region, landscape, and nationalism in the United States and Canada during the nineteenth century. He is the author of *Imagining Niagara: Meaning and the Making of Niagara Falls* (1994) and *Stairway to Empire: Lockport, the Erie Canal, and the Shaping of America* (2009).

Neema Noori
Neema Noori (PhD, Columbia University) is an associate professor of sociology at the University of West Georgia. Prior to his current academic appointment, he taught for three years at the American University of Sharjah in the United Arab Emirates. His publications have appeared in the *International Journal of Culture, Politics, and Society*; *Political and Military Sociology: An Annual Review*; and *Central Asia Survey*.

Luke Peterson
Luke Peterson completed a PhD at the University of Cambridge (King's College) in the Faculty of Asian and Middle Eastern Studies investigating language, media, and knowledge surrounding the Palestinian-Israeli conflict. Dr. Peterson has published in the *British Journal of Middle Eastern Studies*, has chapters in three anthologies, and wrote a monograph titled *Palestine in the American Mind: The Discourse on Palestine in the Contemporary United States*, and his new book, *Palestine-Israel in the Print News Media: Contending Discourses*, is now available through Routledge Publications, London. Dr. Peterson has lived and worked in the Palestinian West Bank as well as in Cambridge, England, and Portland, Oregon, but moved with his wife, his three-year-old son, and his newborn daughter to Pittsburgh (via West Sussex, England) in the fall of 2014 where he took up the post of Visiting Professor of International Studies in the University of Pittsburgh Center for International Studies for the academic year 2014–2015. From Pittsburgh, Dr. Peterson has contributed to local, national, and international media coverage on both television and radio speak-

ing on topics relating to US political and military strategy in the Middle East, the emergence of the Islamic State, the ongoing Palestinian-Israeli conflict, contemporary Islam, and news media and coverage of the Middle East. Dr. Peterson is fluent in Levantine Arabic and has written, spoken, and published in Modern Standard Arabic as well.

Kate Sampsell-Willmann

Dr. Sampsell-Willmann has been on the faculty of the American University in Central Asia since 2011. She holds a Distinguished PhD in history from Georgetown University and a JD from the University of Baltimore. Dr. Sampsell-Willmann's main publication area is intellectual history of the twentieth century, especially the career and times of photographer Lewis Wickes Hine (1874–1940). Her book *Lewis Hine as Social Critic* (University of Mississippi Press, 2009) is the first book-length monograph on the photographer who created the social documentary genre. She is preparing to publish recent research on Lewis Hine. Future research plans include the areas of visual political dissent, African American history, history of the anti-fascist Left, and US Constitutional history. Her published work can be found in the *Journal of the Gilded Age and Progressive Era*, *History of Photography*, *American Quarterly*, and *Reviews in American History*. She is a reviewer for the *Journal of American History*, *American Historical Review*, and the *Journal of Agricultural History* and has presented her research at major conferences in the United States, Egypt, Qatar, Turkey, and the United Kingdom and online at iTunesU, The Saylor Foundation, and the *Journal of the Gilded Age and Progressive Era* (http://www.jgape .org/forum/3).

Index

Abaza, Azeez, 136

Abbas, Mahmoud, 199n21

Abu-Jaber, Diana, 249

Abu Madi, Ilya (poet), 117; American history themes in works by, 123; immigration themes in works by, 119–121; modernity themes in works by, 129–130; natural and cultural beauty of America as theme in works by, 134; Western cultural heritage themes in works by, 130, 132; women as theme in works by, 132–133; work ethic themes in works by, 126–127

Abushady, Ahmad Zaki (poet), 117; American history themes in works by, 124–126; immigration themes in works by, 121–122; natural and cultural beauty of America as theme in works by, 134–136; Western cultural heritage themes in works by, 131–132; women as theme, 133–134; work ethic themes in works by, 128–129

Afghanistan, education in US reconstruction of, 36–37

Ahmadinejad, Mahmood, 22

al-Akhawayn University (Morocco), 40

al-Aqsa Intifada. See Second Intifada

al-Durra, Mohammad, 151

al-Hamra (Beirut), 71

al-Jazeera, 186

al-Khalifa family (Bahrain), 171, 172, 197n3

al-Qaeda, 23, 178

al-Quds University (Jerusalem), viii, ix, 4, 10, 30n3, 251

Alterman, Jon, 46

al-Tikriti, Saddam Hussein Abd al-Majid. See Saddam Hussein

Alwaleed Bin Talal bin Abdulaziz al Saoud, Prince, support for American studies by, 4, 22–23, 72, 183

America: as popular culture construct, 147, 165; positive connotations of word, 24; use of word in naming institutions, 33; use of word to describe United States, 2, 18

American Australian Association, 22

American Center of Oriental Research, ix, 3, 254n18

American exceptionalism, 28, 234, 235

American history as theme in Arab American poetry, 123–126

American Intercontinental University (Dubai), 30n5

American literature as teaching tool in American studies, 241, 249–250

American Middle East University (Jordan), 30n5